Freedom from Our Social Prisons

Freedom from
Our Social Prisons

The Rise of Economic, Social, and Cultural Rights

Anthony George Ravlich

LEXINGTON BOOKS
A division of
ROWMAN & LITTLEFIELD PUBLISHERS, INC.
Lanham • Boulder • New York • Toronto • Plymouth, UK

LEXINGTON BOOKS

A division of Rowman & Littlefield Publishers, Inc.
A wholly owned subsidary of The Rowman & Littlefield Publishing Group, Inc.
4501 Forbes Boulevard, Suite 200
Lanham, MD 20706

Estover Road
Plymouth PL6 7PY
United Kingdom

British Library Cataloguing in Publication Information Available

Library of Congress Cataloging-in-Publication Data

Ravlich, Anthony George.
   Freedom from our social prisons : the rise of economic, social, and cultural rights /
Anthony George Ravlich.
      p. cm.
   Includes bibliographical references and index.
   ISBN-13: 978-0-7391-2286-0 (cloth : alk. paper)
   ISBN-10: 0-7391-2286-X (cloth : alk. paper)
 1. Human rights. 2. Social justice. 3. Liberalism. I. Title.
   JC571.R383 2008
   323—dc22

                                                                        2008002223

Printed in the United States of America

⊗™ The paper used in this publication meets the minimum requirements of American
National Standard for Information Sciences—Permanence of Paper for Printed Library
Materials, ANSI/NISO Z39.48–1992.

To my mother, Dawn Rose: thank you for encouraging me to do what I wanted to do in life and the many years you have devoted to my well-being. I have been very lucky to have such a wonderful mother.

Contents

Preface

The purpose of this book is to provide a human rights belief system more in tune with reality, which can be used to defend, particularly the underclass, against the worst abuses of neoliberalism and hold out the hope of a world where the Universal Declaration of Human Rights prevails. The Universal Declaration of Human Rights has been in existence for fifty-nine years but still over half the world's population live in poverty and powerlessness. Core minimum obligations are presently an integral part of economic, social, and cultural rights which are rising on the United Nations agenda. Under neoliberalism the human rights of the underclass has deteriorated. It is argued that human rights need to be achieved from the bottom-up rather than the top-down. Presently, care minimum obligations such as the right to shelter and primary health are bestowed by the state. It is argued that empowering rights are also required. For example, the empowering right of human rights education which people can use to achieve higher levels of human rights through the democratic process. In addition, the right to development, also an empowering right, is regarded as possessing core minimum obligations. There needs to be a space in society where people can utilize their natural talents and abilities irrespective of the requirements of the dominant ideology. Under neoliberalism many talented, creative, holistic people have been marginalized or forced to leave the country because they do not fit into the budgeting mentality, flexible work force demanded by neoliberalism, and the lack of opportunities due to the emphasis of consumerism over production. Microcredit has proven successfully in helping the poor achieve their dreams. Economic, social, and cultural rights and core minimum obligations will, in my view, civilize neoliberalism. It is considered that financially independent human rights nongovernmental organizations, under the umbrella of civil and political and

ix

economic, social, and cultural rights, can drive such education and development realization.

I am Chairperson of the Human Rights Council Inc. (New Zealand). My university degrees are in politics, statistics, and criminology. Ph: (0064) (09) 302.2761, email: anthony_ravlich@yahoo.com, http://www.hrc2001.org.n2.

Acknowledgments

I would like to thank my family, parents, and brothers, for their patience and the support they have been to me when writing this book. I would also like to thank my friends in the Human Rights Council Inc. and Psychiatric Survivors Inc. especially Mal, Alan, Caroline, and Rex, my holistic friends. Also thanks to Antony Van Den Heuvel for setting up the Human Rights Party and Julian McCusker-Dixon, Chairperson of Psychiatric Survivors Inc., an organization with whom the Council enjoys a very close relationship.

Chapter One

The Rise of Economic, Social, and Cultural Rights

Economic, social, and cultural rights, which are now quickly rising on the United Nations agenda, offers hope to those suffering under the oppression of neoliberalism. But it is up to the people to make the most of this ideological shift, which has been forced on the global elites, to ensure it is not left on their terms.

The rise of economic, social, and cultural rights (see Appendix II) is in response to the divisiveness of neoliberalism displayed by its elitism, large wealth, and power inequalities within and between countries. Also, neoliberalism has resulted in political intolerance, which has exacerbated, if not caused, increasing global conflict in the form of global terrorism, wars, and nuclear proliferation and particularly its use of structural violence, omitting economic, social, and cultural rights from international and domestic laws with its resultant enormous social problems, for example, unemployment, low wage economies, high suicide and incarceration rates, terrorism, and so forth. The economic trend now is toward regional rather than global trade indicating that globalization without social responsibility is self-destructive. There is also an ideological backlash occurring with socialism developing in South America, Islamic Jihadism, and the rise of economic, social, and cultural rights.

Typically the West has an elitist perspective of human rights defining them narrowly as civil and political rights (freedom and democracy, see Appendix I) and have virtually ignored economic, social, and cultural rights (social justice). Both sets of rights are in the Universal Declaration of Human Rights (UDHR, see Appendix III). Noam Chomsky states that economic, social, and cultural rights are "largely dismissed in the West" and in the United States the "contempt for the socio-economic provisions of the Declaration are . . . . deeply ingrained" (Chomsky, 1998: 32–39).

1

However economic, social, and cultural rights were included in the Universal Declaration of Human Rights in 1948 largely as a consequence of the lessons learned in the Great Depression of the 1930s with its massive unemployment. But since the signing of the declaration these rights have been constantly opposed at the United Nations by the American camp of liberal democracies disregarding the benefits these rights would have on the world's poor who make up the bulk of humanity.

Because of the torturously slow progress of these rights at the UN and their negligible education only a small number of countries have included economic, social, and cultural rights as justiciable law (able to be dealt with by a court). Mario Gomez states: ". . .while states both in the North and South, have incorporated civil and political rights in their constitutions, few states have similarly incorporated economic, social, and cultural rights either in their constitutions or domestic legislation. Economic, social, and cultural rights have remained at the level of non-justiciable principles of state policy" (Gomez, 1995: 155–169). Some countries which have are Finland, Norway, and South Africa.

The Western media and human rights NGOs such as Amnesty International, Freedom House, and Human Rights Watch (discussed in later chapters) have largely reflected the Western view of human rights. In 1993 the United Nations Committee on Economic, Social and Cultural Rights noted, in an address to the World Conference on Human Rights, that:

> The international community as a whole continues to tolerate all too often breaches of economic, social and cultural rights which, if they occurred in relation to civil and political rights, would evoke expressions of horror and outrage and would lead to concerted calls for immediate remedial action. In effect, despite the rhetoric, violations of civil and political rights continue to be treated as though they were far more serious, and more patiently intolerable, than massive and direct denials of economic, social and cultural rights (Asbjorne, 2000: 112).

However, the position of the United Nations, at least in terms of rhetoric, is that both sets of rights have equal status (Limberg Principles 1987, Vienna Declaration 1993, Maastricht Treaty 1992). As human rights can be selectively chosen to suit the interests of certain groups, for example, the corporation places considerable emphasis on property rights and the rule of law, the "equal status principle" ensures such prioritization does not occur.

Economic, social, and cultural rights promise a more responsible freedom with greater cooperation within and between countries. At the international level the need for cooperation between states in achieving human rights is contained in Article 2(1) of the International Covenant on Economic, Social and Cultural Rights and is also one of the purposes of the United Nations Charter (Article 1(3)). At the domestic level if economic, social, and cultural rights were included in human rights law, which in addition to civil and political rights theoretically reflects all interests, there is likely to be far greater participation and cooperation between groups in controlling the human rights agenda.

The core beliefs of neoliberalism are the same as for liberalism although the former involves greater economic freedoms and a global political agenda. These beliefs are based on the narrow view of human rights, civil and political rights plus the right to property but with economic, social, and cultural rights excluded. Tony Evans states: ". . . . For neo-liberals, economic, social and cultural rights may be legitimate aspirations but they can never be rights" (Evans, 1999: 33–34). Modern Liberalism, which originated in the early twentieth century as a response to socialism, with its stronger trade unions ensured society was more economically egalitarian and while a liberal elite controlled the human rights agenda there was necessarily a greater degree of political tolerance than under neoliberalism. During the Cold War ideologies were debated in the mainstream rather than being relegated to the margins of society as they are now. Also during the Cold War there were two superpowers: the United States and the Soviet Union. Modern Liberalism was liberalism in a bipolar world. The growth of neoliberalism at the close of the 1970s, the time of Margaret Thatcher and Ronald Reagan, saw a reversion to the Classical Liberalism of the seventeenth century, its minimal state, elitism, minimal democracy, and political intolerance. The collapse of the Soviet Union in 1989 meant that America was the only superpower. Classical Liberalism is liberalism in a unipolar world. While Modern Liberalism was more pluralistic neoliberalism is more oligarchic with societies revolving around the interests of the middle class and professional elite (see later chapters). Minimal government also meant minimal social investment for the future and large private sectors suitable for the Western corporations to constantly perpetuate the status quo. The corporations helped finance the neoliberal's grand scheme of having liberal democratic countries everywhere. But with the huge gap between rich and poor the freedom was to be only for the elites (who traded in their freedom of thought, conscience, and intellectual freedom for the increased benefits offered by neoliberalism). But it is not a socially responsible freedom which is freedom for all. Even on elite terms, that is, only civil and political rights and excluding economic, social, and cultural rights, the former set of rights are far from universal with the poor virtually voiceless and powerless. Neoliberalism, because of its elitism, is very attractive to the global elites who, together with the corporations, have every reason not to want to provide social justice for their people. But it is also important that the poor are not given the opportunity to tell the majority about their situation; rather certain members of the elite are allocated this function to ensure it is done in a controlled fashion acceptable to the establishment. Consequently it is just as important to global elites to minimize civil and political rights for the poor as well as economic, social, and cultural rights.

In recent years economic, social, and cultural rights have gained increasing recognition at the United Nations in discussions on the drafting of a complaints procedure (Optional Protocol) for those suffering social injustices, that is, violations of these rights. Also there is presently discussions on the right to development, which also include economic, social, and cultural rights, and point to the need for socially responsible limits to be placed on economic development such as globalization, privatization, and the corporations. Also, to a certain extent, economic, social, and cultural rights are also gaining greater recognition at the domestic level. For example New Zealand released the New Zealand Plan of Action for Human Rights, which includes economic, social, and cultural rights, in February 2005.

Describing the recent rise of economic, social, and cultural rights on the international agenda, Mary Robinson, former United Nations High Commissioner for Human Rights, and Paul Hunt, United Nations Special Rapporteur for Health, jointly wrote on May 11, 2006:

> A quiet revolution is taking place within international human rights. The traditional focus on civil and political rights—the prohibition of torture, the right to a fair trial, freedom of speech—has been broadened to include economic, social and cultural rights, such as the human rights to education, food, shelter, and the highest attainable standard of health. Both groups of rights are integral elements of the Universal Declaration of Human Rights ("Economic, Social, and Cultural Rights," *The New Zealand Herald*, A13).

And this 'quiet revolution' may get louder at the domestic level. Robinson and Hunt state: "But the most far-reaching change has been within civil society. Today, in every region of the world, including the United States, civil society groups are organising around economic, social and cultural rights. They have understood that a broad spectrum of human rights can empower individuals and humanise the forces of globalisation" (*The New Zealand Herald*, A13).

The addition of economic, social, and cultural rights to the civil and political rights of neoliberalism is likely to decrease political discrimination towards other ideologies such as socialism, social democracy, the Islamic model, and so forth. At present the human rights agenda is controlled by a liberal elite but with a broader range of human rights more reflective of people as a whole there is likely wider participation in the control of this agenda (this is covered in chapter 2). With greater people control the new "people's elite," would be based on ability rather than whether you "fit into" (conform to) the requirements of a liberal, middle-class, professional elite (see following chapters on "closed group monopolies"). The "people's elite" would be more representative of the people as a whole and with the broader ideological dimension allowing for greater tolerance of other ideologies. This increased people participation in the control of the human rights agenda can be achieved through the democratic process. In addition, economic, social, and cultural rights in law will encourage global elites to share in the economic growth with all who contributed toward it including the most disadvantaged who had to sacrifice many years of their life for the sake of the neoliberal's grand schemes. Economic, social, and cultural rights places responsible limits on the free market, for example, immediately addressing the problems of extreme poverty and exploited labor. In my opinion such changes should be driven from the bottom-up as ordinary people and the most disadvantaged are the major beneficiaries of these "bread and butter" rights and are most likely to have the political will. It is this lack of political will on the part of the global elites as evidenced by the long history of neglect of economic, social, and cultural rights means that they cannot be relied upon to act in accordance with the spirit of the Universal Declaration of Human Rights. In my opinion, there is certainly little evidence today of the enlightened leadership which led to the creation of the declaration, most present-day leaders seem unable to rise above their elite interests and represent all the people.

Economic, social, and cultural rights, which have rarely been heard outside of elite circles since the signing of the Universal Declaration of Human Rights in 1948, include the rights to employment, fair wages, health, housing, education, and an adequate standard of living. As previously stated sometimes the debate concerning the relative importance of both sets of rights is called the "food versus freedom" debate but to food should also be added the right to human rights education because poverty and ignorance usually go hand in hand. If people are ignorant of their human rights then they cannot influence the democratic process, cannot access their civil rights and, in fact, there would be no debate at all. It is now increasingly recognized that both sets of rights are of equal importance, that it is not enough just to get necessary food but you have to be able to communicate your needs and protect what you have.

Neoliberalism and neoliberal regimes have largely proven divisive because of their use of structural violence. The reality for the poor is that they very often have minimal choices so when the basic necessities are denied them, that is, economic, social, and cultural rights are omitted by the structure, their only responses can be terrorism, crime, drugs, simply accept the situation and have faith, or make their voices heard but this has heavy costs attached which they can little afford and also there may be little freedom of speech permitted. It is extremely hard to find the cause of your problems when it's a structural "omission" that is, economic, social, and cultural rights. Neoliberalism is generally only concerned with the more direct violence perpetrated by violations of civil and political rights, for example, torture, imprisonment without trial. Structural violence, the omission of economic, social, and cultural rights, may not involve the death squads and the torture of authoritarian regimes but it can relegate millions to a life of poverty with serious affects on their health, high suicide rates, imprisonment, mental illness, and if you have talents and abilities but cannot use them, as is the case with many, then this leads to very unfulfilled lives. Structural violence, which usually involves far greater numbers of people, can still have the same end result as the less sophisticate methods of authoritarian regimes, that is, death or in the words of Samuel Coleridge referring to the poor "And die so slowly that none will call it murder" (Coleridge, 1796).

Neoliberals believe in noninterference by government in the market. Henry Shue states that neoliberals espouse "the classic liberal's main prescription for the good life— do not interfere with thy neighbor" (Shue, 1980). But this is because the elite already have their human rights and are in powerful positions, which can allow them to deny these rights to others. To guard against this government interference is necessary unless the elite adopt the "do no harm" principle of the medical profession. Anyway when people are desperate the liberal's "main prescription" becomes meaningless. As stated by Shue: "It is extremely difficult merely to mind one's own business amidst a scarcity of vital commodities. It is illusory to think that this first commandment of liberalism can always be obeyed" (Shue, 1980: 46).

In addition, even on the elite's own terms, the obligation is on government to ensure the poor get their civil and political rights. It is assumed the poor have choices. But hostile government departments intent on keeping costs low, complaints determined by members of the elite and a user pays society ensure that the poor do not have this access. Consequently the government should "interfere" to ensure this access.

Also, in my view, it is not for the elite to determine what constitutes human rights. If the democratic principle is to have any meaning then this must be a decision of the people but they need to be informed which is also a necessary requirement of democracy. Democracy is the one way of ensuring that human rights are not being manipulated for the benefit of certain interests. David Forsythe states: "It could be said that the one simple notion behind internationally recognized human rights is that the state is not a toy for the enrichment and comfort of the elite, but rather is a tool to be used for the maximum good of the nation as a whole" (Forsythe, 1989: 356).

Structural violence, under the dominance of neoliberalism, has taken various forms: the structural adjustment programs of the IMF and the World Bank involving severe cutbacks to the welfare state which is actually social investment; the role of the leading neoliberal regimes at the UN in severely inhibiting the progress of economic, social, and cultural rights and therefore the alleviation of poverty and the neoliberal regimes refusal to redistribute the benefits of economic growth to all who have contributed toward it. Furthermore, the political intolerance of neoliberalism is increasingly global instability and as trade requires stability this is now leading to an increasing emphasis on regional rather than global trade. There are now increasing conflicts and political divisions evidenced by global terrorism, wars, nuclear proliferation, and the growth of ideologies to challenge neoliberalism such as socialism in South America, Islamic Jihadism, and the promotion, although almost solely at the international level, of economic, social, and cultural rights by an increasing number of states, particularly the poorer regions of Africa and South America. While at the international level it can be described as a "quiet revolution" as the people of the world gain greater awareness of economic, social, and cultural rights it is likely to get much louder. The Optional Protocol (discussed below) is meant to give people an avenue whereby they can seek social justice using the system. Given a genuine hope many of those young men recruited by terrorists may well prefer to seek redress for social injustices through the system (see below). Part of the aims of some these alternative ideologies is social justice, a concept not included in the "freedom and democracy" of neoliberalism. Unlike with individual freedoms there is no plan that ensures that the gains of economic growth should be fair distribution. It is usually at the whim of government and takes the form of a bestowal of a privilege or charity, which can be removed at any time, rather than a human right which allows people sufficient security to pursue their dreams and plan for the future. As the leading neoliberal regime America (which, in my view, together with Britain has the tacit, if not overt, support of most of the world's liberal democracies) has been uncompromising in its opposition to economic, social, and cultural rights ever since the signing of the Universal Declaration of human Rights in 1948. As of December 6, 2006, America remains one of six counties, and the only industrialized country, which have not ratified the International Covenant on Economic, Social and Cultural Rights (Ratifications, Office of the United Nations High Commission for Human Rights).

The dominance of the neoliberal ideology, uninhibited by the socialist challenge during the Cold War, has, in my view, at the domestic level, virtually captured the democratic process and the control of the human rights agenda, the interpretation and implementation of the latter is now in the hands of a neoliberal oligarchy as the system will not countenance a credible alternative to the dominant ideology. For instance, in New Zealand, the mainstream liberal media will only very rarely mention the term economic, social, and cultural rights. I consider that such an oligarchy exists in New Zealand and is likely to be the case in other liberal democracies (see future chapters). For instance, in America both Democrats and Republicans, whatever differences they may have, swear allegiance to the U.S. Constitution, and share its liberal values. Both left and right wing liberalism are concerned to protect the liberal constitution but do so in different ways with the right wing (neoconservatives, Republicans) being prepared to use military force, for example, the War on Terrorism, the war in Iraq to defend itself against terrorism and further the cause of liberal democracy globally while the left wing (liberals, neoliberals, Democrats) are more concerned with peaceful means of upholding the principles of liberalism such as the right to life, freedom from torture. However both left and right will not refrain from using their global dominance to inflict structural violence. Consequently the liberal oligarchy also includes conservatives. It is a bureaucratic business elite although in America the military would be a major influence. But it is not what the Constitution contains that is at issue but what it omits, as Franklin Roosevelt tried so hard to point out in the 1940s, namely economic, social, and cultural rights which are now also included in the Universal Declaration of Human Rights. He wanted a second "economic bill of rights" for America. In my view, the neoliberal oligarchy has cynically used the narrow interpretation of human rights to further their own interests at the expense of the rest. "True liberals," who are relatively few in number may not believe in economic, social, and cultural rights would not discriminate against "the rest" when it comes to applying their principles. They would ensure that the poor had a voice.

Tony Evans states: "Instead of fulfilling its intention of offering protection to the weak and vulnerable, neo-liberal interests have co-opted the idea of human rights as a justification for grabbing 'even more of the world's (and their own nation's) resources than they previously had' and 'to steal back the concessions to social democracy that were forced out of them at the end of the second World War'" (Evans, 2001: 104).

Also, especially with the huge gaps between rich and poor within and between countries, civil and political rights are far from universal with the professional, middle classes drowning out the voices of a powerless poor (see future chapters). Paul Hunt quoted who he described as "the great (African) jurist," Chief Justice Dumbutshena of Zimbabwe, who delivered a speech at the 1990 Commonwealth Law Conference: "Human rights is an ideology used to achieve power. It has been used hypocritically by the middle classes, in efforts only to protect their own rights" (Hunt, 1998: 68).

The freedoms of civil and political rights need to be socially responsible as defined by economic, social, and cultural rights otherwise we are left with a society where people are trapped in their social prisons, and an elite imprisoned in their minds being intellectually captured by a narrow perspective of human rights, and a world in increasing conflict as freedom without responsibility self-destructs. The global elites at the United Nations are now very belatedly addressing this by giving greater recognition to economic, social, and cultural rights in order to give people some protection from structural violence.

In my view, the globalization policies of the 1980s were premature. At the very least economic, social, and cultural rights should have been adopted by all domestic jurisdictions before neoliberal policies were first implemented (see the discussion on rights-based globalization below). However, rather than face up to their social responsibilities, it was easier to take a grand view of a world run by liberal democracies (political globalization) and take an economic gamble on the benefits of efficient corporations, new technology, and the discovery of new markets (economic globalization). But they had no plan as to how benefits, if any, were to be shared. In my view, global elites take the position that it will have to be forced out of them. In my view, the legitimacy of the global elites must be called into question as the bulk of humanity is poor and with sufficient education in economic, social, and cultural rights they would see what is in their best interests.

With the collapse of communism in Eastern Europe in 1989 Fukuyama probably reflected the feelings of the triumphant West when he exclaimed that with liberal democracy humanity had "come to the end of ideological history" Fukuyama, 1992: 49–50. Fukuyama has since altered his viewpoint). The success of the neoliberal ideology is not hard to understand as global elites, particularly liberal elites, and as well as the corporations, usually lack the political will to provide social justice for their people.

In the pursuit of their grand schemes the international and domestic elites did not seek the permission of the many millions who had to suffer immeasurably so neoliberals could achieve their ambitions. This manipulation of the human rights agenda by the global elites, in their own interests, was achieved by deliberately keeping people ignorant of economic, social, and cultural rights. The latter rights in law would have placed limitations on welfare cuts, challenged globalization, privatization, and corporations where they violated these rights, reduced the gap between rich and poor and, most importantly, in my view, given people something to believe in and struggle for rather than being ruthlessly crushed by an ideology for which the ends of ideological dominance and economic growth justifies the means. Neoliberalism is not stopping at structural violence, liberal democracies throughout the world are curbing civil liberties. Democracy has already been minimized. Where structural violence is perpetrated it is not hard to see how terrorism could be a last resort where there is no peaceful way of getting social justice (such a peaceful way is discussed below, that is, the Optional Protocol for the International Covenant on Economic, Social and Cultural Rights). The inclusion of economic, social, and cultural rights in domestic human rights law would have been a more civilized approach to globalization and privatization. As Reins Mullerson points out: ". . . such rights as the right to employment, education and health care, if claimed as rights in the strict sense of the word i.e. if they could be legally formalized and enforced by courts, would conflict with the logic of freedom and of the market. However, this is a conflict, or rather a contradiction, the resolution of which makes the market more perfect, more civilized" (Mullerson, 1995: 59).

In my experience of many years mixing with the poor in New Zealand there are many able-bodied and intelligent individuals whose lives have been cut short because of the immense destructive effects of neoliberalism. Unfortunately, there are many who are not just materially impoverished but also spiritually impoverished. Neoliberalism can crush the human spirit because the social exclusion is such that often no matter how hard you try to improve your life it can make no difference. Often they live in isolation and poverty, and without a voice. The lucky ones have a belief they can cling to. If absolute poverty, for example, food deficiency is a major problem in the developing countries in the developed countries it is relative poverty being in close proximity with a hostile elite with a "them versus us" attitude who still want to control you coupled with the huge wealth differences while you could not hope to have so many choices and such luxuries. In the West this relative poverty leads to a high level of mental illness. In a recent major study by the New Zealand Ministry of Health it was found that "one in two New Zealanders will have some kind of mental disorder during their lives' and 'some 20 per cent had a disorder in the last 12 months." The study involved interviewing nearly 13,000 people (Hinengaro, 2006).

As indicated by the extensive study of the World Bank, "Voices of the Poor," the poor in the developing countries may have a more holistic view of well-being although may be materially worse off than their Western counterparts. The report states: "The poor describe ill being as lack of material things—food especially but also lack of work, money, shelter, and clothing—and living and working in often unhealthy, polluted, and risky environments. They also defined ill being as bad experiences and bad feelings about the self. Perceptions of powerlessness over one's life and of being voiceless was common; so was anxiety and fear for the future." The report adds: "Poverty is much more than income alone. For the poor, the good life or well-being is multidimensional with both material and psychological dimensions. Well-being is peace of mind; it is good health; it is belonging to a community; it is safety; it is freedom of choice and action; it is a dependable livelihood and a steady source of income; it is food" (World Bank Series, Voices of the Poor).

In the West if you are poor you are all classified as the same and all have to "get by" on "survival level" welfare as best one can. While there are those who because of the immense hurdles involved in trying to progress while enduring considerable insecurity (the global economy could not work without stability) give up trying but there are many who keep struggling to pursue their dreams, despite immense odds, to reach their maximum potential in their talents and the perennial hope of having "a job, a family and a house." It is from this group that many of societies' most original ideas come because unlike the mainstream they are not in the grip of the mind limiting and numbing neoliberal ideology. In my experience the elite use these ideas where it suits to further their own wealth and power without any reward to those who may have suffered considerably to arrive at these ideas. And the elite, who merely obey the neoliberal ideology, do not discriminate against the poor any less.

Without a more civilized freedom (i.e., including economic, social, and cultural rights) societies are given to violent extremes: elitism develops to the point of oligarchy leaving the people feeling powerless; wealth inequality ensures civil and political rights are far from universal; where people become nothing but a means to the ends of grand political ambitions and economic growth and virtually worthless in themselves; where social responsibilities are reinvented as individual responsibilities even though the most disadvantaged have minimal choices to exercise such responsibility; where there are huge social problems such as extreme poverty, terrorism, crime, mental illness, excessive gambling, and drugs, large influxes of economic refugees, political discrimination, and huge increases in immigration without any consideration for the economic, social, and cultural rights of citizens.

Thomas Hobbes, a famous seventeenth century English philosopher, stated in the *Leviathan*: "Ignorance of remote causes, dispose men to attribute all events, to the causes immediate, and instrumental; for these are all the causes they perceive." Knowledge of economic, social, and cultural rights, violations of which are often regarded as the underlying cause of social problems, would enable people to make a leap in the imagination and see that the cause of their own suffering and many global and social problems such as poverty, terrorism, crime, mental illness, economic refugees, wars, and even nuclear proliferation can have their origin in "remote causes," that is, domestic and international structures that have failed to include economic, social, and cultural rights. In other words, it would enable people to see that these social problems are much more the responsibility of government (because with human rights the obligation rests with government) than the individual and that freedom without social responsibility is self-destructive. Only in a society where people have their human rights can the concept of individual responsibility be considered valid. Presently, it may be valid at the elite level but certainly not at the level of the most disadvantaged. Western elites, reflecting the narrowness of their thinking, have generally attributed social problems to immediate, inner causes—hence terrorists and criminals are just evil, the mentally ill are weak, poverty is the fault of the poor, that is, their lack of hard work, innate inadequacies, and lack of talent, and North Korea and Iran are renegade states and part of the Axis of Evil. The emphasis of neoliberalism has been to regard unemployment, low wages, health, housing, education, and standard of living as increasingly an individual responsibility requiring the user to pay rather than as a social responsibility, that is, economic, social, and cultural rights to be ensured by government. Neoliberals take the view that everyone is independent and responsible for their own lives but are often completely blind to the enormous advantages of their positions of power in society and their high salaries which enable them to make far better use of their civil and political rights. Many are often oblivious to the fact that many have minimal choices, are voiceless and powerless. One of the "Voices of the Poor," Adoboya of Ghana in the World Bank study made an observation on poverty. He states: "Poverty is like heat; you cannot see it; so to know poverty you have to go through it." (Voices of the Poor, 2000). In my opinion secular liberal elite perceptions of many social problems are often dictated by their fear of the unknown—poverty, violence, spirituality, and suffering—and consequently many seem incapable of dealing with problems like extreme poverty, terrorism, and Islamic countries like Iran. They simply lack the understanding. Paradoxically while they extol the virtues of freedom many actually fear being civilized and being in the words of Roosevelt "truly free" and prefer to cling to their liberal past and relatively comfortable social prisons and keep reliving the same social problems over and over again. Now some are seeing parallels between the war in Iraq and the war in Vietnam. The need for economic, social, and cultural rights was a lesson from the Great Depression but they ignored it. It was George Santayana who said "those who cannot learn from history are doomed to repeat it."

In my view it is this fear of the unknown that caused them to over react to September 11. It should have occurred to the Bush administration to ask the terrorists why they did it—was it because they hate freedom or because they hate freedom without responsibility. This is certainly not to say that America should not defend its people from terrorists but balanced judgment can avert making matters worse, for example, the U.S. failure in Iraq. This lack of understanding is described very well by Benjamin Disraeli, the nineteenth century British prime minister because in my experience it reflects today's world: "[The rich and poor are] two nations, between whom there is no intercourse and no sympathy, who are as ignorant of each other's habits, thoughts and feelings, as if they were . . . . inhabitants of different planets."

In December 2006, a United Nations (UN) survey by the World Institute for Development Economics Research has found that 2 percent of adults command more than half of the world's wealth, while the bottom 50 percent possesses just 1 percent. While income is distributed unequally across the globe, the geographical spread of wealth, which includes property and financial assets, is even more skewed, the study showed. The authors say it is the most comprehensive study of personal wealth ever taken. Institute director Anthony Shorrocks said, "The super-rich are even more grotesquely rich than 50 years ago." The study says wealth is heavily concentrated in North America, Europe, and high-income Asia-Pacific countries like Australia and Japan. "People in these countries collectively hold almost 90 percent of total world wealth," the survey said.

This increasing gap between rich and poor reflects the failure of "trickle down" (the market left alone to redistribute the proceeds of economic growth). But with nothing to force the elites to share the proceeds of economic growth that everyone contributed to it does not happen. This has led to the United Nations preparing the Millennium Development Goals as a way of ensuring some redistribution to address extreme social needs. These goals were signed by all countries in September 2000 and range from halving extreme poverty to halting the spread of HIV/AIDS and providing universal primary education all by the date of 2015. However these goals are not defined in human rights terms and consequently show a lack of ideological commitment so the goals amount to little more than charity. It may not be surprising that according to the Human Development Report 2005: ". . . . most countries are off track for most of the targets. The world is heading for a heavily sign-posted human development failure. . .". This may have hastened the rise of economic, social, and cultural rights on the UN agenda to provide greater ideological impetus as these rights in domestic law are likely to speed up the achievement of the Millennium Development Goals.

Economic, social, and cultural rights have much less relevance to the dominant elite, already wealthy and powerful, than civil and political rights which can protect their dominant position and wealth from government intervention. Consequently such rights as freedom of the press, the rights to association and property, the right to protest, protections against search and seizure, torture, and discrimination are much more important to the elite than the rights to employment, fair wages, housing, health, and so forth (the politics of human rights will be discussed more fully in later chapters). The latter more "bread and butter" rights have more relevance to the general population, especially the most disadvantaged for whom government intervention can mean ensuring an adequate lifestyle and protection from the oppression and exploitation of the dominant elite. Particularly under neoliberalism the dominant elite has had no qualms about using their high level on the social structure to their own advantage even if it means the ruthless treatment of the weak and the sick. But it is not this image of the dominant elite that is projected to people who only see civilized lifestyles they would like themselves. Well-known New Zealand historian, Keith Sinclair when talking about New Zealand workers stated: "Only a few workers were convinced by Marxian dogma that the state could never promote their welfare. The majority still seemed to regard their 'historic mission' as the achievement of bourgeois living standards, of bourgeois respectability, rather than the abolition of the bourgeoisie" (Sinclair, 1991: 203–4).

For fifty-eight years economic, social, and cultural rights have been confined to discussion among elite circles with the liberal democracies, led by the United States, mainly responsible for the torturously slow progress of these rights at the United Nations (see later chapters) and their negligible education around the world.

The United Nations Committee on Economic, Social and Cultural Rights, a UN body monitoring the implementation of the Covenant on Economic, Social and Cultural Rights, was created in 1985. One of the major achievements of the Committee has been the concept of the core minimum obligations of the state with respect to economic, social, and cultural rights (see the General Comments). However, a major flaw has been its failure to regard human rights education, including economic, social, and cultural rights, as a core obligation (this is further discussed in chapter 2). Core minimum obligations with respect to the right to development should also be devised (see later chapters). Another flaw stems from the division of the Universal Declaration of Human Rights into two covenants whereby one set of rights can be prioritized over another (see chapter 2).

Since 1990 the United Nations Committee on Economic, Social and Cultural Rights has been contemplating the adoption of a complaints procedure (Optional Protocol) for the International Covenant on Economic, Social and Cultural Rights to enable those suffering social injustice to take their complaint to the United Nations (Arambulo, 1999:199). Over the past three years, open-ended working groups discussed whether to draft the Optional Protocol. During most of this time there was strong resistance to drafting an Optional Protocol from the American camp, including Australia, Britain, and Canada and American allies Japan, Egypt, and Saudi Arabia. Unlike these states, which prioritized civil and political rights New Zealand promoted the equal status of both sets of rights (in line with the position of the United Nations) but tried to steer a middle course being against immediate drafting but happy to continue with discussions. Another reason New Zealand did not want to be allied too closely with the American camp may be because many of these states have been subjected to major terrorist attacks in recent times, indicating the ideological nature of global terrorism (this is discussed more in later chapters). While, at the United Nations, the leading liberal democracies refused to make a long-term, ideological commitment to help the poor, domestically they supported short-term, charitable gestures such as the G8's debt relief, the Make Poverty History campaign and Band Aid. However, in June 2006, eventually receiving the considerable support of states, the United Nations Human Rights Council issued a mandate to draft the Optional Protocol. The procedure in making a complaint to the United Nations under an Optional Protocol has required that the complainant must exhaust all domestic remedies first. In 1989 when New Zealand acceded to the Optional Protocol for the International Covenant on Civil and Political Rights and domestic remedies were quickly put in place in the form of the New Zealand Bill of Rights Act 1990, the Human Rights Act 1993 as well as a number of human rights commissions where complaints could be made. So it could be anticipated that when the Optional Protocol for economic, social, and cultural rights is ratified by states there will be some domestic remedies available for violations of economic, social, and cultural rights. This could enable potential terrorists to seek social justice through the system.

Economic, social, and cultural rights provide a challenge to economic globalization. Yash Ghai states: "The regime of rights provides the nearest thing to a coherent challenge to economic globalization. It emphasizes the importance of human dignity, the right to work in just conditions and in return for fair wages, the right to welfare. . . . Contemporary economic globalization is self-evidently inconsistent with these objectives" (Ghai, 1999: 250). However, as Reins Mullerson has pointed out, it is the resolution of such contradictions that create a more civilized society. This is another reason why core obligations are important to allow some flexibility when contradictions have to be reconciled. For example, trade-offs may be required to ensure core obligations are fulfilled.

In my view, these economic, social, and cultural rights should have been included in domestic law before globalization was embarked upon however the right to development had received little attention.

On December 10, 1998, Mary Robinson, former High Commissioner for Human Rights remarked, when reflecting on the fiftieth anniversary of the Declaration, "we must be honest and recognize that there has been an imbalance in the promotion at the international level of economic, social and cultural rights and the right to development on the one hand, and of civil and political rights on the other." She adds that this imbalance is not only evident at the international level. At the regional and national levels, there has also been greater recognition of civil and political rights in comparison to economic, social, and cultural rights (Discussion Paper Re-evaluation of the Human Rights Protections in New Zealand, October, 2000, 21–22).

However in the same year, 1998, working groups and high-level task forces met at the United Nations to discuss the right to development. The mandate of the open-ended working group is "to monitor and review progress made in the promotion and implementation of the right to development." What is particularly unusual about this declaration is that it is the first United Nations international instrument to recognize the equal status of both sets of rights. It regards violations of these rights and the prioritization of one set of rights over another as impeding progress. The Declaration on the Right to Development (1986) states: "Concerned at the existence of serious obstacles to development, as well as to the complete fulfillment of human beings and of peoples, constituted, inter alia, by the denial of civil, political, economic, social, and cultural rights, and considering that all human rights and fundamental freedoms are indivisible and interdependent and that, in order to promote development, equal attention and urgent consideration should be given to the implementation, promotion, and protection of civil, political, economic, social, and cultural rights and that, accordingly, the promotion of, respect for, and enjoyment of certain human rights and fundamental freedoms cannot justify the denial of other human rights and fundamental freedoms."

Similarly the United Nations Committee on Economic, Social, and Cultural Rights stressed the importance of not marginalizing economic, social, and cultural rights in the free market in its statement to the 1993 World Conference on Human Rights:

> The increasing emphasis being placed on free market policies brings with it a far greater need to ensure that appropriate measures are taken to safeguard and promote economic, social, and cultural rights. Even the most ardent supporters of the free market have generally acknowledged that it is incapable of its own accord of protecting many of the most vulnerable and disadvantaged members of society (UN Doc E/1993/22, para.10).

Consequently, globalization as a form of development should have taken account of economic, social, and cultural rights as well as civil and political rights but according to Margot Saloman such a rights-based globalization has not been the approach of most international development institutions. She states: "The Task Force is concerned with the disregard for human rights inherent in most global strategies for the creation and distribution of wealth. Its consensus on the matter asserts that the primary utility of growth is as an instrument in ensuring the right to development, thus the search for economic growth is approached from a distinctly different angle to that prevailing in most international development institutions. The notion that human rights exist to serve instrumental functions in the achievement of economic ends is now being subordinated. The conclusions of both the Task Force and the Working Group are unequivocal: 'development has to be grounded in sound economic policies that foster growth with equity. . .' and '. . . has to be grounded in economic policies that foster growth with social justice' (Salomon, 2006).

The United States ignores the economic, social, and cultural rights provisions in the right to development. Felix Kirchmeier quotes members of the U.S. delegation: Joel Danies, U.S. Delegation to the 61st Commission on Human Rights, on April 12, 2005 stated that the United States understands the term right to development "to mean that each individual should enjoy the right to develop his or her intellectual or other capabilities to the maximum extent possible through the exercise of the full range of civil and political rights." Also, Lino Piedra, Public Member of the U.S. Delegation, March 22, 2005 states that "the U.S. is willing to talk about an individual's right to development", but not a "nation's right to development, [. . .]. for the simple reason that nations do not have human rights." Kirchmeier adds that "the U.S. also rejects, consequently, the elaboration of a legal binding instrument on the right to development [for example the universal declaration was elaborated into the covenants which are legally binding instruments]" (Kirchmeier, 2006). However, in my opinion, the U.S. position demonstrates a lack of understanding of economic, social, and cultural rights because both sets of rights are meant to represent the interests of all the people of the nation; consequently, it is possible to talk about the human rights of a nation if the nation is conceived as being all the people. Therefore, the right to development can be attributed to the nation and policies such as globalization have to abide by the limitations imposed, that is, economic, social and cultural rights.

There is, I consider, a need for a core minimum obligation with respect to the right to development. This will be discussed more in later chapters but briefly, as States have a right to choose which ideology they follow and usually, this means, where they focus development this should not mean that it totally neglects other sectors. Consequently the State should have a core minimum obligation to foster the individual development of talented and creative individuals within society under the umbrella of both sets of rights, in other words, without any political discrimination. For example, under neoliberalism the focus of development is in the middle class, professional sector, and the Corporations, however, this should not mean that talented and creative people should be totally ignored elsewhere, which often can mean individuals are forced to leave the country to reach their full potential or have to live on the margins of society. Arrangements should be made for the independent funding of such individuals.

It took thirty-eight years for the Declaration on the Right to Development (see Appendix IV), with its recognition of the equal status of both sets of rights, to come into being. Originally it was conceived that there would be only one covenant for the universal declaration but in 1951 it was divided, at the West's insistence, into two covenants thereby separating the two sets of rights (Shue, 1980). This enabled the West to define human rights only in terms of civil and political rights and able to prioritize these rights domestically and internationally. Focusing on a single covenant can lead to overlooking the other so, for example, while, at the United Nations, greater recognition may be given presently to economic, social, and cultural rights and addressing poverty but because of the War on Terror liberal democracies around the world are curbing civil liberties such as the Patriot Act in the United States, the anti-terrorism laws in Britain over the past six years, and the Terrorism Suppression Act 2002 in New Zealand. So food can be given with one hand while freedom is taken away with the other. In my view, there is a need to have only one covenant combining both sets of rights as originally conceived, and the United Nations should work in this direction.

With neoliberal dominance, and its narrow human rights perspective, it could be said that people are being indoctrinated into one side of the truth, that is, only civil and political rights and excluding economic, social, and cultural rights. As a famous nineteenth century liberal philosopher John Stuart Mill said in his book *On Liberty*:

> Not the violent conflict between parts of the truth, but the quiet suppression of half of it is the formidable evil.

One of the measures of the success of the United Nations, in my view, will be not only the achievement of the Millennium Development Goals but also the extent to which they are able to educate people in economic, social, and cultural rights. The violations of these rights are often said to be the underlying causes of many of the world's major problems, wars, nuclear proliferation, terrorism, and so forth. And without such education people will not be able to make informed decisions at election time and have these rights included in human rights law and promoted by their government internationally.

The extent of this education will, in my view, determine the success or failure of the new United Nations Human Rights Council, which recently replaced the discredited United Nations Commission on Human Rights (see later chapters). Article 1 (3) of the United Nations Charter requires states to educate their people in human rights: ". . . in promoting and encouraging respect for human rights and for fundamental freedoms for all without distinction as to race, sex, language, or religion." Sir Geoffrey Palmer states that under the Charter states have a legal duty to promote and encourage respect for human rights and fundamental freedoms. He states: "Although not often acknowledged, members of the United Nations are under a legal obligation to act in accordance with the purposes and principles of the Charter" (Palmer, 1998: 9). The exclusion of economic, social, and cultural rights which are more relevant to ordinary people's everyday lives has meant there is often little interest shown in human rights and sometimes people's reactions can be quite negative.

While the United Nations has implemented various programs involving education of these rights, States have shown little interest in doing so outside of elite circles. A recent initiative by the United Nations was the United Nations Decade of Human Rights Education (1995–2004). States provided a "summary of national initiatives undertaken within the decade." However, examining the responses of these ninety countries reveals human rights are not defined, that is, there is no way of knowing whether or not they include economic, social, and cultural rights. The only States that mentioned these rights were Colombia and the Holy See and with Mexico only referring to health-related rights, which are economic, social, and cultural rights. In April 2000 as part of the "Decade," the Office of the High Commissioner and the United Nations Educational and Scientific and Cultural Organization (UNESCO) launched a world-wide survey on human rights education by addressing two questionnaires to respectively, heads of governments and other principle actors. The purpose of the survey was "to take stock of the human rights education programs . . . . since the launching of the Decade, and to request the principal actors to highlight educational needs, accomplishments and obstacles, and recommendations for the remainder of the Decade." However, it proved to be a failure. While the surveys were sent to 191 countries only 35 replied, and of these, only 26 extensively. The High Commissioner for Human Rights presented a full report on the survey to the United Nations General Assembly on September 7, 2000. The report states that guidelines for national plans of action for human rights education were developed in 1997 but the evaluation "reveals that effective national strategies for Human Rights Education have very rarely been developed" (Report of the High Commissioner for Human Rights to the UN General Assembly on September 7, 2000, "a mid-term global evaluation," A/55/360, 20). The review indicates that "international organizations, both governmental, and non-governmental, have not fully appreciated and utilized the potential for mobilization offered by the Decade" (Report of the High Commissioner A/55/360, 20 (f)). The feedback from nongovernmental organizations describe "a lack of public awareness of and interest in human rights issues, and the difficulties encountered by, and dangers to the physical integrity of their staff and supporters in some countries. The lack of human resources and political will on the part of Governments to support greater and wider knowledge of human rights are also seen as impediments to their efforts and as factors that need to be addressed" (Report of the High Commissioner A/55/360, 19 (126)). Nils Rosemann describes the considerable lack of interest of States in educating their people in human rights. He adds: "The lack of political commitment to the aims of the UN Decade is one reason—among others—for requesting further studies of implementation and follow-up by the United Nations High Commission for Human Rights" (Rosemann, 2003). In 2005, described "as a follow-up" to the unsuccessful "Decade" the UN embarked on the World Programme for Human Rights Education which as a first step focuses on human rights education in schools, however, in response to my request for information from the UN High Commission for Human Rights regarding human rights education. I was informed by the Methodology, Education, and Training Unit that, "according to our records, a statistical data on countries teaching economic, social and cultural rights and civil and political rights in schools is not available"(personal correspondence, March 14, 2006). In

1998 New Zealand developed a human rights module for primary, intermediate, and secondary schools, however it is not known how many schools have chosen to take up the option in their social studies curriculum. I am informed by Rosslyn Noonan, the Chief Human Rights Commissioner, that research is presently under way to find out the extent of human rights education in New Zealand schools.

In New Zealand, the Human Rights Commission admits that while they have a responsibility under Section 5(a) of the Human Rights Act 1993 to educate people in economic, social, and cultural rights, successive governments have refused to fund it. Also, at the international level (e.g., the United Nations, the Asia Pacific Forum), New Zealand promotes the equal status of the two sets of rights but says nothing domestically (see chapter 5). Since the Vienna Declaration and Program of Action was adopted in June 1993 only fourteen countries (including New Zealand) have developed action plans which often include economic, social, and cultural rights and require consultation with NGOs. New Zealand released its national plan of action in February 2005. The education is very limited with the Consultation Facilitator for the action plan reporting that 4,558 people were approached. However, the action plan received very little publicity with Index New Zealand, only citing twelve articles and to my knowledge its inclusion of economic, social, and cultural rights was barely mentioned. Index New Zealand is located in the New Zealand Public Library and lists articles written in New Zealand and covers New Zealand popular periodical literature, professional and trade journals, scholarly journals in the arts and humanities and the social sciences, and New Zealand newspapers. From 1988 to 2006 only seventeen articles on economic, social, and cultural rights were cited (approximately one per year) in Index New Zealand compared to about 1,547 articles on civil liberties in the same period. However, despite this lack of education the action plan represents a milestone for economic, social, and cultural rights in New Zealand.

The action plan was released fifty-seven years after former Prime Minister Peter Fraser and the New Zealand delegation at the "Great Debate" in 1948 upset their Western allies when they promoted the inclusion of both sets of rights in the universal declaration. At the "Great Debate," the West, led by America, only wanted civil and political rights (traditional civil liberties and democracy) included, the East European Communists only wanted economic, social, and cultural rights (social justice) included while the Latin American states wanted both sets of rights (Craven, 1995: 17). Consequently human rights were to be a political football, although only at an elite level, until the collapse of communism in 1989. Professor Gordon Lauren of University of Montana, USA, who came to New Zealand in 1998 to research New

Zealand's involvement in 1948 stated: "In launching this revolution, New Zealand was far out in front of other nations, though its role is not generally known and certainly not appreciated" (Lauren, *Herald*, 1998).

In my opinion, the failure to educate people in economic, social, and cultural rights since 1948 reflects the dominance of the liberal democracies. People were deliberately kept ignorant of these rights irrespective of the fact that such education is the legal duty of these global elites under the UN Charter. Richard Nordahl states:

> Dominant elites in nearly all societies have a vested interest in maintaining their privileges, and thus in giving their own biased/self-interested interpretations about what the international standards should be and what rights are required for their societies. In order for there to be genuine dialogue, people from all sectors of society, especially those from the less privileged sectors, should be involved in the discussions. Ideally, this dialogue would be theoretically informed, including Marxian theory (Nordahl, 1992: 179).

I consider these elites are concerned that such education will replace liberal elite control with people control of the human rights agenda through the democratic process. For instance, our council (the Human Rights Council Inc., New Zealand) helped set up the Human Rights Party, promoting both sets of rights in the New Zealand Plan of Action for Human Rights, and stood candidates in the last two elections. Because of such possibilities elites prefer to keep the people ignorant of economic, social, and cultural rights.

By refusing people this peaceful avenue for achieving social justice means that some may resort to violence such as terrorism as a last resort. In the words of the Universal Declaration of Human Rights: "Whereas it is essential, if man is not to be compelled to have recourse, as a last resort, to rebellion against tyranny and oppression, that human rights should be protected by the rule of law."

The rise of economic, social, and cultural rights does not mean that liberal elites will implement these rights in full, in fact, they can be manipulated to serve the purposes of the elite. There has been much discussion at the UN on piecemeal approaches to the covenant on economic, social, and cultural rights which may not reflect the spirit of the covenant (for a full discussion on the a la carte versus comprehensive approaches to economic, social, and cultural rights, see later chapters). But this is why education is necessary from the bottom-up to keep the elites honest.

According to The Social Report 2006 published by the New Zealand Ministry of Social Development, voter turnout of the eligible population in 2005 was 77 percent. Voter participation in general elections declined sharply from 89 percent in 1984 to 78 percent in 1990, increased slightly to 81 percent in

1996, then declined again to a new low of 72.5 percent in 2002. In 2005 the turnout recovered to the level recorded in the 1999 election. The decline in voting over the past two elections may indicate people feel increasingly powerless to influence their governments. This is indicated by Massey University's New Zealand Value Surveys with many respondents, 85.4 percent in 1998 (New Zealand Human Rights Commission, 2004: 101) and 74 percent in 2005 (Rose, Perry, et al, 2005, 32) believing that "the public had little control over what politicians did in office." In September 2004, following facilitated consultation events involving 3,144 New Zealanders around the country, the Human Rights Commission stated: "There is dissatisfaction with the perceived responsiveness of government and political institutions in New Zealand" and identified it as an area "we could do better" (New Zealand Human Rights Commission, Human Rights in New Zealand Today, 104). Robin Gwynn, former associate professor in history at Massey University, who relinquished academic life "in order to oppose the damage being done to education and society in general throughout New Zealand," stated in his book *The Denial of Democracy* in 1998: "The wishes and opinions of the people have become of little account. Politicians, civil servants and heads of State Owned Enterprises freely make decisions with scant regard for the long-established traditions of democratic government" (Gwynn, 1998).

It seems the decline of democracy and the experience of powerlessness by the general population may also be the case in other liberal democracies. The Power Commission, led by Helena Kennedy QC, a member of the House of Lords, was set up in the United Kingdom in 2004 to understand the reasons for the decline in participation in "formal democracy" and to propose solutions to reverse the trend. In 2001, only 59 percent of the British public turned out to vote—the lowest since 1918. It published its report in February 2006, and the Power Commission concluded that people feel they lack a voice and lack choices because the political parties were too similar. The report states: ". . . citizens do not feel that the processes of formal democracy offer them enough influence over political decisions—this includes party members who feel they have no say in policy-making and are increasingly disaffected . . . . the main political parties are widely perceived to be too similar and lacking in principle" (The Power Inquiry, 2006: 17). The report adds that the democratic process is becoming increasingly elitist. It states: "Politics and government are increasingly slipping back into the hands of privileged elites as if democracy has run out of steam" (The Power Inquiry, 9–10).

With the introduction of neoliberalism governments no longer listened to the people, elite rule was legitimized not by democracy, which only consisted of periodic elections, but by human rights narrowly defined as civil rights.

For instance, in New Zealand immediately following the collapse of communism in East Europe in 1989, civil and political rights were prioritized in the form of the New Zealand Bill of Rights Act 1990 and the Human Rights Act 1993 plus a number of commissions promoting individual freedoms (and ignoring social responsibility) and acting as a watchdog on government (this is analyzed in more detail in later chapters). It was no longer the people watching government, it was the elite watching their fellow elite in government. Using these selective human rights, which were far more in elite interests, they misled people into thinking that the rights chosen reflected the interests of all equally simply by using the term human rights. In addition the people had no way of knowing that economic, social, and cultural rights had been omitted or even that they existed. Even the electoral rights included in section 12 of the bill of rights were limited to formal requirements. For example, not mentioned but contained in the International Covenant on Economic, Social and Cultural Rights was the right "to take part in the conduct of public affairs, directly or through freely chosen representatives" (Article 25(a)) and "to have access, on general terms of equality, to the public service in his country" (Article 25(c)). It seems clear that it was civil rights rather than democracy that was being prioritized in order to legitimize the government's pursuit of neoliberal policies at the domestic level in line with other liberal democracies.

Chapter Two

Political Tolerance and
Core Minimum Obligations

It is not often realized that economic, social, and cultural rights first gained its most significant recognition not in socialist countries but in America. During the 1930s Great Depression former United States president Franklin Roosevelt's New Deal introduced a new age of social responsibility. Perkins describes this as

> a positive conception of responsibility never emphasized before . . . responsibility . . . to relieve want and unemployment through the federal agencies, responsibility for providing for the farmer a larger part of the national product, responsibility for the development of national resources on a more grandiose scale, responsibility for the maintenance of industrial peace, enlarged responsibility for the operation of the nation's credit system (Perkins, 1965: 2).

The Roosevelt era also involved greater participation in economic development. Perkins states: "The balance of power between the most important groups was substantially changed. Unionism, especially industrial unionism, attained a much greater importance. The farmer, neglected in the twenties, attained a new political power. The less fortunate economic groups became more self-conscious than ever before and disposed to exert their influence." Previously suppressed by narrow self-interest Roosevelt's broader vision unleashed a flood of new, original ideas. "And paradoxically," adds Perkins, ". . . along with all this went an immense increase, in the second half of the period, in the scope and sweep of American business enterprise, in the magnitude of the tasks performed by the industrial machine, in technological advance. Never before, as the epoch closed, had men faced a future so brightly illuminated with the hope of scientific progress and widening productivity" (Perkins, 965).

The social responsibility exhibited by the liberal democratic system in the Roosevelt era was a leading example of Modern Liberalism. However, it was not revolutionary because the liberal elite whose ideology reflects the Constitution were not challenged. Perkins states: "The story of the Roosevelt years in domestic affairs is a story of adjustment, not of revolution." However, after his "Four Freedoms Address" in 1941: freedom of speech and expression, freedom of religion, freedom from want and freedom from fear (The "Four Freedoms," Franklin D. Roosevelt's Address to Congress (Internet, January 6, 1941), Chapter 36), Roosevelt went down a revolutionary path.

Toward the end of his twelve years in office Roosevelt in his 1944 State of the Union address proposed the introduction of economic and social rights in a second "economic bill of rights." Such rights with equal status to civil and political rights posed a direct threat to the elite and consequently all those who had benefited from the status quo. He considered the inclusion of this second bill of rights would result in "true" freedom. Roosevelt recognized that people cannot be free if they do not have sufficient opportunities in life and that it was only socially responsible to ensure this was the case. Without such opportunities you could not make use of your civil and political rights. For Roosevelt "true" freedom meant freedom for everyone, not just primarily an elite. And it was not about income equality it was about equal rights which includes the provision of sufficient opportunities to improve one's income status if one so desires.

Roosevelt states:

> We have come to the clear realization of the fact that true individual freedom cannot exist without economic security and independence. 'Necessitous men are not free men.' People who are out of a job are the stuff of which dictatorships are made. In our day these economic truths have become self-evident. We have accepted, so to speak, a second bill of rights, under which a new basis of security and prosperity can be established for all—regardless of station, race or creed" (Steiner and Alston, 1996: 258–259).

Roosevelt recognized that even the poorest person has something to say and needs to have his/her voice heard and when individuals are reduced to nothing so are their rights which are then no longer universal but merely serve the interests of the rich and powerful. The second economic bill of rights signaled a wider participation in the control of the human rights agenda and co-operation rather than competition between groups. The Constitution, with its high standards for individual freedoms, had been a major barrier to social responsible policies such as welfare. Steiner and Alston state:

Let there be no doubt. The United States is now a welfare state. But the United States is not a welfare state by constitutional compulsion. Indeed, it became a welfare state in the face of powerful constitutional resistance: federalism and, ironically, notions of individual rights—economic liberty and freedom of contract—held the welfare state back for half a century; and a constitutional amendment was required to permit the progressive income tax which was essential to make the welfare state possible . . . . Jurisprudentially, the United States is a welfare state by grace of Congress and of the states . . . (Steiner, 272).

A year before Roosevelt's death in 1945 a draft international bill of rights was prepared by a committee of the American Law Institute in 1944 and included the rights to education, work, reasonable conditions of work, food and housing, and social security. Roosevelt's vision was so radical it was removed from the people's domain to the elite domain, including the United Nations. The dialogue on economic, social, and cultural rights was to remain at the elite level ever since and thereby ensure the liberal elite's hegemony was hidden from the people.

Although the Soviet states championed economic, social, and cultural rights at the United Nations during the Cold War the initiative for their inclusion in the Universal Declaration of Human Rights came from elsewhere. Hunt states their origins include the American Law Institutes draft international bill of rights which was completed in 1944, President Roosevelt's proposal for an "Economic Bill of Rights" in the same year, the President's Four Freedoms Address given in 1941, the Atlantic Charter adopted by Roosevelt and Prime Minister Churchill also during 1941, and the work of the International Labor Organization founded in 1919 (Paul Hunt, *Reclaiming Social Rights*, (Dartmouth Pub.1996), 4).

Hunt describes the major contribution to the declaration made by America, quoting John Humphrey, head of the UN Division on Human Rights responsible for preparing the Universal Declaration. Humphrey stated, "The best text from which I worked was the one prepared by the American Law Institute, and I borrowed freely from it" (Hunt, 4).

Steiner and Alston state that "in the drafting of the relevant provisions (Articles 22-27) in the declaration, strong support for the inclusion of economic, social, and cultural rights came from the United States (a delegation led by Eleanor Roosevelt), Egypt, several Latin American countries (particularly Chile) and from the Communist countries of Eastern Europe. Australia and the United Kingdom opposed their inclusion, as did South Africa . . ." (Steiner and Alston, 1996), 260).

However, America then completely reversed its support for these rights. Perhaps when confronted with the strong Soviet support for economic, social, and cultural rights but no support for civil and political rights, America may have considered it necessary to only promote traditional civil liberties and democratic freedoms to ensure these rights were not minimized. Hunt quotes Philip Alston who argues that the Cold War changed what was a rational and balanced debate between 1944 and 1947 into "a struggle that encouraged the taking of extreme positions and prevented objective consideration of the key issues raised by the concept of economic and social rights" (Hunt 8). But perhaps more likely America's liberal elite had regrouped following Roosevelt's death and regained control of the human rights agenda. For the past fifty-eight years America has been the major opponent of economic, social, and cultural rights even after the collapse of communism in Eastern Europe in 1989.

Tyson and Aziz Said describe what has typically been the Western elite position. They state: "The model of the modern democratic state was—and still is—a capitalist, mercantilist, middle-class system and society, emphasizing civil and political rights, and arguing that cultural, economic and social rights will come later, that they will have to wait, because after all, 'these things take time,' as old segregationists in the South of the United States used to say" (Tyson and Said, 1993: 591).

The attitude toward the International Covenant on Economic, Social, and Cultural Rights has varied from administration to administration. David Forsythe states:

> Although both the Carter and Clinton administrations have endorsed the UN Covenant on Economic, Social and Cultural Rights, it remains especially controversial in Washington. The Republican Party [including Ronald Reagan and George H.W. Bush] and conservatives in general remain strongly opposed to the notion that the U.S. government should be obligated, without the fundamental discretion to choose otherwise, to provide such things as food, clothing, shelter, and medical care to those who cannot purchase them in private markets. (Forsythe, 2000: 29).

America made its ideological position clear at the United Nations Commission on Human Rights discussion of the Optional Protocol for the International Covenant on Economic, Social and Cultural Rights in March 2004. The United States sees economic, social, and cultural rights only as aspirations to be attained progressively while civil and political rights are immediate. The U.S. representative stated: "Economic, social and cultural rights does, however, not fall under international decision making. While all rights are universal, there is a clear distinction between civil and political rights and economic, social and cultural rights. Economic, social and cultural rights must be progressively realized while civil and political rights are immediate."

However, this is not the view of the United Nations and given the considerable support given by states to draft an Optional Protocol for the International Covenant on Economic, Social and Cultural Rights (which America opposed) suggests the majority of states consider many economic, social, and cultural rights can be immediately addressed.

Francis Fukuyama states that the number of liberal countries in 1990 was sixty-one and about double that in 1975 indicating that the neoliberal ideology was growing in strength prior to the collapse of communism in Eastern Europe in 1989 (Fukuyama, 1992: 49–50). But the collapse of the Soviet bloc was a major impetus to neoliberalism. Tony Evans states:

> With the end of the Cold War, all resistance to the neo-liberal approach to human rights seems to have vanished. The now unmatched dominance of civil and political rights derives from a set of principles that emphasizes the freedom of individual action, non-interference in the private world of economics, the right to own and dispose of property, and the important principles of laissez-faire and free trade. The move to reduce state support for economic and social programs in all Western countries during the last two decades, a trend which is now accepted as desirable globally, is indicative of the predominance of the neo-liberal approach to rights. . . . For neo-liberals, economic, social and cultural rights may be legitimate aspirations but they can never be rights (Evans, 1999: 33–34).

It had been hoped that the collapse of the Soviet bloc would see the end of using human rights as a political football and the West would adopt both sets of rights but this was not to be the case.

David Beetham adds that

> although in theory the end of the Cold War could have provided an opportunity for ending the sterile opposition between the two sets of human rights, in practice it has reinforced the priorities of the United States, the country which has been most consistently opposed to the idea of economic and social rights. And the more general loss of credibility of socialism in any form has deprived the poor everywhere of an organizing ideology for political struggle and the politics of redistribution (Beetham, 1995: 43).

Instead human rights was to used to legitimize the globalization and privatization policies of global elites which may not have reflected the democratic will of the people.

This same 'them versus us' approach at the domestic level is being reflected at the international level toward countries which are not liberal democracies. For instance, President George H.W. Bush's Address to the

Nation on January 10, 2007, divided the world into moderates and extremists. He states:

> The challenge playing out across the broader Middle East is more than a military conflict. It is the decisive ideological struggle of our time. On one side are those who believe in freedom and moderation. On the other side are extremists who kill the innocent, and have declared their intention to destroy our way of life. In the long run, the most realistic way to protect the American people is to provide a hopeful alternative to the hateful ideology of the enemy, by advancing liberty across a troubled region.

Yet America fails to see its own extremist position with respect to economic, social, and cultural rights whose omission helped result in the structural violence inflicted on, for example, Arab states by the structural adjustment programs of the IMF and World Bank in the late 1980s and early 1990s, which resulted in considerable poverty and left many disenchanted unemployed youth. It will be shown later had the democratic policies of the Bush administration included economic, social, and cultural rights it may have been more effective in getting the support of domestic religious elites and offer some genuine hope for a better future for the many disenchanted unemployed youth in the Arab states.

However, it seems the neoliberal ideology has had some ideological success. This is illustrated by the doubling of liberal democracies around the world since 1977. For example, in 1977 there were forty-three liberal democracies (28 percent of countries) but by 2007 there were 90 (47 percent of countries) (Rummel, 2005). While there has been some ideological success this has not seemed to translate into better quantity and quality of lives apart from the elites.

According to the Human Development Report (2005) extreme poverty fell from 28 percent in 1990 to 21 percent today (2005) (Human Development Report 2005, 20) but "this improvement has been uneven." The Human Development Report states: "Amid the overall progress, however, many countries suffered unprecedented reversals. Eighteen countries with a combined population of 460 million people registered lower scores on the HDI (Human Development Index) in 2003 than in 1990" (Human Development Report 2005, 21). The report states this was particularly the case in sub-Saharan Africa and the former Soviet Union.

The unevenness of development in terms of quantity of life is compounded by a serious, almost global, decline in quality of life. As the gap between rich/powerful and poor/powerless within and between countries increases so the hope of the poor, which sustains them as much as food, diminishes considerably leading to lives of seemingly never ending humiliation.

The Human Development Report 2005 states that of the 73 countries for which data are available, 53 (with more than 80 percent of the world's population) have seen inequalities rise, while only 9 (with 4 percent of the population) have seen it narrow. The report adds that this holds true in both high- and low-growth situations (such as China in the first case and Bolivia in the second) and across all regions (Human Development Report 2005).

The New Zealand experience reflected this global trend. The Social Report 2006 states that income inequality rose between 1988 and 1991, then plateaued, and has been rising since 1994. The report states that most of the observed increase in income inequality has been due to a larger overall rise in incomes for those in the top 20 percent of incomes than for those in the bottom 20 percent of all incomes. The latter have only increased a little, once adjustments for inflation are made, whereas those in the top 20 percent of incomes have climbed by more than a third (The Social Report 2006, New Zealand Ministry of Social Development).

Comparisons with other OECD countries are available using a different measure, the Gini coefficient. The latter measures income inequality, with a score of 100 indicating perfect inequality and a score of 0 indicating perfect equality. Around 2000, New Zealand's score of 33.9 indicated higher inequality than the OECD median (30.1) and a ranking of 18th out of 25 countries. New Zealand's score was slightly higher than those for Canada (30.1), Australia (30.5), and the United Kingdom (32.6) and lower than that for the United States (35.7). The 2004 figure for New Zealand was 33.5.

The effects of such income gaps on the poor's civil and political rights is indicated by the major study of the World Bank (2000 to 2002) entitled Voices of the Poor which consists of three books that bring together the experiences of over 60,000 poor women and men. Although the study does not define poverty in human rights terms (which is also the case with the Millennium Development Goals), it is apparent that the world's poor are not only often severely deprived of their economic, social, and cultural rights (economic security) but also their civil and political rights (individual freedoms). The report states: "Poor people use metaphors of a trap, of prison and of bondage"; "Poor people repeatedly stress the anxiety and fear they experience because they feel insecure and vulnerable. Most say they feel less secure and more vulnerable today than in previous times"; "Poor people frequently describe problems with accessing information about government, market and civil activities, particularly outside their communities";

Poor people are disadvantaged by lack of information, education, skills and confidence. Many factors contribute to limited personal capability, including physical isolation, being cut off from the powerful and the wealthy, lack of access to media and limited schooling. . . ."; " Insecurity has increased. Violence is on the rise, both domestically and in the society. And the poor feel they have been by-passed by new economic opportunities.

In addition, as shown in chapter 1, the lack of human rights education leads to ignorant populations unable to take advantage of their civil and political rights and articulate their problems in a language the elite can understand. While lack of economic, social, and cultural rights leads to high illiteracy and a desperate struggle to fulfill immediate needs there is little time or money to make use of individual freedoms in the hope of reaping some future benefits. The voices of the poor are increasingly drowned out by an increasingly wealthy and powerful elite.

It is the increasing powerlessness, a result of minimal human rights, that is causing a huge decline in quality of life. While one can come to terms with one's reality, no matter how unjust, it is extremely difficult to constantly endure the humiliation of powerlessness. A report titled "Human Rights and Poverty Reduction—A Conceptual Framework"—published by the Office of the United Nations High Commissioner in 2004 states: "Fundamentally, a human rights approach to poverty is about empowerment of the poor. One of the clearest and most persistent themes in the series Voices of the Poor is the powerlessness of the poor. For example, the second volume, Crying Out for Change, is organized around an examination of the 'ten interlocking dimensions of powerlessness and ill-being [that] emerge from poor people's experiences.'" The report provides a top-down solution: "The challenge for development professionals, and for policy and practice, is to find ways to weaken the web of powerlessness and to enhance the capabilities of poor women and men so they can take more control." The report considers that human rights can help empower the poor, "expanding their freedom of choice and action to structure their own lives." It states: "Provided the poor are able to access and enjoy them, human rights can help to equalize the distribution and exercise of power both within and between societies. In short, human rights can mitigate the powerlessness of the poor." It adds: "To use the language from Crying Out for Change, human rights provide one way of weakening 'the web of powerlessness' and enhancing 'the capabilities of poor women and men so that they can take more control of their lives.'"

In my experience the powerlessness stems largely from being locked out from positions of influence—government-funded community organizations, government departments, the mainstream news media, inability to influence politicians, and lack of representation for the poor. This plus the overwhelming social conformity created by a neoliberal ideology which reaches into every aspect of society gives one a constant sense of powerlessness. People are also loath to make complaints because of the hostile attitude of the bureaucracy intent on cutting costs and because their complaints are heard by professionals with every reason to want to uphold the status quo. In addition, the economic struggle for survival plus ignorance of human rights makes matters far worse. In short, the elite has found a myriad of ways to crush hope and without hope you simply cannot persevere at anything. These bureaucratic and business organizations operate in the words of T.H. Marshall as "closed group monopolies." They are "one into which no man can force his way by his own efforts; admission is at the pleasure of the existing members of the group," (Marshall, 1950: 19). With this emphasis on "fitting in," ability is of much less importance. This not only nullifies hope for those for whom ability is a way out of their social prison but it induces considerable conformity to the neoliberal ideology (left or right wing) amongst the elite. This "mind control" is best described by Noam Chomsky, as follows:

"In his preface to *Animal Farm*, Orwell turned his attention to societies that are relatively free from state controls, unlike the totalitarian monster he was satirizing. 'The sinister fact about literary censorship in England,' he wrote, 'is that it is largely voluntary. Unpopular ideas can be silenced, and inconvenient facts kept dark, without any need for any official ban.' He did not explore the reasons in any depth, merely noting the control of the press by 'wealthy men who have every motive to be dishonest on certain important topics,' reinforced by the 'general tacit agreement,' instilled by a good education, 'that "it wouldn't do" to mention that particular fact.' As a result, 'Anyone who challenges the prevailing orthodoxy finds himself silenced with surprising effectiveness.' As if to illustrate his words, the preface remained unpublished for thirty years." (Chomsky, 1998: 25). In my experience, the same process operates throughout the professional, middle-class sector of society. Fear for their positions ensures they are silenced.

The fraudulent nature of civil and political rights, namely their serious lack of universality, is carefully concealed. For instance the above study, Voices of the Poor, is not defined in human rights terms, nor are the Millennium Development Goals. Also, in my experience I have never come across statistical research that looks at the civil and political rights of the poor. Although our Council has the expertise to do such research we have been rejected for funding assistance by organizations which promote these rights. It is obvious that such research is regarded as "too political" and together with the refusal to educate in economic, social, and cultural rights this amounts to deliberate deception of the people.

With minimal choices in life civil and political rights are virtually unattainable. Henry Shue states: "It is fraudulent . . . to promise liberties in the absence of security, subsistence and any other basic rights" (Shue, 1980: 69).

Steiner and Alston also describe how society discriminates against the poor:

It is important to realize that traditional distinctions between classical or negative rights (civil and political rights), and social or positive rights (economic,
social, and cultural rights), and the willingness to provide for judicial enforcement of one but not the other, operate in fact to discriminate against the
poor. To be in a position to complain about state interferences with rights, one
has to exercise and enjoy them. But without access to adequate food, clothing,
income, education, housing and medical care it becomes impossible to benefit from most traditional human rights guarantees. . . . (Steiner and Alston,
1996: 303).

Yet under Classical Liberalism civil and political rights are required for
economic development. T. H. Marshall described civil rights as necessary to
the maintenance of capitalist inequality. He states: "And civil rights were indispensable to a competitive market economy. They gave to each man, as part
of his individual status, the power to engage as an independent unit in the economic struggle and made it possible to deny to him social protection on the
ground that he was equipped with the means to protect himself" (Marshall,
1950: 33–34). It is exceedingly difficult for the poor to engage in economic
development when not only faced with lack of economic security, instability,
and elite oppression but also with minimal civil rights.

The recent comments of Nelson Mandela on "true freedom" and poverty
are in a similar vein to Roosevelt's. He states: "Overcoming poverty is not a
gesture of charity. It is an act of justice. It is the protection of fundamental human rights. Everyone everywhere has the right to live with dignity, free from
fear and oppression, free from hunger and thirst, and free to express themselves and associate at will. Yet in this new century millions of people remain
imprisoned, enslaved and in chains. Massive poverty and inequality are terrible scourges of our times—times in which the world also boasts breathtaking
advances in science, technology, industry and wealth accumulation.

"While poverty persists, there is no true freedom."

And on the subject of powerlessness Mandela states: "People living in
poverty have the least access to power to shape policies—to shape their future. But they have the right to a voice. They must not be made to sit in silence as 'development' happens around them, at their expense. True development is impossible without the participation of those concerned" (Mandela,
2006).

Human rights can be seen as a nonviolent means of achieving freedom,
peace, and social justice in the world. Each violation of human rights can be
seen as an act of violence on that individual while addressing the most seri-

ous acts of violence such as torture and extreme poverty can be regarded as the core obligations of the State (see below). The most well-known and ardent advocates of nonviolence in recent history are Mahatma Gandhi and Martin Luther King, Jr., for whom nonviolence is deeply spiritual. They also maintain that the ends do not justify the means so, for example, you cannot use violence even to achieve just ends. Violence can be inflicted by an act or omission. The former may involve state or nonstate terrorism while the latter may involve depriving people of the means of subsistence when there is enough for everyone. The innocence of the people subjected to structural violence is no less than the innocence of the people subjected to terrorism. Consequently neoliberal policies, which involved the sacrifice of millions of the most disadvantaged for the ends of economic growth and ideological goals could not be justified, even on the elite's own terms, because of the huge deprivation in terms of civil and political rights that is involved, that is, voicelessness and powerlessness. If the ends of the neoliberals justify the means then they may not be surprised when terrorists take the same attitude.

It is rarely discussed but the duty of citizens to their society is spelled out in Article 29 of the Universal Declaration of Human Rights:

"Everyone has duties to the community in which alone the free and full development of his personality is possible."

While some duties can be fulfilled by the private citizen or business sector the final responsibility for ensuring human rights remains with government, as the elected body. Henry Shue describes three types of government duty: ". . . a right can be enjoyed only where individuals and institutions avoid deprivation, protect against deprivation, and aid any who are nevertheless deprived" (Shue, 1980: 81). These duties are now in common usage throughout the United Nations system and human rights organizations. The duty to promote human rights is a modern addition but only occasionally used. These duties are described as 1) the duty to respect—the state respects a person's life and means of a livelihood, 2) the duty to protect—the state is involved in protecting individual's physical security and protecting against forced evictions, 3) the duty to fulfill—the state provides prisons at the appropriate standard and primary education, 4) the duty to promote human rights. For example, the New Zealand Human Rights Commission states that being a State party to the International Covenant on Economic, Social, and Cultural Rights, New Zealand has a duty to respect, promote, protect, and fulfill the rights to housing (New Zealand Human Rights Commission, 2004: 227).

While in terms of international law States generally recognize the equal status of both sets of rights, most having ratified both sets of rights, this is far from the case at the domestic level where only a small number have included economic, social, and cultural rights in domestic law. Of the 188 member states of the United Nations, 156 have ratified the International Covenant on Civil and Political Rights while 153 have ratified the International Covenant on Economic, Social and Cultural Rights (Human Rights Development Report 2006). New Zealand ratified both covenants under international law in 1978 but only bought civil and political rights into domestic law in the form of the Human Rights Act 1993 and the New Zealand Bill of Rights Act 1990. With the greater recognition being given, economic, social, and cultural rights at the United Nations may result in more countries including these rights in domestic human rights law. To achieve equal status with civil and political rights, economic, social, and cultural rights need to be included in the human rights law of States. Greater choice and economic security will enable people to make use of their civil and political rights. There is an immediate need, in my view, for governments to fulfill core obligations with respect to both sets of rights. Equal status of both sets of rights is important because human rights should not favor certain interests over others. It is preferable, in my view, to have equal status at the level of core obligations and only these met than the present high level of legal recognition of civil and political rights on the one hand and the failure to recognize economic, social, and cultural rights on the other. Under the latter circumstances, the poor themselves have an almost nonexistent voice in society, much less than what would be determined as the core obligations of the state. By contrast to the poor the elite benefit considerably from the present situation (see the next chapter on the liberal oligarchy). Some countries, like America, which do not believe in economic, social, and cultural rights, should at least ensure that all people have the civil and political rights promised in the Constitution on the basis of equal rights not just in law but in reality. If you cannot use your civil and political rights then they might as well not exist, and this is often the case with the most disadvantaged. Criminals in the criminal justice system are a special case because the courts are used by the elite to uphold the civil rights in human rights law. In the New Zealand Bill of Rights 1990 under Part II, Civil and Political Rights, seven out of twenty-one sections are devoted to protecting the criminal—"Search, Arrest, and Detention" (New Zealand Bill of Rights Act 1990, chapter 4) sometimes to the dismay of the general public but with human rights education some may take a different view considering that being deprived of economic, social, and cultural rights is a major cause of crime.

America, with its long admirable tradition of respect for freedom of speech and intellectual freedom, could well do much better than any other country in being able to permit their poor a voice. And by a voice I mean a voice in the mainstream, not just at the margins of society. Sometimes it is said that civil and political rights only require the duties to respect and protect but not fulfill (Robertson, 1997). However, the government does fulfill certain civil and political rights. Paul Hunt states: "It is misleading to suggest that civil and political rights require only non-interference by the state. The prohibition against torture, inhuman and degrading treatment, for example, obliges the state to provide places of detention which conform to international standards and to establish training programs for prison and police officers" (Hunt, 56).

To achieve the "full realization" of economic, social, and cultural rights, Article 2(1) the International Covenant on Economic, Social and Cultural Rights requires international assistance, for the state to use the "maximum of available resources" and that the rights are to be realized progressively with a "core content" realized immediately (see the interpretation of the United Nations Committee on Economic, Social and Cultural Rights General Comment 3 below). In addition, this would also include the best ideological and/or economic development model to realize the rights or at least the one chosen by the people. Article 2(1) states: "Each State Party to the present Covenant undertakes to take steps, individually and through international assistance and co-operation, especially economic and technical, to the maximum of its available resources, with a view to achieving progressively the full realization of the rights recognized in the present Covenant by all appropriate means, including particularly the adoption of legislative measures."

The term "by all appropriate means" is interpreted by United Nations Committee on Economic, Social and Cultural Rights which regards any ideological and/or economic development model that best realizes these rights as being the best model (although this would depend on the democratic choice). The Committee states: "In terms of political and economic systems the Covenant is neutral, and its principles can not accurately be described as being predicated exclusively upon the need for, or desirability of, a socialist or capitalist system, or a mixed, or centrally planned or laissez-faire economy, or upon any other particular approach" (UN Document E/C. 12/1990/8).

The addition of economic, social, and cultural rights in law would allow for far greater tolerance when it comes to political and economic development and given that countries will then promote this equal status at the international level it is likely to result in greater cooperation within and between countries.

Consequently, such current development models as Classical Liberalism, Modern Liberalism, Socialism, Asian Values, the Islamic model may be accommodated within the human rights framework so long as the core obligations are met.

Whether it involves state or private ownership/control is of little consequence if it achieves the human rights objectives. Consequently, for example, the private sector will not have an advantage over the public sector in terms of efficiency because it is able to exploit its workers since the private sector will have to be as socially responsible as the public sector. Similarly, at the international level, countries should not use sweatshop working conditions to gain advantages. Nearly all countries have ratified the covenant on economic, social, and cultural rights under international law and should be held to them. An option to deter countries from engaging in such practices is to require such products to be labeled—made under sweatshop working conditions, made with child labor, and so forth.

Such an approach would allow for a much greater degree of political tolerance as it is unencumbered by reliance on liberal elite dominance. The latter no longer favored by the narrow interpretation of human rights will have to compete at the level of equality with other ideologies for the vote of the people.

People may choose a particular elite to take a leadership role, to prioritize certain human rights over others (within limits), or to drive a certain economic model. As stated in chapter 1, in the West, under the narrow interpretation of human rights, people have found that their political parties are too similar and they have little by way of choice. The inclusion of economic, social, and cultural rights will widen the range of political choice.

Such an approach may increase the appeal of democracy worldwide. For example, in countries where the majority is Muslim they may prefer to vote for a Muslim elite. This would not preclude liberal representation or different religions as nondiscrimination with respect to religion, political opinion, and so forth would certainly be a core obligation. The greater political tolerance would mean that more extreme political groups would be less likely to be marginalized and can play a part in the political affairs of the country and consequently be less likely to resort to terrorism.

The United Nations Committee on Economic, Social and Cultural rights was created in 1985. Only the United States opposed the establishment of this new Committee (Felice, 1996: 169). From 1989 to 2005 the United Nations Committee on Economic, Social and Cultural Rights formulated eighteen General Comments including the rights to work, water, health, education, adequate food, and adequate housing. General Comments are produced by the UN Committee on Economic, Social and Cultural Rights to clarify and provide detail on procedures related to its work and, primarily, about the content of specific economic, social, and cultural rights. Some of these General Comments also describe the core obligations of the State. The minimum core content of a right has been described as a "floor" below which conditions should not be permitted to fall (Chapman and Russell, 2002: 9). Fulfilling the core content of a right is the minimum core obligation of the State. The Committee's General Comment No. 3, adopted in 1990, confirms that States parties have a "core obligation to ensure the satisfaction of, at the very least, minimum essential levels of each of the rights" enunciated in the Covenant. As the Committee observes, without such a core obligation, the Covenant would have little relevance explaining that it "would be largely deprived of its raison d'être." Also Section 9 of the Maastricht Guidelines on Violations of Economic, Social and Cultural Rights (1997) maintains that "a state party in which any significant number of individuals is deprived of essential foodstuffs, of essential primary health care, of basic shelter and housing or the most basic forms of education is, prima facie, violating the Covenant." More recently, the Committee has begun to identify the core obligations arising from the "minimum essential levels in relation to the rights to health, food and education." For example, General Comment 14 on the right to the highest attainable standard of health asserts that all States have immediate obligations, including minimum core obligations which are intended to ensure that people are provided with, at the very least, the minimum conditions under which they can live in dignity; enjoy the basic living conditions needed to support their health; and be free from avoidable mortality. They serve, in other words, as a minimum or bottom line for responsibilities of States. They require governments to take the basic measures that are needed to enable people to achieve minimum standards of health, including the provision of essential primary health care. Chapman states that since the opening years of the new millennium the commitment to a right to health for all, once heralded for the year 2000, seems ever more remote. She states:

> Global trends reflect greater gaps and inequalities in access to basic health care. The gap between the availability of health care in developed countries and the least developed countries is widening and there are growing gaps between rich and poor and between different areas within countries. Even in wealthier countries commercialization of the health sector is transforming health services into an expensive commodity increasingly out of the reach of the poor members of the community (Chapman and Russell, 2002: 214–215).

Stephen Lendman states:

> An example of such a wealthy country is America where 47 million people can't afford basic health insurance; over 80 million in total have no health coverage during some portion of each year and most of them are employed; where the Bush administration just proposed sweeping cuts in payments to pharmacies to reduce the Medicaid benefits 50 million poor in the country rely on, can't afford to make up the difference on their own, and may have to forgo medications they vitally need if pharmacies won't fill prescriptions at lower prices.

Lendman adds that the United States ranks 41st in infant mortality, and the World Health Organization (WHO) ranks the country 37th in the world in "overall health performance" and 54th in the fairness of health care despite spending at a current level overall of around $2 trillion a year or about double the amount per capita of the OECD countries that deliver superior health care overall to their citizens as a national priority (Lendman, What lies ahead in the age of neocon rule?, 2007). The introduction of Roosevelt's vision of a second bill of rights would ensure that core obligations with respect to health are immediately fulfilled, for example, the reduction of maternal mortality to levels agreed at the 1994 Cairo International Conference on Population and Development and the 1995 Bejing Fourth World Conference on Women (Maastricht Guidelines, Part II, Section 7). Also any retrogressive measures by the State should, in my view, be subjected to a public referendum (although national security may need to be dealt with more quickly. A vote requiring a super majority of representatives is possible here). According to paragraph 14(e) in the Maastricht Guidelines, the adoption of any deliberately retrogressive measure that reduces the extent to which a right is guaranteed amounts to a violation of such a right.

In addition a nationwide program of human rights education would ensure that people use the democratic process and the courts to gain higher levels of the right to health.

Chapman and Russell state that the problem for many human rights activists is that the "floor" will become a "ceiling," in other words, "That states will do that minimum and nothing more." However, by guarding against retrogressive legislation and ensuring human rights education this problem may largely be overcome. Chapman, in relation to the right to health, states: "Safeguarding the gains already achieved and promoting greater equity and respect for the right to health will require a renewal of public commitment to this goal and the investment of appropriate human and financial resources. This is unlikely to occur without increased public mobilization on the part of the citizens. Like all human rights the realization of the right to health is dependent on a citizenry aware of its rights and willing to fight for them" (Chapman and Russell, 2002: 215).

When applied domestically in the West these core obligations could include the state addressing the problems of long-term unemployment, the use of food banks, serious cases on the hospital waiting list, homelessness, illiteracy, those living well below the poverty line (particularly children), ignorance of human rights, sweatshop working conditions, child labor. Also there is an urgent need to arrive at core obligations with respect to civil and political rights. Between 1981 and 2004 the United Nations Human Rights Council have formulated 31 General Comments on the United Nations Covenant on Civil and Political Rights but have not arrived at any core obligations for these rights. In my experience in New Zealand the elite, the trade unions, and most churches, who are all captured by the neoliberal ideology control the more radical elements by isolating them and refusing to allow funding to ensure there is no challenge to the human rights agenda. To ensure core obligations with respect to civil and political rights requires, in my view, an independently funded radio station, national newspaper, and television channel run by beneficiaries. These could be meeting places for beneficiaries who have no elected representatives in the same way as elite organizations have elected representation as do trade unions, farmers, and superannuitants.

Global terrorism has shown that the United States will even violate their most deeply held beliefs; for example, the treatment of prisoners at Guantanamo Bay and Abu Ghraib violated America's constitutional prohibition against torture and cruel and unusual punishment and habeas corpus. This has undermined the elite's legitimacy and America's international credibility. Core obligations, for example, with respect to torture and cruel and unusual punishment would introduce a firm bottom line. As stated at the beginning of this chapter, the U.S. Constitution provided strong opposition to the welfare state. Although ideally it would be preferable to maximize all human rights, rigidly held high standards prevent compromise with necessary social responsibilities and national security. Of course, by requiring such high standards the liberal, middle-class, professional elite is protecting their interests as it also disregards the equal status principle in order to prevent such compromises. While it is necessary to aspire to high standards there should be a firm bottom line, the core obligations, which is kept. There needs to be a balance between principle and reality while the former always should remain uppermost. As America learned from the aftermath of September 11 it is pointless having high standards if the reality is such that it results in ending up with almost no standards at all at least as far as torture is concerned. Some work on finding the core obligation with respect to freedom of speech is being done in New Zealand. The Human Rights Commission states: "While the significance of the right to freedom of expression has been treated differently in national jurisdictions there is a broad consensus that emerges from the international human rights framework; while some restrictions on expression (not opinion) are proper there is a core to freedom of expression that should not be restricted at all (Rishworth, forthcoming)" (Status report, New Zealand Plan of Action for Human Rights, New Zealand Human Rights Commission, 4).

International cooperation was a contentious issue during the discussions at the United Nations over the past three years on whether to draft Optional Protocol for the International Covenant on Economic, Social and Cultural Rights. Those countries which are economically incapable of providing core obligations need international assistance. According to the NGO Coalition for the Optional Protocol, developing countries argued that the Optional Protocol must include provisions on international cooperation while Western states argued that international law must not be amenable to adjudication regarding the international cooperation requirement in Article 2(1) (see above) as it constitutes a moral rather than a legal requirement. However, this attitude may change if an increasing number of states include economic, social, and cultural rights in law, and if poor countries can reduce the gap between rich and poor (in accordance with 'using the maximum of available resources') and educate their people in human rights (which costs little).

Core obligations were considered in the case of *South Africa v. Grootboom* in October 2000. The court derived the core obligations from the needs of the most vulnerable group. Chapman and Russell state: "The minimum core obligations approach is woven through the Court's opinion, both explicitly and implicitly" (Chapman, 18). The case involved a group of 500 children and 400 adults who were squatting on land in the Western Cape and who brought a case under the constitution challenging their eviction. They argued that the South African government was required to provide them with adequate basic shelter or housing under the Bill of Rights. The South African Constitutional Court unanimously decided that the Bill of Rights required the State to devise and implement a program to realize progressively the right of access to reasonable housing. Given the crisis situation with so many people living in intolerable conditions, the court held that the programs in place were clearly inadequate. The court looked to the parallel provisions in the ICESCR and to international jurisprudence on the right to housing. It decided that there was no doubt that the economic, social, and cultural rights were justiciable and that the government was required to act to fulfill them. The court ordered the government to devise and implement a program within available resources to realize progressively the right of access to adequate housing (Charlesworth, 2002: 68–69). Chapman and Russell state: "The Constitutional Court said also that 'minimum core obligation' is determined generally by having regard to the needs of the most vulnerable group that is entitled to the protection of the right in question. It is in this context that the concept of minimum core obligation must be understood in international law (Chapman and Russell, 2002: 19).

Often a concern expressed with respect to economic, social, and cultural rights is that the judiciary should not make political decisions, however, this problem can be circumvented by using negative judicial review. Paul Hunt suggests that negative judicial review could have been used to address the severe benefit cuts which took place in New Zealand. He states: "In April 1991, the New Zealand government introduced cuts in welfare. According to the Human Rights Commission, the reduced rates brought some beneficiaries below the Treasury's own 'income adequacy' level. If New Zealand law provided that individuals have a right to an adequate standard of living, why could a court not declare that the cuts were unlawful because they violate this right?" (Hunt, 1996: 68). He adds that a ministerial decision could be measured by the court against social rights enshrined in statute. If the court finds the decision inconsistent with a statutory social right, it may quash the decision—but not substitute its own view by telling the minister what to do (Hunt, 1996: 67). The problem could also have been dealt with earlier after the introduction of the bill (e.g., the Finance Bill which resulted in the benefit cuts) in the same way that civil and political rights are dealt with in the New Zealand Bill of Rights Act 1990. For example, Section 7 of the New Zealand Bill of Rights Act 1990 requires that the Attorney-General "as soon as practicable after the introduction of the Bill, bring to the attention of the House of Representatives any provision in the Bill that appears to be inconsistent with any of the rights and freedoms in this Bill of Rights." If also applied to economic, social, and cultural rights, this would avoid much unnecessary litigation.

Some consider economic, social, and cultural rights to be too unrealistic. For instance Maurice Cranston states that a duty must be possible to do. He states: "A right is like a duty in that it must pass the test of practicability. It is not my duty to do what is physically impossible for me to do" (Cranston, 1973: 66). Further, he adds: "Another test of a human right is that it should be a genuinely universal moral right. Thus the so-called human right to holidays with pay plainly cannot pass" (Cranston, 1973: 67).

However, I maintain that at the level of core obligations it is possible to implement economic, social, and cultural rights, and this can be universal. Of course, what is a core obligation in one country may differ from another. For example, some countries place much more emphasis on family than others, and this would affect the core requirements. Focus groups could determine what are the core requirements for each country. Statistical research can be employed to find out whether core requirements are being met and also whether human rights education is being conducted. Microcredit is an example of how core obligations can be fulfilled. Microcredit, where the poor are loaned, without security, a very small amount of money which they invariably repay, offers millions a way out of extreme poverty. According to the Microcredit Summit Campaign Report: "As of December 31, 2005, 3,133 microcredit institutions have reported reaching 113,261,390 clients, 81,949,036 of whom were among the poorest when they took their first loan. Assuming five persons per family, the 81.9 million poorest clients reached by the end of 2005 affected some 410 million family members." In awarding the Nobel Peace Prize in 2006 to Muhammad Yunus and the Grameen Bank for their 30-year involvement in providing microcredit to the poor helping to bring many out of poverty, the Norwegian Nobel Committee commended their efforts to create economic and social development from below and furthering the cause of human rights. The Committee states: "Lasting peace cannot be achieved unless large population groups find ways in which to break out of poverty.

Micro-credit is one such means. Development from below also serves to advance democracy and human rights."

Contrary to the prevailing social mores of the West, which view poverty a person's individual responsibility, microcredit clearly demonstrates that most of the poor, if given the slightest opportunity, will make the most of it. It helps to fulfill the poor's right to development, and empowerment right. The State could well get more involved in microcredit by providing more interest-free loans to beneficiaries to be paid back by slight reductions in the benefit. The fact that States are not also fully involved in providing such microcredit clearly indicates that extreme poverty has little to do with limited resources and much more to do with deliberate social control ensuring a rigid top-down society and a culture of fear ensuring people's silence (I will discuss "divide and rule" in a future chapter).

Some criticize the inclusion of economic, social, and cultural rights as putting too much power in the hands of government but in my view any increased state control of behavior is preferable to the excessive mind control, which is a consequence of the narrow view of human rights.

The major problem facing the human rights activist and the concerned citizen is the elite capture of the economic, social, and cultural rights discourse. Even though these rights are gaining greater recognition at the United Nations and in civil society, the silence of NGOs can be bought. So it is really left up to you to think of novel ways of educating people in these rights.

Chapter Three

The Politics of Human Rights and the Liberal Oligarchy

We are now seeing a swing from elitism to populism at both the domestic and international level. I use the term populism to refer to the majority rather than a people's country, which is for everybody, including minorities such as the elite and the most disadvantaged, and which New Zealand thought itself to be for about thirty years after the Second World War. With populism an underclass and social hierarchy is still very likely to remain. It is not the bipolar world that existed during the Cold War where there was considerable "bottom-up" input from people politicized by socialism, rather neoliberalism completely dominates both internationally and domestically, and there is little challenge from the socialism developing in South America largely because the Western trade unions no longer have credibility having "sold out" to neoliberalism and the human rights agenda as defined by the global elites. Certainly in New Zealand religion has also "sold out" so it is very difficult to see how a non-Christian religion such as Islam, especially Islamic Jihadism, can offer any credible challenge to neoliberalism in the West. Without any ideological challenge the domestic and global elites "call the shots." Chapter 5 will show how economic, social, and cultural rights can be manipulated to suit the purposes of the elite and how the draft OP for the International Covenant on Economic, Social and Cultural Rights ensures that the most disadvantaged are deprived of a belief system—core minimum obligations— which would enable a meaningful "bottom-up" input to limit the excesses of neoliberalism and in conjunction with the right to development ultimately holds out the hope of a united world based on the UDHR where all people can pursue their dreams. The emphasis on democracy represents the majority, largely home owning, working families, and independent individuals. Left wing liberals, in particular, link with the elites of other minorities and global elites to further the human rights agenda. The present shift of emphasis from civil liberties to democracy represents a shift from this particularism (or group interest) to majority interests.

Whereas for most of the past twenty years government was legitimized by civil rights now there is a move away from civil rights to democracy under-lying the legitimacy of government or, it could be said, before government was "good" because it abided by human rights (or at least the narrow version defined by the West) to now, government is "good" because it listens to the people.

Chapter 5 shows how this political shift is occurring at the international level but at the domestic level two recent incidents, which involved what could be described as a moral panic among the left wing liberal middle classes, bear this out. These incidents which involve greater containment of the left wing liberal opposition, with democracy now increasingly likely to le-gitimize government, indicates that the right wing liberals are intent on pur-suing their neoliberal policies despite growing global resistance.

Recently New Zealand experienced a major terrorism scare. On October 15, 2007, after a year of surveillance by police, the Terrorist Suppression Act 2002, in case there were potential breaches, and the Arms Act were used to carry out a raid on those who had attended an alleged "terrorist training camp" in the Urewera mountain ranges in the North Island. The seventeen people who were apprehended come from anarchist, environmental, and Maori sovereignty groups with the latter playing, by far, the leading role. The incident, which is very rare in this country, received worldwide coverage and much domestic media coverage. However, the Solicitor General David Collins, although describing the activities as "very disturbing," decided that the Terrorist Suppression Act 2002 proved to be "unnecessarily complex," "incoherent" and "almost impossible to apply in practice" consequently it was decided not to press on with charges under the antiterror law only under the Arms Act 1983. It was the left wing liberals, lead by Global Peace and Justice, Auckland, which was at the forefront of the protest movement in sup-port of those arrested and wanting a repeal of the antiterror laws and were par-ticularly concerned that most of those appearing before the court failed to get name suppression and consequently bore the terrorist label. This indicates "the goal posts" have shifted with the liberal middle classes who were once regarded as "freedom fighters" are now seen as "friends of terrorists." Such antiterrorist laws have the effect of containing the left-wing liberal middle classes who view these laws as authoritarian although the Terrorism Sup-pression Act 2002 was passed under urgency by 106–9 (the Green Party, de-fending civil liberties, voted against) in parliament ("Terror Law 'faulty,' ad-mits Clark," *New Zealand Herald*, November 9, 2007). The act was passed about one year after the U.S. Patriot Act and would have been very unlikely, given the climate, that if subjected to a public referendum the result would have been much different. However, there are limits to the denial of civil liberties simply because democracy cannot function without some essential civil liberties such as freedom of speech and freedom of the press as people need to be informed and also freedom of movement, association, security of the person, and nondiscrimination are necessary. Referring to September 11, Noam Chomsky does not see any serious curbing of civil liberties in the United States. He states: "I do not think it will lead to a serious restriction of rights internally in any serious sense. The cultural and institutional barriers to that are too firmly rooted, I believe" (Chomsky, 2001).

The second incident in November 2007 involved the Electoral Finance Bill, which "will put caps on spending by lobby groups during election year" (*New Zealand Herald*, November 17, 2007). The intent of the bill is to make the democratic process more fair. Prime Minister Helen Clark said there was "a need for a level playing field" because of "the intrusion of *very* [her stated emphasis] big money in our election campaigns of the kind that wouldn't be tolerated in other liberal democracies" (Newstalk ZB, Mike Hosking talks with Prime Minister Helen Clark about the Electoral Finance Bill, November 19, 2007). The national newspaper, the *New Zealand Herald*, took the rare step of putting the editorial on the frontpage under the heading "Democracy under Attack," considering the bill to be an assault on freedom of speech. It led to sizable street protests against the bill in the three major centers in New Zealand. Under section 7 of the New Zealand Bill of Rights Act 1990, the Attorney-General must advise Parliament at the introduction of a bill if that bill is inconsistent with the New Zealand Bill of Rights Act. The Crown Law Office, which undertook the review, concluded that the Electoral Finance Bill was consistent with the Bill of Rights. The National Business Review described the Crown Law's opinion as ". . . one of the worst, most politically expedient calls on New Zealand human rights legislation in memory" (*National Business Review*, November 17, 2007). Also the New Zealand Human Rights Commission, which rarely criticizes government, described it as a "dramatic assault" on freedom of expression and the right to participate in an election and concluded emphatically that it breached the Bill of Rights Act 1990. The Commission states: "Section 14 of the Bill of Rights states that 'everyone has the right to freedom of expression, including the freedom to seek, receive and impart information and opinions of any kind in any form.' As the [Electoral Finance Bill] seeks to limit election advertising and electoral activity it clearly infringes section 14" (Human rights agency's outcry gains it new respect on the Rights, *New Zealand Herald*, November 13, 2007, A4). It

demonstrates that the move toward a more democratic system is undermining the civil liberties of a section of the elite, and the politicians are now listening more to the ordinary people. As the New Zealand prime minister
stated, most people do not want big money intruding in the democratic
process (Newstalk ZB, November 19, 2007). While this is evidence of more
populist policies the purpose seems primarily to gain the support of the majority in order to pursue neoliberal policies.

Now it seems that the left wing liberals who were at the forefront of the
changes that took place in New Zealand with the Labor Government in 1984
are themselves now being contained by the same "monster" that they created
at the outset—neoliberalism—in the change of emphasis from civil liberties
to democracy. Consequently it is largely the high standards, which protect
their interests, of the left wing liberals that are under assault. Their arguments
would be far more convincing if they also demanded the same high standards
of civil liberties for the voiceless poor and oppressed. For those "true liberals" that stood up for the latter's rights it is unfortunate that they will also get
caught up in the "blame game" which can have devastating consequences at
a personal level.

If the IMF and the World Bank, with the United States a major influence (see
chapter 5), largely controlled the economic policy of States it was largely the
U.S. State Department which determined the human rights agenda. This
agenda, which was to a certain extent inclusive of the trade unions but largely
omitting the most disadvantaged, also lends itself to a populist approach.

The State Department's Country Reports on Human Rights Practices
(2006) are administered by the Bureau of Democracy, Human Rights, and Labor (2007). These Country Reports were initiated in 1993 four years after the
collapse of communism in Eastern Europe and demonstrate how the trade
unions have been assimilated and the poor excluded. The stated purpose of
the reports is to "cover internationally recognized individual, civil, political,
and worker rights, as set forth in the Universal Declaration of Human
Rights." However, economic, social, and cultural rights, also part of the declaration, are almost completely overlooked. Also with respect to civil and political rights the poor are not treated as a special category, rather, the special
categories are women, children, disabled, and indigenous groups irrespective
of class and poverty status. Also the reports focus on the law, government restrictions, and respect for human rights but ignore the human rights violations
of the professional middle classes, who have considerable support at governmental level. For example, while the Country Reports are concerned about
freedom of the press there is no information on whether the media reflects the
interests of society as a whole and whether discrimination is occurring in the
media who could be promoting their own interests.

To what degree the most disadvantaged have a voice is not addressed. For example, if it was found the most disadvantaged were not having their voice heard by the liberal media why couldn't it be required that they have their own national newspaper, radio, and television channel with a mainstream audience? Or, to keep costs down, this could involve some sharing by the present mainstream media. This would be a better approach than that taken by some authoritarian regimes which close down the liberal press. Even if the latter are only promoting their own interests they still have a right to their opinion. Extending freedom of speech by giving a greater voice to the poor would not involve violation of human rights. Also the country reports do not consider whether the human rights establishment in their prioritization of certain human rights and special categories are less than enthusiastic about complaints which challenge the establishment such as discrimination on the grounds of political opinion, for example, universities which fail to uphold intellectual freedom and bureaucrats and the business elite who can discriminate on political grounds. In addition, there is no recognition of nondiscrimination on the grounds of class, property, or social origin although these are included or implied as prohibited grounds of discrimination in Part II, Article 2(1) of the International Covenant on Civil and Political Rights. Rather, the Country Reports seem mainly concerned with the human rights of the middle-class, professional sector and its relationship with government than the relationship between the people and the most disadvantaged with the middle-class, professional sector. However, the trade unions, decimated by neoliberalism, have been accommodated to a certain extent. Workers rights in the Country Reports go beyond the basic requirement of the right to association in the covenant on civil and political rights (Article 22, the International Covenant on Civil and Political Rights) to also include some economic, social, and cultural rights, that is, acceptable conditions of work (Article 7, International Covenant on Economic, Social, and Cultural Rights) and the right to organize and bargain collectively (implied in Article 8 of the International Covenant on Economic, Social and Cultural Rights). These country reports focus almost exclusively on civil and political rights and in so doing considerably favor the interests of the middle-class, professional sector. For example, noninterference by government and the emphasis on minimal government has allowed for a redistribution of the wealth from the bottom to the top and, by default, expands economic freedoms favoring private rather than public control and the elimination of government-controlled protectionism, that is, the promotion of privatization and globalization. Consequently, what was once controlled by the people is now controlled by the private sector thereby further empowering the middle classes generally as the professional sector requires a degree of lifestyle equality between the public and private sectors.

The public sector is concerned to promote the human rights agenda and so legitimize this process. However, Michael Ignatieff, in his analysis of the U.S. State Department's annual report on human rights practice around the world, disputes that "human rights is a style of moral individualism that has some elective affinity with the economic individualism of the global market"; rather he points to "the campaigns by human rights activists against the labor and environmental practices of the large global corporations" (Ignatieff, 2001: 7). He states: "The NGO activists who devote their lives challenging the labor practices of global giants like Nike and Shell would be astonished to discover that their human rights agenda has been serving the interests of global capital all along" (Ignatieff, 2001: 71). He also states: "Human rights has gone global not because it serves the interests of the powerful but primarily because it has advantaged the interests of the powerless" (Ignatieff, 2001: 7). However, in my opinion, while the trade unions have certainly been very harshly treated by neoliberalism they still form part of the capitalist system so both workers and employers have a vested interest in it. And, as shown in chapter 3, the fact is the trade unions have joined the establishment. It is no longer the capitalist versus socialist world of the past. For example, the situation in the nineteenth century was described by Marx as follows: "Society as a whole is more and more splitting up into two great hostile camps, into two great classes directly facing each other: bourgeoisie and proletariat" (Marx and Engels, 1959: 49). This ideological battle continued until the collapse of communism in Eastern Europe in 1989. Since then most socialist groups have been relegated to the fringes of society and play little part in the trade union movement. The "two great camps" now are the establishment led by the dominant liberal elite and the great mass of poor, to which I would also add, those working on very low wages because they can barely play a part in society. The poor's exclusion from society, irrespective of race and gender, represents discrimination on a massive scale. Louis-Edmond Pettiti et al. state: " . . . since 1950, the widening gap between rich and poor has become a form of discrimination as serious as that on ethnic grounds" (Pettiti and Meyer-Bisch, 1998: 164). In my opinion the growing mutual hostility of the two groups is evidenced by global terrorism, who often recruit the poor, and the spread of socialism in South America, the mass protests worldwide against globalization and privatization, and the increasing hatred being felt by many people in the world toward America and, to a lesser extent, Britain for their involvement in Iraq. The situation has been reached where trust in the leading liberal democracies and even the United Nations has plummeted and the people are likely to look to other belief systems, particularly those which incorporate social justice. Thomas Pogge indicates how we in the West fail to make the connection between our actions and global poverty and this could also include even the poverty in our own countries. He states: ". . . it would be unthinkable to us that we are actively responsible for this catastrophe. What could be more preposterous?" If we were, then we, civilized and sophisticated denizens of the developed countries, would be guilty of the largest crime against humanity ever committed, the death toll of which exceeds, every week, that of the recent tsunami and, every three years, that of World War II, the concentration camps and gulags included. What could be more preposterous? (Pogge, 2005).

For the past twenty-three years human rights and development revolved around the liberal middle-class, professional sector and the corporations. The elite has far superior human rights with these rights far from equal as the gap between rich and poor grew. Particularly following the collapse of communism in Eastern Europe in 1989 a large human rights establishment was created to promote civil rights and elite interests. When the State promotes the interests of the elite it also emphasizes civil rights to legitimize its power. It is the elite who are the major beneficiaries of civil liberties (see below). And when it wishes to promote the interests of the majority it emphasizes democracy to legitimize its power. However, it excludes economic, social, and cultural rights, which would also be in the interests of many people so the "rules of the game" are always heavily slanted in favor of the dominant elite. Yet the Universal Declaration of Human Rights is often used by the latter as the authority for liberal rights (i.e., only civil and political rights) but this document should not, in my view, be used as the authority when economic, social, and cultural rights are subject to exclusion from human rights law. For instance, the preamble of New Zealand's Human Rights Act 1993 refers to being "in general accordance with the United Nations Covenants or Conventions on Human Rights" and the preamble to the New Zealand Bill of Rights Act 1990 states "To affirm New Zealand's commitment to the International Covenant on Civil and Political Rights," however, both Acts only include civil and political rights. It would be more accurate to base these Acts on our common law inherited from Britain or even the American constitution (which only deals with civil and political rights) but references in the Acts to the United Nations and the Universal Declaration of Human Rights cannot be justified. As Asbjorne Eide states: "Anyone who wants to pick out some parts of human rights but deny the validity of others cannot refer to the Universal Declaration as the source of validity of the right they refer to. What is left, therefore, is only a reference to their own particular subjective opinions" (Eide, 2000: 110).

The human rights institution, which has developed in recent times to further civil rights, if seen in the light of the equal status principle, it means that human rights have become grossly politicized. The human rights institution now consists of the Human Rights Commission (1993), Race Relations Office (1972) (the latter two commissions are now combined), the Health and Disability Commission (1994), the Ombudsman (1962), the Privacy Commissioner (1993), the Mental Health Commission (1998), the Commissioner for Children (2003), the Retirement Commissioner (1995), the Human Rights Act 1993, the New Zealand Bill of Rights Act 1990 as well as Habeas Corpus Act (1679), the Magna Carta (1297), the English Bill of Rights (1689), the New Zealand Constitution Act (1852) replaced by the New Zealand Constitution Act (1986); there is also NGOs promoting only civil rights: the New Zealand Council for Civil Liberties, the Human Rights Foundation, the Human Rights Network, and Amnesty International. New Zealand inherited its common law rights from Britain. Sir Ivor Richardson describes the common law protections of human rights: "Common law protections of the freedom of person and property are provided by habeas corpus and other civil and criminal remedies. The right to a fair trial according to law is a fundamental element of the criminal justice system. Other human rights, such as liberty of expression and freedom of speech, freedom of assembly and freedom of the press, are protected by the common law. . . ." (Richardson,1995: 63–64).

New Zealand's constitution, unlike the American constitution, is "unwritten," meaning it is not contained in any one document but rather is scattered so New Zealand is still described as a constitutional monarchy. As in many liberal democracies it has a parliamentary system of government that is founded on the principles of representative democracy and an independent judiciary. The powers of the Crown are limited by law and are exercised on the advice of Ministers or by Ministers in the name of the Crown.

The above "constitutionally significant" changes took place with few of the general population knowing about it. Shortly after the collapse of communism in Eastern Europe in 1989 the New Zealand government enacted the New Zealand Bill of Rights Act 1990 and created a number of new human rights commissions. The change in the global balance of power may have given added encouragement to the liberals to force through the Bill of Rights Act. Rishworth states: "Enactment of our Bill of Rights coincided with a spring tide of judicial enthusiasm for the enforcement of fundamental rights and control of government power" (Rishworth, 1995:, 76). However, in disregarding the equal status principle (which New Zealand promotes at the international level), human rights were politicized still further. That this was not necessary is indicated by a Ministry of Foreign Affairs and Trade report: "In the field of human rights, it has been unnecessary for New Zealand to engage in massive legislative change in order to give effect to newly assumed international obligations. The reason for this is that New Zealand, with its strong common law tradition together with the separation of powers and independent judiciary has provided the necessary safeguards for the protection of most civil and political rights" (Inquiry into the Role of Human Rights, (Ministry of Foreign Affairs and Trade, August 2000), 5).

In addition the submissions did not support the bill and the people had little interest in it. By early 1987 according to the Justice and Law Reform Select Committee: "It would be fair to say that the concept of a Bill of Rights has not yet gripped the imagination of the wider public of New Zealand" (Rishworth, 1995: 19). Rishworth adds: " . . . the White paper debates [on the bill of rights] had shown that the bill of rights was largely irrelevant to the concerns of ordinary working people" (Rishworth, 1995: 23).

In addition Hunt states: "The majority of submissions was not in favor of the bill of rights proposal. Nonetheless, the Committee's interim report, tabled in the House of Representatives in July 1987, found "there is substantial merit in a bill of rights" and recommended that the proposal proceed" (Hunt, 1996: 45).

It seems that because of the lack of support for the original intention to have an entrenched bill of rights it was decided to pass the bill as ordinary law. Entrenchment requires greater democratic support than ordinary law, for example, a super majority of Parliament or a public referendum. An example is Section 268 of the Electoral Act 1993 and its entrenchment of certain voting rights. Despite not being entrenched Rishworth describes the bill as "constitutionally significant": " . . . the bill of rights and the Human Rights Act are in a special category of legislation, marked out by the importance of the values which they seek to protect and advance. There are other statutes which fall into the category of the 'constitutionally significant.'" The Constitution Act 1986 and the Official Information Act 1982. . . ." (Rishworth, 1995: 78). While ordinary law would take precedence over the bill Section 6 allowed some influence: "Whenever an enactment can be given a meaning that is consistent with the rights and freedoms contained in the Bill of Rights, that meaning shall be preferred to any other meaning." By 1995 Rishworth stated: "By this time there was little doubt that the Bill of Rights was much more significant than had been thought of by opponents and proponents alike" (Rishworth, 1995: 27). However, the real purpose of the Bill of Rights was, in my view, to create a culture of individual responsibility in Parliament and government departments and ensure that as far as possible people were to take responsibility for their own situation as evidenced by large hospital waiting lists to encourage people to use the private sector, the welfare department referring people to food banks, the emphasis placed on private charities and community-based treatment for the mentally ill (although it would be fair to say the former institutionalization of the mentally ill was far from satisfactory).

Often poor people would be thrown back on the kindness of their fellow poor who would often oblige despite having so extremely little themselves. During this time government was almost completely dominated by liberal elites and the middle-class, professional sector were well-taken care of so had little need for these rights. Complaints from those in other sectors of the economy would be dealt with by professionals who abide by the human rights agenda. For instance, if it is a complaint with respect to women or race it would receive their immediate attention but complaints relating to political discrimination would be low on their priorities.

The purpose of encouraging a culture of individual responsibility is indicated by the Bill of Rights being limited only to the public sector. General Provision 3 states: This Bill of Rights applies only to acts done—

(a) By the legislative, executive, or judicial branches of the government of New Zealand; or

(b) By any person or body in the performance of any public function, power, or duty conferred or imposed on that person or body by or pursuant to law.

Also a Code of Health and Disability, containing many civil rights, became part of the culture of all health bodies and patients who considered their individual freedoms infringed could lay a complaint with the Health and Disability Commission. Those working in government bodies realized that they could be held to account. This reinforced the culture of individual responsibility in the public bodies who wherever possible would avoid providing assistance and when they did it was as little as possible.

In Parliament this culture was promoted by requiring "the Attorney-General to report to Parliament where a Bill appears to be inconsistent with the Bill of Rights" (General Provision 7).

Bedggood states that when the Justice and Law Reform Committee was considering the White Paper's proposal for a Bill of Rights its final report suggested that a bill of rights should include key economic, social, and cultural rights. These were the right to an adequate standard of living, to work, education, property, and participation in the cultural life of the country which were "to be included as something akin to the Principles in Part 1V of the Indian Constitution (Constitution of India (1949))" where such rights are listed as constitutional principles for the State to take into account, but are judicially unenforceable. This recommendation was, however, rejected in the parliamentary debate on the Bill (Bedggood, 1998: 345–346). Hunt states: "This is not surprising since Geoffrey Palmer [the then Labour Party prime minister] the main architect of the legislation, was firmly against their inclusion" (Hunt, 1996: 49).

However, Hunt points out there was little political interest in their inclusion:

. . . . it should be noted that the White Paper's brief and superficial consideration of second-generation rights [economic, social and cultural rights] reflected
the lack of support, at least within the higher ranks of the Labour Party, for their
inclusion in a bill of rights. The inclusion or otherwise of second generation
rights was far from the dominant issue in New Zealand's bill of rights debate
(More dominating and controversial were the issues of entrenchment, supreme
law and Treaty of Waitangi incorporation) (Hunt, 1996: 44).

Furthermore Hunt adds: "(The Justice and Law Reform Select) Committee
rejected the approach of enshrining second-generation rights as directives and
set out its views about how such rights could best be protected." The Committee stated: "In our view the preferable approach would be to try to
heighten the awareness of New Zealand about the existence and the content
of the international instrument and its use both as a goal to aim at and as a
standard against which legislation can be measured" (Hunt, 1996: 46). However as stated in chapter 1 such education, apart from a small number of people concerned with the action plan, never took place.

In addition, Rishworth pointed out that neoliberalism and economic, social
and cultural rights are not very compatible. He states: ". . . New Zealand's
bill of right debate coincided with a Treasury-driven shift away from the welfare state and towards classic liberalism, an ideology ill-suited to the legal
protection of second-generation rights [economic, social and cultural rights]"
(Hunt, 1996).

The concept of individual responsibility (and user pays) was made popular
in New Zealand by Roger Douglas, Finance Minister under the 1984 Lange
Labour government, in his book '*There's Got to Be a Better Way*' (Douglas,
1980). This meant that individuals and groups had to take responsibility for
themselves as government help would be less than forthcoming. In relation to
health Douglas stated: "Almost everyone expects too much of modern medi-
cine and not enough of themselves. The cure for many ailments that plague
us is in our own hands. Attention to lifestyle and environment are a necessary
first step towards self responsibility for health" (Douglas, 1980). Individual
responsibility was seen as being made possible by the choices provided by
civil rights, which in turn guarded against "government interference." Following the collapse of communism in Eastern Europe in 1989 the New
Zealand government disregarding the "equal status principle," greatly expanded civil rights in human rights law with more human rights commissions
to promote these rights (see below). This promoted a culture of individual responsibility in the state sector whereas before it had been one of public service. The effect was that government departments and agencies pushed the responsibility for help back onto the individual and the community. And the
concept of individual responsibility became deeply embedded in the social

mores of much of society disregarding the fact that individuals in the underclass often had paltry choices. This concept was sometimes described as
"tough love," for example, "people have to learn to stand on their own two
feet." This, in the past, was the attitude of mind reserved for criminals and
used only as a last resort. Individual responsibility made it possible to blame
the individual for perceived irresponsibility. Pierre Bourdieu states: "The return to the individual is also what makes it possible to 'blame the victim' who
is entirely responsible for his own misfortune, and to preach the gospel of
self-help, all of this being justified by the endlessly repeated need to reduce
costs for companies" (Bourdieu, 1998: 7). In my experience, equally insidi-
ous is the zero tolerance for anger that has also become ingrained in the social mores particularly of the middle classes. As individuals are to blame for
their own problems they are regarded as being in no position to get even a little angry about anything unless they belonged to the liberal sanctioned radicals, that is, Maori and feminists. But it is extremely difficult not to get angry
when one is saddled with blame for society's ills simply by virtue of belonging to a certain class. The lack of understanding and intolerance of the establishment prevented many of the poor from ringing talkback, getting involved
in politics and attending meetings, in fact, many do not even bother to vote as
they feel society is not meant for them. This concept of individual responsibility is in contrast with the view of Thomas Paine, a famous nineteenth century philosopher often credited with inventing the term "human rights," who
considered that "instead of seeking to reform the individual, the wisdom of a
Nation should apply itself to reform the system" (Thomas, 1997: 137).

   In 1984 the state decided New Zealand needed to face global realities—the
growing dominance of neoliberalism and the need to accept that the "poor
will always be with us." The poor were given the hope of trickle down (that
was twenty-three years ago!) because their social and economic rights did not
exist in the neoliberal belief system so there was nothing to oblige the establishment to redistribute any wealth. New Zealand, which had a long history
of being at the forefront of social justice, and respecting the interests of all,
became elitist and ignored the plight of the underclass. By contrast New
Zealand historian Keith Sinclair, when describing early twentieth century
New Zealand, stated: "If the colony was not yet 'God's Own Country,' as
most of mankind seek in one respect it touched greatness; in its care for the
poor and the laggard" (Sinclair, 1991: 192).

   Sinclair describes what a lot of New Zealanders used to feel proud of:
"That democratic and egalitarian aspiration, that yearning for what was later
called 'social justice' . . . . is the main element in the New Zealand tradition"
(Sinclair, 1991: 188). He also describes the vision of the early colonists from
Britain to be free from poverty: "The new colonial society would consist of a

vertical section of English society, excluding the lowest stratum. It would form, not a 'new people,' but an extension of an old, retaining its virtues, but eliminating its poverty and overcrowding" (Sinclair, 1991: 60–61).

From my experience many New Zealanders now feel there are two New Zealands—rich and poor. This separation was the result of a vicious attack on the trade unions and beneficiaries. Groups such as trade unions, churches, community groups, and the special categories such as women, Maori, Pacific Islanders, and the mentally ill, all had to abide by the human rights agenda for fear of becoming isolated and vulnerable to the vicious attacks of the dominant elite. They all had to copy the elitist hierarchical model of sharp divisions between leaders, members, and the underclass. This contrasted with the egalitarian model of the past when leaders, members, and any others often mixed together. In my opinion, the present outward appearance of tranquility between the groups hides the reality of virtual complete submission to the dominant elite. The churches and the trade unions have succumbed to the human rights agenda as defined by the domestic and global elites and consequently have little credibility when it comes to offering an alternative model to neoliberalism. Both socialism, as developing in South America or Islamic Jihadism, would find it difficult to find roots or credibility in this society and this probably applies to many other liberal democracies whereas human rights, coupled with the economic dimension of the right to development, is part of Western tradition and would represent a far more civilized improvement to neoliberalism.

The separation and division between groups was largely achieved by two major pieces of legislation: the Employment Contracts Act 1991 and the severe Welfare Benefit Cuts of 1991, with their emphasis on individual choice and responsibility. From a society where there was mutual respect between employers and employees (e.g., often drinking in the same bar), professionals were to be separated from workers. The Employment Contracts Act placed severe restrictions on the right to strike, removed compulsory union membership, and required individual rather than collective contracts. This move more than halved the membership of the trade union movement by the late 1990s. Trade union membership dropped from 683,006 (December 1985) to 302,405 (December 1999) (Trade Unions, Membership and Union Density 1985–2003, Household Labour Force Survey, Industrial Relations Centre, Victoria University, Wellington). While the Employment Contracts Act was in operation the 1990s saw strike action fall from 26,800 in 1992, to 7,600 in 1997, to 2,600 in 2000 (Boraman, 2006).

The trade unions turned inwards guarding its interests. The then president of the Combined Trade Unions (CTU), Ken Douglas, wrote that the "focus is on workers rights." Although regarding economic, social, and cultural rights as "complementary to the CTU's campaign on workers rights," he added, "we do not have any plans to broaden our campaign" (personal letter, June 9, 1997, copy available). In addition, particularly with the collapse of communism in Eastern Europe in 1989, socialism, which had played a major part in the trade union movement prior to 1984, was largely marginalized to the fringes of society.

According to Toby Boraman, in 1991 the National Party cut social spending by one third. It savagely cut the rates of all benefits, including invalid and sickness benefits. The harshest cuts were for the unemployed. The unemployed benefit was cut by 25 percent for young people, 20 percent for young sickness beneficiaries, and 17 percent for solo parents. They abolished the family benefit and made workers ineligible for the unemployment benefit for a stand-down period of six months. Toby Boraman considered that these policies represented the harshest attacks upon beneficiaries since the depression of the 1930s (Boraman, January 26 2006). Yet a Ministry of Foreign Affairs and Trade report in justifying the noninclusion of economic, social, and cultural rights in New Zealand law was to state that: ". . . the state's commitment to social welfare rights has ensured that no specific legislative action was required to give effect to the rights protected by the International Covenant on Economic, Social and Cultural Rights" (Inquiry into the Role of Human Rights (Ministry of Foreign Affairs and Trade, August 2000), 5). Rather, given the above benefit cuts, the introduction of student loans and fees, the requirement to pay market rentals for Housing New Zealand homes, and other user pays policies, indicates that legal rights, for instance with respect to benefits, housing, and education, which are ordinary legislation, can easily be changed by government and that only economic, social, and cultural rights included in human rights law with the same status as civil and political rights and the education of the people will provide an adequate safeguard. Modern Liberalism can easily revert to Classical Liberalism without the safeguard of these rights as demonstrated in 1984 in New Zealand.

Despite such severe cuts and unemployment reaching 10 percent in the early 1990s, to my knowledge, the churches were involved in only one significant political protest on behalf of the poor in the past sixteen years: the "Hikoi [walk] of Hope," which involved a walk from either end of the country to the New Zealand Parliament in December 1999. While they "made a difference" by helping people who might not have been helped by the state in their charitable organizations they were not prepared to address the underlying causes and the system change that would be required. Like the majority of New Zealanders, they did not want to "rock the boat." Yet the Catholic Church, which through a small organization called Pax Christi was able to, although to a very limited degree, promote economic, social, and cultural rights. The lowering in the lifestyle of beneficiaries helped prepare the country for the low waged economy which was to come (see below) and even the lifestyles of middle New Zealand became more vulnerable as a result.

Any community group which engaged in political protest threatened to have their funding cut. For instance the Unemployed Workers Rights Centre, which often engaged in political protests in the 1990s, had to form the People's Centre, Auckland, in order to gain funding while Psychiatric Survivors Inc. had their funding withdrawn about six years ago largely because, in my view, of its promotion of economic, social, and cultural rights (see my article on the internet Psychiatric Survivors on the beach). Unlike the other groups the beneficiaries have no generally recognized elite. If there had been the political will beneficiaries could at the time of registering on the unemployment benefit, invalids benefit, domestic purposes benefit, and so forth with the Ministry of Social Development could at a very small sum, each week, join a beneficiaries union which would enable them to vote for representatives of the union at the same time as the national elections. This is an idea that I think should be pursued. This union would then be able to link with the international poor, have representatives at the United Nations, the World Social Forums, and so forth and gain the support of some of the world's most highly regarded intellectuals (many of whom in my experience would only be too pleased to lend support) with international television debates on human rights and poverty and the televised investigation of poverty in various parts of the world all possible especially with the Internet. And yet how extremely little of this is being done by the major international human rights NGOs.

Now New Zealand has a growing underclass consisting of the homeless, those begging on the streets, using food banks, living well below the poverty line, long-term unemployed, often including invalids and sickness beneficiaries, the illiterate and often suffering a mental illness. New Zealand has eight parties in Parliament but Labour and National are by far the most dominant so it is essentially still a two party system. The National Party (the main opposition party) leader John Key, in his State of the Nation address, said National will make tackling New Zealand's growing underclass a policy priority this year and in government. He adds: "We are seeing a dangerous drift toward social and economic exclusion" (Press Release: New Zealand National Party, January 30 2007). No official figures on the numbers involved are available but a recent poll found that "more than eight out of ten people polled say there is such a problem in New Zealand" (One News/Colmar Brunton Poll, February 19, 2007). The numbers in the underclass, which can be perceived as a subclass of the beneficiary sector, often including many who have "fallen through the cracks," who often do not have the core obligations with respect to economic, social, and cultural rights (or civil and political rights for that matter), may have increased if the numbers on sickness/invalid beneficiaries can be used as a rough indicator. In 1985 the total number on sickness and invalid beneficiaries was 31,090 (Broken Welfare, *North and South Magazine*, May 2000). By 2006 this figure reached 145,908 (2006 Census, Statistics New Zealand, Sources of Personal Income, Table 37). Although this also includes the community-based mentally ill, it represents a massive increase of 114,818 in a small country of only four million. In addition New Zealand has experienced high suicide rates. A compilation of statistics between 1978 and 1998 reveals that New Zealand males had the second highest suicide rate of twelve selected countries behind Finland while New Zealand females had the fifth highest suicide rate of twelve selected countries (Suicide Trends in NZ 1978–1998, New Zealand Health Information Services, Ministry of Health). Now that the dominant elite has consolidated their power they feel they can admit an underclass exists and afford to be a little more generous. John Key stated that National policy will give "big boost to the giving tradition in New Zealand" by increasing the amount charities can receive with tax exemptions. Key placed considerable emphasis on providing food for those children who often go to school hungry. The UNICEF Innocenti Research Centre Report Card 7 in its press release on February 15, 2007, places New Zealand in the bottom third of the OECD (so-called group of thirty rich countries) in terms of child well-being. New Zealand is at the bottom of twenty-four OECD countries when it comes to deaths from accidents and injuries under nineteen years old. It is also at the bottom of twenty-three OECD countries for the percentage of fifteen- to nineteen-year olds in education or part-time education.

The low unemployment rate of 3.6 percent (40,000) in 2006, the second lowest of the twenty-seven OECD nations, may reflect more the large numbers of New Zealanders now working for minimal wages in the low wage economy. Although official figures cannot be obtained at Statistics New Zealand, the leader of the National Party opposition John Key stated: ". . . we are a low-wage economy and we have been for a long period of time" (Post-Budget 95bFM Interview 24 May 2005 when Key was finance spokesperson). In addition Key states: ". . . we have a brain drain which is starting to become excessive" (Post-Budget 95bFM Interview 24 May 2005 when he was finance spokesperson). In an article in the *New Zealand Herald*, "Quarter of NZ's brightest are gone," on March 12, its social reporter, Simon Collins, states that "almost a quarter of New Zealand's most highly skilled people have left the country." This is the biggest exodus of skilled workers from any developed nation, according to a report by the Organization for Economic Cooperation and Development (OECD), which takes official statistics from its thirty member nations to produce data on the numbers of expatriates from all countries. It shows that 464,465 people born in New Zealand were living in twenty-six other OECD countries at the last censuses in 2000 and 2001. The figures also show that 24.2 percent of all New Zealand-born people with tertiary educations now live overseas.

Collins adds that "only two other nations come anywhere near this level of 'brain drain'—Ireland (also 24.2 per cent, though marginally behind New Zealand) and tiny Luxembourg (22.2 per cent)." He adds that New Zealand's brain drain is nearly ten times worse than Australia's. Only 2.5 percent of tertiary-educated people born in Australia live outside their homeland. There are 355,765 Kiwis in Australia but only 56,142 Australians here. But expatriates who leave both countries are even more highly educated than the immigrants and better qualified than expatriates from anywhere else, except the United States and Japan. Furthermore, he adds, both countries have a lot more foreign-born immigrants than emigrants. Even if New Zealanders are excluded, Australia has 3.7 million foreign-born residents (21 percent of its population), while New Zealand has 624,405 foreign-born (18 percent), excluding Australians.

Often this "brain drain" is attributed to economic reasons, for example, as a way to avoid paying student loans. However, I consider research would reveal that many of these New Zealanders, particularly professionals, are unhappy with the social direction the country has taken and also feel that the "tall poppy syndrome" and the injunction against "rocking the boat" that exists in this country is a serious curb on their personal development. Consequently, they either have to leave the country or remain, often unemployed, in the margins of society. Also a large number of immigrants were allowed into the country with almost complete disregard of the fact that many New Zealanders were on welfare and had to compete with immigrants for rental accommodation and treatment at the public hospitals. If economic, social, and cultural rights were law, government would have been required to focus on the most disadvantaged in New Zealand first. While such policies reflect the liberal elite's ethnic tolerance it also, in my view, reflects its extreme political intolerance.

With such emphasis on individual responsibility any attempt to change the system became futile because it was 'your' fault, not the system's. There was a dramatic decrease in democratic participation designed to silence people and prevent any challenge to neoliberalism and so ensure the power of the dominant elite. This decline in democratic participation was not just confined to New Zealand. Norman Lewis states: "During the 1990s, it is no exaggeration to suggest that the majority of western society has been squeezed out of public life—the diminishing numbers of people participating in political parties, trade unions, churches, and all kinds of cultural organizations—demonstrates as much. People's lives have, as a consequence, become more individualized and privatized" (Lewis, 1998: 98).

Toby Boraman describes the initial resistance to neoliberalism in New Zealand during the 1990s:

> Even if it is true that the majority of Pakeha [a Maori term for white New Zealanders] did not overtly attempt to resist neo liberalism, a significant minority did. . . . The 1990s, far from being a period of working class passivity [as some commentators claim], witnessed a multiplicity of largely working class struggles against the imposition of neo liberalism. These include . . . . the near general strike in 1991 against the introduction of the Employment Contracts Act [see below] and a wave of land occupations by largely working class Maori in the mid-1990s. (Boraman, January 26 2006).

However this resistance, which lacked real conviction, died out towards the end of the 1990s. Boraman states:

> Nonetheless, this resistance failed. The movements that attempted and still attempt to resist neo liberalism in Aotearoa have been isolated and defeated, and have not led to a more widespread opposition to capitalism. For example, these movements never developed into riots, insurrections, workplace occupations, general strikes and near revolutions (such as in Bolivia and Argentina) that have characterised opposition to neo liberalism overseas. Indeed, resistance in Aotearoa never reached the level of even the miner's strike and the Poll Tax riots of the Thatcher years in Britain (Boraman, January 26, 2006).

A notable exception here has been and still is the Water Pressure Group. He adds: "The late 1990s saw significant working class community based struggles emerge that opposed water privatisation in Auckland. The Water Pressure Group received much popular support through its reconnection squads that reconnected water supply to those homes who refused to pay for the commodification of water."

Jane Kelsey states that in New Zealand the changes were implemented "with no explicit mandate" by a Labour government from 1984 to 1990 and was continued by right wing National Party administrations since. She quotes the English *Economist* magazine as describing the "economic experiment" experienced by New Zealand as "out-Thatchering Mrs Thatcher," and creating "a paradise for free-marketeers—if not for those New Zealanders who have lost their jobs" (Jane Kelsey, "Hatched, Thatched, and Dispatched." That many New Zealanders were not happy with the changes is strongly suggested by the rejection of the first-past-the-post system (FPP) in favor of a mixed-member proportional system (MMP), increasing the number of parties, by voters in a referendum in 1993 although the two major parties, Labour and National, are by far the most dominant—there is now a further six small parties.

Colin James states: "The vote for MMP in 1993 can be read in large part as an attempt to reassert popular sovereignty against what many felt to be an un-mandated policy revolution after 1984 by single-party majority governments" (James, 2000: 5).

While it may be said that New Zealanders should have struggled more against the changes, the fact was that the majority of New Zealanders had little idea what their rights were. In my view, without a belief system you are easily defeated. The political intolerance of the neoliberals is because of their concern at the threat posed by different belief systems.

The Human Rights Commission states: "Among the general population there is little knowledge and understanding of human rights, their relevance to everyday life. . ." ("Human Rights in New Zealand Today," New Zealand Human Rights Commission, September 2004, 376). For instance, in 1978 New Zealand ratified the International Covenant on Economic, Social and Cultural Rights under international law and has to report periodically to the United Nations Committee on Economic, Social and Cultural Right. In 1994 the latter Committee expressed "its concern that no reference is made to economic, social and cultural rights in the text of the Bill [of Rights]" and expressed its concern that "recent extensive reforms in the social security and labor relations system may negatively affect the enjoyment of economic, social and cultural rights. In particular, the Committee notes that reforms introduced by the Employment Contracts Act of 1991, raise questions of compatibility in relation to the rights recognized in articles 7 and 8 of the Covenant." In addition, concern was expressed at "the failure to keep statistical information as to the extent of malnutrition, hunger and homelessness in New Zealand" (Conclusions and Recommendations of the Committee on Economic, Social and Cultural Rights, New Zealand, U.N. Doc. E/C.12/1/Add.88 (2003)). Also as discussed in chapter 2 the likely decline in access to the civil and political rights, particularly for the most disadvantaged due to neoliberalism was not considered in the report. Even if the majority did support the "economic experiment," the underclass, a minority, had as much right to access their civil and political rights as the dominant elite, also a minority.

The separation that took place between groups can be described as "divide and rule" by the dominant elite. The Human Rights Act 1993 deals with nondiscrimination with respect to special categories such as race and sex. New Zealand ratified the Conventions on the Elimination of Discrimination with Respect to Race (1972) and the Convention on the Elimination of Discrimination with Respect to Women (1984). Affirmative action was also included in the Human Rights Act 1993 (Section 73(1)) and the New Zealand

Bill of Rights Act (Section 19(2). These were assisted by the Equal Employment Opportunities Trust. It was regarded that affirmative action policies were necessary because of past discrimination toward these groups. However, it was the elites of these groups which benefited most while the most disadvantaged of these groups, which would have been worse affected by past discrimination, ended up far worse off.

Affirmative action took place in the public service: in 1986, Maori (approximately 15 percent of the population) made up approximately 10 percent of the Public Service, increasing to 15 percent in 2001 and 17.3 percent on June 30, 2004. Women also increased—in 1986 there were 48 percent in the Public Service, 56 percent in the year 2000, and 59 percent by June 30, 2004. Also affirmative action took place in Parliament: "The number of MPs who identified as being Maori has tripled since the introduction of MMP, the representation of women in Parliament has reached record levels achieving 32% in 2005" (Final Results 2005 general election New Zealand Parliament). While the number of Maori and women were increasing in the bureaucracy and Parliament, Maori unemployment rate rapidly rose to 16 percent (and oscillated around that level for 21 years until recently decreasing to 8 percent (now that New Zealand has achieved a low wage economy)). With respect to women, the numbers on Domestic Purposes Benefit increased considerably from 1984 to the present: from 56,548 in 1985 (Broken Welfare? North and South, May 2000) to 93,090 in 2006 (2006 Census, Sources of Personal income, Statistics New Zealand, Table 37). As a consequence the most disadvantaged, who really needed their human rights, drastically increased in numbers. In the community the division between special categories meant that women, Maori, Pacific Islanders, and the mentally ill organizations were all separated and competing for resources even though their clients were usually beneficiaries with similar wants and needs and consequently, in my opinion, did not need to be separated. In fact if economic, social, and cultural rights had been law and implemented, an underclass is unlikely to have been created at all. But given the present reality it would be positive for these groups to adopt these rights and struggle for social justice as a common cause.

The concept of individual responsibility required that blame not be directed at government, the problem was your own. "Divide and rule" meant that people were inclined to channel their anger toward the least powerful and according to prejudice, for example, common targets were beneficiaries or immigrants and, in the case of Maori and women, condoned by successive governments, toward the ordinary white males. The dominant elite conceals its hegemony by such divide and rule tactics. There were strong prohibitions against the general public, such as the human rights nondiscrimination legislation which received much publicity, expressing anger or protest. This allowed government to increase immigration at will. Unable to direct anger toward government or racial groups the anger was turned inwards and, in my opinion, resulting in increased mental illness, increased domestic violence, and increased child abuse. Police Minister Annette King released figures in August 2006 showing the number of recorded family violence occurrences over the past ten years have increased from 31,654 in 1996 to 63,685 in 2005, with arrests increasing over that period from 9,311 to 18,305. This represents a doubling of domestic violence in nine years although Ms. King seems to attribute this solely to greater reporting. She states: "An increase in domestic violence call-outs and arrests over the past decade shows society is becoming much more open in terms of reporting and exposing the level of such violence." However, the increase in child deaths from maltreatment seems to suggest that violence is being turned inwards. John Bowis, executive director of Save the Children stated: "The annual number of deaths from maltreatment in New Zealand in the 1990s was 1.2 per 100,000 children, compared to 0.9 between 1971–1975." Also, according to a UNICEF report, New Zealand is third from the bottom of the OECD countries for such deaths ("Child Abuse Figures Unacceptably High in New Zealand," *Scoop*, September 19, 2003).

Non-State sanctioned political protests such as the Water Pressure Group backed by many ordinary New Zealanders were treated harshly with their leader, Penny Bright, having been arrested nineteen times in the past thirteen months. Also the Unemployed Workers Rights Centre, their leader, Sue Bradford, now a Green MP, was involved in many street protests in the 1990s with the center subjected to police raids. By contrast state-sanctioned activism, such as the Maori occupation of what they regarded as their land, the feminist assault against the "white, middle class, male" was, in my opinion, encouraged. The elite portrayed themselves as supporters of these groups so the "enemy" was the ordinary people of New Zealand. Typically terms are muddied with the media and politicians describing ordinary New Zealanders as part of the middle class. In fact the majority of New Zealanders are "lower middle class" in origin although could be described as part of "middle New Zealand," ordinary New Zealanders, or "aspiring middle class," or perhaps working class. So while these state-sanctioned radicals were also reluctant to attribute blame to the system or their professional work colleagues, the "real" middle class, their prime target was the "white, lower-middle class, male." The exclusion of the most disadvantaged reflected the strict conformity to the human rights agenda and its elitist model. Such conformity was also required in Parliament and MPs such as Jim Anderton, Hamish McIntyre and Gilbert Miles, who opposed the direction New Zealand was taking left their parties. Jane Kelsey states: "Complementing this hegemony of the political, bureaucratic and business elites is an intolerance of dissent. In the parliamentary arena, strict party discipline has seen MPs who publicly attacked their government being censured, expelled from their caucus or forced to resign. With National and Labour in control of the whips, those who might embarrass them or the corporate elite have had difficulty securing a platform" (Kelsey, 1996).

Once the "divide and rule" process—vertically (classes) and horizontally (special categories)—had been completed the "truth," apart from the human rights agenda, became relative to the group you belonged to or your own personal situation. In the "me" society each individual's opinion was seen as no better or worse than anyone else's. Truth became relative. There was no universal truth except that uttered by the dominant elite. Individuals who had a belief system which did not conform with that of the establishment were dismissed as having "a hobby horse," "an agenda" or "a chip on their shoulder" and really needed to learn that "life is unfair" and they should really "just get on with it" (repeated ad nauseam by the elite!). But as stated at the outset of this chapter it is extremely hard to "just get on with it" when you have virtually nothing and society gives you barely enough for survival whether you are on a benefit or part of the low waged economy.

For civil and political rights to have any credibility as universal rights everyone must have the means of access to at least the core content (see chapter 2) of these rights. The failure of the underclass to make use of their rights should be a strong indicator that they do not have the means, either resources and/or information and education.

David Beetham states:

"It is clear that civil and political equality does not require complete economic leveling. But it becomes severely compromised if, on the one hand, the privileged can use their wealth or status, to purchase undue political influence; or if, on the other, the poor are so deprived that they are incapable of exercising any basic civil or political rights, and are effectively excluded from any common citizenship" (Beetham, 1999: 77).

However, the nature of the social structure ensures that these rights greatly favor the dominant elite. Particularly such rights to property, freedom of the press, liberty, enable the middle class, professional elite to own and/or control the mainstream media and consequently the power to censor what people read.

Yash Ghai states: "As the power of many states declines and that of corporations rises, the capacity of the latter to violate the rights of others, or to create conditions in which rights become harder to exercise or protect, has increased vastly. Freedom of expression is now largely in the hands of corporations, which effectively determine what is published. They have enormous powers of censorship. In pursuit of profitable ventures, they are prepared to make deals or establish understandings with states as to what kind of television programs they will not show or books they would not publish (as publisher Rupert Murdoch has done with China, and many foreign publishers with Singapore)" (Ghai, 1999: 260).

The dominant elite also often own and/or control the mainstream employment sector—both business and bureaucracy—and consequently the means of a livelihood of many. They can exclude those who are considered "politically suspect," those who might "rock the boat" or those who are "over qualified." As Yash Ghai states: "Through their employment practices, corporations are in a position to negate norms of equal opportunity and nondiscrimination. Their employment practices may have more impact on people's health and sense of security than policies of governments" (Ghai, 1999: 260).

Also these businesses often have independent funding and escape some State control with their income deriving from the market. In addition the middle-class, professional sector are able to form numerous powerful associations such as the New Zealand Business Round Table described as "an adjunct policy agency for government" for much of the 1990s by Jane Kelsey (Kelsey, August 13th 1996). Such associations extend to the international level with New Zealand's elite (bureaucratic) meeting with fellow elites at the United Nations, Asia-Pacific Forum, World Trade Organization, the Commonwealth, and many others. Few doors are closed to them domestically or internationally. William Felice said that Marx saw that the international ruling class had a general common interest that went beyond national boundaries. Marx wrote, using rather colorful language, "the wolf as a wolf has an identical interest with his fellow wolves, however much it is to the interest of each individual wolf that he and not another should pounce on the prey" (Felice, 1996: 65). These international associations meant the dominant elite had much less need for support from the domestic majority and consequently the latter had much diminished influence. From my experience these elite bonds are far greater than exist between the elite and the people. By comparison workers have relatively few international associations, for example, there is the International Labour Organization, the World Federation of Trade Unions, and International Trade Union Confederation. To my knowledge the world poor, who make up the bulk of humanity, do not have any internationally recognized organization of their own. Our council, the Human Rights Council, Inc., made up mostly of beneficiaries, is unfunded and there is very little possibility of our being represented among the so-called independent civil society NGOs at the United Nations. This is likely to apply to many other unfunded truly independent NGOs. In my view, there is a need for such an international organization that can represent the poor at the United Nations.

Classical Liberalism coincided with a Parliament considerably dominated by MPs who came from the middle-class, professional sector. In the early days of Modern Liberalism there was a strong working-class representation. An example of this middle-class, professional dominance is given by Jack Nagel in the *British Journal of Political Science* (1998) who provides statistics on the occupations of NZ Labour MPs:

	1935	1984	2000 (my figures)
Professional, semi-professional	17.9%	73.2%	77.1%
Business, other white collar	26.8%	12.5%	6.3%
Manual workers, farmers, union officials	55.3%	14.4%	14.6%

As can be seen, the background of MPs in the 1935 Labour Party included 55.3 percent manual workers, farmers, and union officials but by the year 2000 this had declined to only 14.6 percent while the professional, semi-professionals increased from 17.9 percent to 77.1 percent. At the same time public support for politicians declined. Colin James states: "Combined support for the mainstream Labour and National Parties dropped from a peak of 99.8 percent in 1951 to 69.7 percent in 1993 (62.0 percent in 1996)" (James, 2000: 163).

To illustrate how unrepresentative this is there are approximately 191,000 professionals (1996 Census of Populations), 327,800 trade unionists (December 1997, New Zealand's Second Report under the International Covenant on Economic, Social and Cultural Rights, 32), the total self-employed or business sector was 453,189 (2001 Census, Source of Person Income, Table 27) and 726,196 beneficiaries and superannuitants (2001 Census, Source of Personal Income, Table 27)). As these figures of the backgrounds of MPs are very unrepresentative of society as a whole I consider that greater efforts should be made to have more MPs with backgrounds in small business, trade unions, religion, voluntary work, and beneficiaries/superannuitants. Improved representation in Parliament would protect human rights, including economic, social, and cultural rights, by ensuring no ideology and/or socio-economic group gets too much of an upper hand.

At public meetings during the election campaign in September 2005 in New Zealand the representatives of the political parties generally refused or were very reluctant to reply when asked where they stood on the economic, social, and cultural rights which were included in the Human Rights Commission's New Zealand Plan of Action for Human Rights in February 2005. Only the Green Party included economic, social, and cultural rights as part of their policy, but it was never publicized in the media.

The meetings were held at Auckland University (eight parties represented) and the Mt. Roskill War Memorial Museum (nine parties represented), the former on August 16 and the latter on September 3, 2005. While all refused outright to respond at the first meeting of political representatives on August 16 to answer questions related to economic, social, and cultural rights, at the second meeting on September 3 they were a little more forthcoming but still very reluctant. The Maori Party and the Communist League, neither of whom had been elected to Parliament, were supportive of economic, social, and cultural rights. Hine Harawera, representing the Maori Party, said his party would support greater legislative protection for the areas dealt with by economic, social, and cultural rights, that is, employment, fair wages, health, housing, education, and an adequate standard of living. Two other party representatives responded reluctantly with Phil Goff, the then Labour government Minister of Foreign Affairs, while admitting the importance of economic, social, and cultural rights, sidestepped the issue of the need for economic, social, and cultural rights in law and instead talked of the existence of legal rights under ordinary legislation to protect social justice. However, he overlooked the fact that legal rights are at the whim of successive governments whereas with economic, social, and cultural rights social justice would be protected by the courts in the same way as are traditional liberties and democratic rights (and governments do not like to be seen violating human rights). The Green Party representative, Keith Locke, was also rather muted in his response though indicated his party recognized the importance of economic, social, and cultural rights.

Apart from the Green Party, none of the parties presently represented in Parliament promote economic, social, and cultural rights in their policy as evidenced by their web sites and Index New Zealand at the public library, which lists articles written in magazines and newspapers, reveals no public statements by any member of Parliament on the subject of economic, social, and cultural rights. From my experience, although sometimes economic, social, and cultural rights are mentioned by members of the establishment in public, the media does not report it. In addition many professionals in the bureaucracy and community groups are fully aware of these rights but say nothing publicly. Even Amnesty International, Auckland, whose principles are based on the Universal Declaration of Human Rights will not discuss them publicly (although they promote it at the elite level, e.g., the United Nations). Consequently, there is an elite collusion to keep these rights from the public of New Zealand. In the words of Noam Chomsky, there is a "general tacit agreement" that it "wouldn't do" to mention that particular fact (Chomsky, 1998: 25). So political choices at elections fall within the narrow range of left wing liberalism and right wing liberalism. Hence the democratic process has been captured by the liberals and although while in law we are a democracy in reality we are a liberal oligarchy.

The human rights agenda, defined by the domestic and global elite, and more particularly, the American State Department, bore little relationship to the true human rights abuses taking place in society, that is, the increasing growth of an underclass and the exclusion of creative and talented people. Richard Nordahl states: "They [the dominant elite] have an unjustified belief in the autonomy of the concepts and principles, together with a related unjustified belief in the power of abstract thinking to generate practical solutions from them." He adds: "They do not see that the concepts and the principles—or, at least, their specific formulations—are tied to a particular social order. They think they are playing a disinterested role in promoting free, fair, or just society, that society which is in accord with their general principles" (Nordahl, 1992: 165). Consequently the end result is what Jack Donnelly describes as "culpable social science malpractice" (Donnelly, 1989: 180).

Chapter Four

The History of Economic, Social, and Cultural Rights and the Most Disadvantaged

The Philosophical Argument

Throughout history the most disadvantaged have lacked a belief system which would engender a hope which would allow them to persevere against insurmountable odds and act as a rallying point for others to get involved in pursuit of social justice. While religious charity, the trade union's promotion of economic, social, and cultural rights in the nineteenth century, and Modern Liberalism in the twentieth century did improve the lot of the poor it was driven by elites with mainly their own interests at heart and where it was convenient they could withdraw this support. Core minimum obligations reflects more closely the needs of the most disadvantaged and will not be able to be co-opted to solely serve the interests of the elites as economic, social, and cultural rights can be. The lack of a belief system is, in my view, the reason the most disadvantaged have been so easily oppressed and why the majority of the world's people live in poverty. Their lives have been determined in a top-down fashion and they have had virtually no input into their own destiny. Core minimum obligations, which are universal with human rights education for all, the right for people to reach their full development, the equal status of both sets of rights at both the core level and progressively at higher levels and nonretrogression with respect to human rights can be driven by those who have also suffered most from neoliberalism: particularly the underclass, but also the romantics, the creative artists and intellectuals, independent entrepreneurs, volunteer workers and, generally, the more altruistic in society—individuals for whom life is more of a balance between "me" and "we" rather than the enormous dominance of the former that we see in Western society. The universal core obligations approach to human rights discussed in chapter 2 is an attempt to provide an empowering ideology for the most disadvantaged which would

71

initially limit the excesses of neoliberalism and later, in a progressive fashion, will transform neoliberalism into a world where both sets of rights have equal status at the higher and lower levels providing a human rights culture where coupled with the economic dimension, the right to development, people are able to pursue their dreams. It is such a dream that has been missing in the antiglobalization movement. Not everything about neoliberalism is detrimental to human kind—you would not want to remove civil and political rights and even globalization has much to recommend it if it was to take the whole of society with it rather than just consolidating the wealth and power of the domestic and global elites. Ishay states: "Theoretically, while the anti-neo-liberal globalization movement provides new hopes and opportunities for the development of a more vibrant global civil society and integrated human rights dialogue, it still lacks a common progressive political, economic, and social agenda, an important denominator needed to unite more effectively, a variety of human rights interests" (Ishay, 2004: 349). As global conflict increases it becomes in everyone's interests to have a peaceful way of achieving social justice as would be the case if economic, social, and cultural rights were included in domestic human rights law and the core obligations agenda is immediately addressed and higher levels of economic, social, and cultural rights achieved progressively. To date only a very small number of countries have included economic, social, and cultural rights in domestic human rights law.

As so much in our society revolves around money people frequently overlook the importance of belief systems, the individual's and the nation's, yet this can determine "who gets what," your limitations, your responsibilities, where the system needs to be improved but, more importantly, a commitment to a dream can help an individual persevere against seemingly impossible odds. Attempts to subvert the Constitution are sometimes regarded by States as sedition, a criminal act. This reflects the importance the State attaches to its basic principles. People, whereas they might not die for money, may often be prepared to die for their country and what it stands for. In addition, because of what the country stands for people are often prepared to give their consent to be governed, which means that usually the State has less need to resort to force. Al Qaeda may prove a formidable force not because of its military might or financial assets but rather because of the strength of its convictions as evidenced by its suicide missions. Steiner and Alston describe the significance of a belief system enshrined in a constitution: "[A] constitution is more than a legal document. It is a highly symbolic and ideologically significant one—reflecting both who we are as a society, and who we would like to be. Inclusion of certain rights and principles in the constitution says a great deal about their stature and importance; omission of others have the same effect" (Steiner and Alston,1996: 304).

While spreading the belief system is relatively inexpensive people might think fulfilling core minimum obligations is far from inexpensive even though the needs of the poor are small. To a large extent this is an attitude problem as even so-called "primitive societies" provided essential needs. The attitudes are a consequence of a lack of understanding of the realities. Shue states: "If subsistence rights seem strange, this is more likely because Western liberalism has had a blind spot for severe economic need. Far from being new or advanced, subsistence rights are found in traditional societies that are often treated by modern societies as generally backward or primitive" (Shue, 1980: 28). Also regarding the cost of subsistence rights Pogge considers that "this problem is hardly unsolvable, in spite of its magnitude." He states:

> Though constituting 44 percent of the world's population, the 2,735 million people the World Bank counts as living below its more generous $2 per day international poverty line consume only 1.3 percent of the global product, and would need just 1 percent more to escape poverty so defined. The high-income countries, with 955 million citizens, by contrast, have about 81 percent of the global product. With our average per capita income nearly 180 times greater than that of the poor (at market exchange rates), we could eradicate severe poverty worldwide if we chose to try—in fact, we could have eradicated it decades ago (Pogge, 2005).

Thomas Jefferson, who was the principle author of the American Declaration of Independence (1776), states: "We hold these truths to be self-evident, that all men are created equal, that they are endowed by their Creator with certain unalienable Rights, that among these are Life, Liberty and the pursuit of Happiness." The "self evident truths" described by Jefferson were to be found in natural law, according to which the universe is infused by principles laid down by God. But what constitutes "self evident truths" can differ from one person to another. Jerome Shestack states: "In short, the principle problem of natural law is that the rights considered to be natural can differ from theorist to theorist, depending on their conception of nature" (Shestack, 1998: 208).

At the time arable land was plentiful and according to Francis Fukuyama Jefferson perceived happiness as the accumulation of property: "The right to 'the pursuit of happiness' proclaimed in the American Declaration of Independence was conceived largely in terms of acquisition of property" (Fukuyama, 1992). The institution of property can, to some extent, be seen as acting as a buffer against the vagaries of nature and as encouraging development which was very much needed in America at the time. The right to property was eventually included in the American Bill of Rights (1791) (whose principle author was James Madison).

However, rights to subsistence were not included in the American Bill of Rights. But you cannot "pursue happiness" when you have virtually nothing and live in a society which prevents you from getting enough to survive. Also under such circumstances of scarcity, severe insecurity, and lack of choice your "life" and "liberty" can also be in constant jeopardy. Even John Locke, the seventeenth-century liberal English philosopher whose ideas formed the foundation of liberal democracy and greatly influenced both the American and French revolutions, recognized that while there was a duty to respect private property in land that its enclosure did not prejudice the livelihood of others, because "enough and as good" was left for them (Beetham, 1995: 54). Also subsistence rights, such as the right to food, shelter, and health, could also be seen as "self-evident truths" that can be derived from nature, as Cranston points out scarcity is sometimes a part of nature and there would be a need for sharing: "Scarcity prevails in nature. Man is not only vulnerable in the sense that he is very easily killed or injured. He is also bound by his own needs to work for a living. Food does not grow abundantly on every tree. Natural caves do not provide adequate shelter for every human being" (Cranston, 1973: 48).

Asbjorne Eide considers that the concept of human rights developed to include economic, social, and cultural rights because of the scarcity of property in the modern world:

> The transformation from an agricultural to an urban and industrial society requires a more complex system of rights in order to ensure livelihood in dignity for all. The right to property therefore has been supplemented by at least two other rights: the right to work with a remuneration which ensures an adequate standard of living for all those who are willing to work and are able to find work, and the right to social security which is a substitute for work for those who either cannot find work or are unable to work, and a substitute for insufficient income derived from property or from work: insufficient, that is, in regard to the enjoyment of an adequate standard of living" (Eide, 120).

However, economic, social, and cultural rights may have also developed not simply because of the scarcity of property but also to protect people from the increasing oppression and exploitation of a growing powerful elite, the major beneficiaries of civil and political rights (see below). As stated above you may not only lack the means of subsistence but also be prevented from getting it, that is, sufficient to survive with some dignity.

The mid-nineteenth century saw Classical Liberalism at its height during the Industrial Revolution with its appalling working conditions and wide gap between rich and poor. Karl Marx provided a class perspective of the American Declaration of Independence 1776 and Bill of Rights (1791) and the

French Rights of Man and of Citizens 1791–1793 which he described as "securing the rights of the bourgeoisie" (Ishay, 2004: 129–130). For Marx, 'the rights of man' were "bourgeois, property-based and egoistic" (Scott Davidson, *Human Rights*, Open University Press 1993, p. 174). Marx viewed the human as a "species-being" or social being rather than an isolated individual only responsible to him/herself. The latter encourages a "me" society, where the individual takes priority over the collective, rather than a "we" society, which is the reverse, whereas the ideal society, according to modern human rights theory, is where there is a balance between the two with individual and collective rights being of equal importance. Where, for example, people will vote not only for themselves but also for what is best for the country. In the present day extreme liberal "me" societies, individuals, and groups will usually only think of themselves and results in particularism with individuals who belong to such groups severely limited in terms of personal development and social conscience, trapped in their social prisons, unable to transcend their own self-interest or their class and separated from the community because of the division between the public and the private. Marx states: ". . . Thus none of the so-called rights of man goes beyond the egoistic man, the man withdrawn into himself, his private interest and his private choice, and separated from the community as a member of civil society. . . The only bond between men is natural necessity, need and private interest, the maintenance of their property and egoistic persons." (Ishay, 1997: 196).

According to Karl Marx, it was civil rights plus the right to property, with their emphasis on liberty, which separated people from the state and society. This is the separation with its isolated individuals, which is evident in today's world. Economic, social, and cultural rights and universal suffrage were still in their formative stages of development in the mid-nineteenth century, and Modern Liberalism was to come later. Micheline Ishay describes how the lower classes had little say in government at the time, bearing some similarity to the minimal democracy that exists today (although this emphasis on democracy is now returning). "In principle, the Enlightenment offered all white men the option to become voting members of society should they acquire enough property, earn a sufficient income, and pay adequate tax. In the industrial reality of the nineteenth century, however, the gap between the rich and the working class had grown so wide that this opportunity had become a mere chimera" (Ishay, 2004: 135).

The rights to liberty and property, in particular, led to a large private sector and, in the case of Classical Liberalism, a huge gap between rich and poor. This represented "the separation of man from man." Marx states : ". . . liberty as a right of man is not based on the association of man with man but rather on the separation of man from man. It is the right of this separation, the right of the limited individual limited to himself." Further Marx adds: "The practical application of the right of liberty is the right of property. . . . the right of self-interest. . . . It lets every man find in other men not the realization but rather the limitation of his own freedom."

These rights ensured noninterference by the State, which also meant minimal social responsibility and maximum individual responsibility. Weaker groups were isolated and unprotected and this allowed the most wealthy and powerful groups in society to dominate with little restraint. What was once publicly controlled, the formation of the private sector enabled control by the bourgeoisie or middle-class, professional sector. Under such circumstances the profit motive dominated and there need be little social responsibility.

Tony Evans, describing the modern origins of human rights in the seventeenth century, states: "The separation of private and economic life from public and political life, which is central to natural rights, was presented as a moral imperative in the interests of all the people, not the outcome of new power relationships that served the interests of particular groups (Evans, 2001: 17).

While the class nature of human rights was much less apparent under Modern Liberalism, which was to come later, under Classical Liberalism, describing the present-day situation, the classes were sharply separated into the bourgeoisie, the ordinary people, and the underclass while the special categories such as women and race were also separated, thereby dividing the sexes and races. It is a society where particularism dominates by contrast with a society which emphasizes democracy and the independent individual. Under Classical Liberalism all other groups follow the dominant elite with many independent individuals and underclass at the bottom of the social structure. This divide and rule approach can be seen at the higher level in the separation of powers—in America between the executive, Congress, and the judiciary—in the liberal constitution. Philip Joseph states: "It is based on the notion that if a power is divided it will be less dangerous" (Joseph, 2000: 185). For liberals the major fear is the 'tyranny of the majority' (de Tocqueville, *Democracy in America* (1835, 1840)) or populism, a society where the independent individual dominates, and this had to be made less "dangerous." Civil rights are meant primarily to protect minorities such as the dominant elite but without democracy there is little protection for the majority.

The neoliberal requirement of noninterference by government is based on the assumption that there is always a conflict between the individual and the State but this need not always be the case. For instance, in America, there were many who regard Franklin Roosevelt as a great leader because he rose above his class and took into account the interests of the whole nation. Similarly, New Zealand leaders such as Michael Joseph Savage, Peter Fraser, and

Norman Kirk were regarded as great leaders by many New Zealanders. Susan Mendes states:

> Where human rights are asserted, they are asserted as claims by individuals and against the power of the state, or against other individuals. But to assume that rights are needed against the state is to assume there must always be antagonism between the interests of the state and the interests of individuals, and this is a denial of the kind of ideal society envisaged by socialists. . . (Mendes, 1995: 12–13).

But to a considerable extent the philosophical argument regarding whether the development of economic, social, and cultural rights is due to the scarcity of property in the modern world or the increasing oppression of an dominant elite or both has been largely overcome by a global consensus as to what constitutes human rights in the modern era. Michael Freeman describes the view of Jack Donnelly: "There is, in his view, not only a consensus that human rights exist, but also an enumeration of rights in international law. He admits that he cannot defend a particular list of rights with direct philosophical arguments, but maintains that the actual consensus makes this problem unimportant (Freeman, 1994: 491). Given its support, at least in principle, worldwide the Universal Declaration of Human Rights can be regarded as the most fully developed description of human rights that humankind has devised. However, there is a vast difference between acceptance in principle of the declaration and its implementation with a number of liberal democracies still clinging to human rights as it was defined in the seventeenth century, that is, Classical Liberalism. For instance, only a small number of countries have included economic, social, and cultural rights in domestic law as justiciable rights. The Western liberal democracies only give recognition to economic, social, and cultural rights at the elite level. Tony Evans states: "The western, neo-liberal coalition, both in the United Nations (UN) and the wider global community, has succeeded in acknowledging formal parity between the two sets of rights while simultaneously promoting only civil and political rights through rhetoric, policy and action" (Evans, 1999: 33).

It is perhaps not surprising that many global elites, not just liberal democracies, do not want to give social justice to their people. David Beetham states: "There is general agreement among commentators on economic and social rights that for them to be effectively realized would require a redistribution of power and resources, both within countries and between them. It is hardly surprising that many governments should be less than enthusiastic about such an agenda. . . ." (Beetham, 1995: 43).

Yet as shown in previous chapters it may not cost much to fulfill the core obligations of economic, social, and cultural rights which from a human

rights point of view are very much the priority. Rather, it is argued, the problem is much more ideological as these rights pose a direct threat to the dominant liberal elite and, it will be shown, its ability to "divide and rule."

The human rights agenda is determined by the liberal elite (in and outside
government) both at the domestic level and through the United Nations. As
stated elsewhere the ordinary people have very little knowledge of the subject
and are largely kept ignorant of it. And in my experience many members of
our Parliament have little knowledge of human rights. With these rights in law
or as United Nations conventions it was the role of the middle-class, professional sector (bureaucratic) to promote the human rights agenda and so legitimize the private sector and the social divisions in society. In this way, as indicated by T. H. Marshall in chapter 2, ideology and the capitalist economy
operate in sync. As the protectors of the human rights agenda the public service is more concerned than the private sector to maintain high standards
while the private sector could operate at a lower level, involving less social responsibility, and was in a situation where it could exploit workers only limited by a minimum wage which may not be much above the unemployment
benefit. This ensured the nation's international competitiveness. But the heavy
focus of economic development on the dominant elite and the corporations
rather than a more balanced approach to development meant the rest of the
population became a mere means to economic and ideological ends—the individual is no longer seen as important in themselves. Erich Fromm describes
the capitalist mode of production and the dominance of the profit motive:

> The subordination of the individual as a means to economic ends is based on the
> peculiarities of the capitalist mode of production, which makes the accumula-
> tion of capital the purpose and aim of economic activity. One works for profit's
> sake, but the profit one makes is not made to be spent but to be invested as new
> capital; this increased capital brings new profits which again are invested, and
> so on in a circle (Fromm, 1984: 96).

A History of Economic, Social, and Cultural Rights

Throughout history groups have required a belief system to achieve or maintain power. The ancient Greeks and Romans had a belief in natural law.
Monarchy was legitimized during the medieval period by the divine rights of
kings and later the middle classes were elevated to political power and protected by the natural rights (renamed human rights but were actually only
civil rights) of liberalism. Later still, socialism gave the working class the
promise of political power while the church and religion were inclined to give
divine sanction and insist on duties to various powerful groups. While the ideologies mentioned and religion all claimed to be universal, in reality the in-

terests of the poor were marginalized or their interests recognized only when it suited the elites. Often the most disadvantaged depended on an elite to find it delivered little. While historically the range of duties have broadened from the duties first owed to the monarchy, then extended to middle-class rights holders, then further extended to a certain extent to the working class, however, the only duties owed the most disadvantaged in the West are legal rights such as ordinary law protecting welfare benefits, employment, and so forth, but unlike human rights, can be changed at the whim of governments.

Economic, social, and cultural rights, which first gained some prominence in the nineteenth century, promised to give to the poor the material means and education whereby they could have a voice in society and make use of their civil and political rights. However, a major difficulty with these rights is that given the realities of the world they actually amount to false hopes. This is reflected in the comment of a former U.S. ambassador Jeane Kirkpatrick when she described economic, social, and cultural rights as "a letter to Santa Claus" (Chomsky, 1998: 32). In short these rights are too unrealistic for the obvious reason it would be extremely difficult to contemplate ensuring a job for everyone who wanted one in India or as Cranston states "to provide periodic holidays with pay" for all Indian workers. Human rights need to be attainable otherwise they will lack credibility in the eyes of people whose support is essential. ESC rights are of a constitutional nature, affecting future generations, so should be subjected to the vote of the people, not a version bestowed from above, if they are to be included in a constitution. For these rights to be attainable it makes sense to focus on those who suffer the worst human rights violations which the "core obligations agenda" attempts to do. But it is also necessary to protect the rights already achieved and empower people with human rights education and the right to development to achieve higher levels of rights. The empowerment will ensure a bottom-up participation. Economic, social, and cultural rights, rather than focusing on the most disadvantaged, can easily be manipulated to suit elite groups. For example, trade unions may only focus on the economic and social rights of the workplace just as middle- class professionals are more concerned with their own economic and social rights. In my view, the most disadvantaged cannot rely on elite groups to give them their rights. They must do it themselves, which essentially means educating the people and finding ways to further their own right to development.

In human rights history the emphasis was first on duties to one another, for example, natural law and religion, while later, under liberalism, the emphasis was on natural rights (which were first renamed, it is said, by Thomas Paine as human rights (see below). Paul Lauren states: "For centuries most of these early philosophical theories of natural law—just like those of religious doctrine—focused on universal responsibilities and duties rather than what are now described as rights" (Lauren, 2003: 13).

The Universal Declaration of Human Rights (UDHR), although by reciprocity includes duties emphasizes rights, is based on the view that people should have human rights simply because they are human. William Felice states: "Human rights are moral claims to a certain standard of treatment that derive solely from the very fact of being human" (Felice, 2003: 159).

It could be said we all have a right to a share in this world and this is a duty to some higher law, in the nature of things or just intuitively obvious and where sharing among families, species occurs despite competition. Freedom would require such a share. In addition, all of us have a duty or social responsibility to ensure this share for every individual. The "core obligations agenda" can be seen as the very least required to fulfill this share while governments can be chosen to ensure and fulfill most of these duties on our behalf although we still have duties to the community. Consequently, in my view, there is a higher law than the Universal Declaration of Human Rights. There is little mention of duties in the UDHR, which probably reflects its Western origins where natural rights were emphasized over duties. Johan Galtung states, referring to the universal declaration: "The western historical stamp on the process whereby a bourgeois class replaced the power of a clergy by faith, and an aristocracy by birth, is unmistakable" (Galtung, 1998: 213). Ideally our duty is to all people, not to some vested interest or dominant elite. This, as stated in an earlier chapter, is articulated in Article 12 of the UDHR, that is, "everyone has duties to the community in which alone the free and full development of his personality is possible." From this duty can be derived the rights contained in the declaration, that is, essential duties to be performed which are then defined as individual rights which enable individuals to make claims. Also, reflecting the lack of emphasis on duties by the declaration while economic, social, and cultural rights protects people from oppression and exploitation it does not reinforce this by explicitly requiring associations, including political associations, "to do no harm" although such a duty by associations to the wider community could be inferred from Article 12. Article 20 of the declaration simply states: "Everyone has the right to freedom of peaceful assembly and association. No one may be compelled to belong to an association." Consequently, the declaration gives the impression that, for example, it is up to the poor to seek social justice with little requirement that elites refrain from oppression. To move forward the poor need not only the material means but also to be free from oppression. In addition, freedom of speech and freedom of the press are contained in Article 19 of the UDHR. It states: "Everyone has the right to freedom of opinion and expression; this right includes freedom to hold opinions without interference and to seek, receive and impart information and ideas through any media and regardless of frontiers." There are limits—most jurisdictions disallow the promotion of violence and the spreading of hatred toward people; however, the duty to inform people of matters of considerable importance including necessary information to be able to properly play a part in the democratic process is largely ignored. For example, it has been shown in former chapters how economic, social, and cultural rights are rarely mentioned by the media. This duty to inform is also not included in Article 21 of the UDHR in relation to elections. This article states:

> Everyone has the right to take part in the government of the country, directly or through freely chosen representatives. Everyone has the right to equal access to public service in his country. The will of the people shall be the basis of the authority of government; this will be expressed in periodic and genuine elections which shall be by universal and equal suffrage and shall be held by secret vote or by equivalent free voting procedures.

In my view, all associations could adopt, as a guide, the equivalent of the medical profession's Hippocratic Oath, that is, "keeping myself far from all intentional ill-doing." Also, in particular, all associations should be "Human Rights Transparent" (as should government and political parties) with respect to where they stand in relation to the Universal Declaration of Human Rights (their human rights position could be included in their mission statement)—people need to be informed whether the association adopts, for example, a political position—in terms of belief and practice—on human rights. People need to know the human rights position of who they are voting for, donating to, the human rights position of the media and whether the business they are dealing with is socially responsible with this defined in human rights terms.

The idea that we owe a duty to a higher law than that of the State originates in ancient Greece and Rome. In ancient Rome statesman, Cicero, defined this higher law called natural law (*ius naturale*) stating: "Law is the highest reason, implanted in Nature, which commands what ought to be done and forbids the opposite" (Ishay, 1997: 24).

Paul Lauren states that "a tradition began with a number of classical Greek philosophers who argued that a universal law of nature pervaded all of creation." He adds: "This law was eternal and universal, and thus placed well above and beyond the narrow and self-serving dictates of a particular state, the rules of a specific society, or the will of a single lawmaker. It governed every aspect of the universe and provided a framework for rights. Human conduct should be bought into harmony with this law of nature and judged according to it" (Lauren, 2003: 12).

This natural law could be appealed to where the State acted unjustly. It was an appeal to an "imaginary," though often deeply believed, universal law of nature or God. An example, described by Lauren, often given comes from the Greek literature of Antigone, who, on being reproached by the king for denying his command not to bury her slain brother, considered she had a duty to natural law which gave her brother a right to be buried. She asserted: "I did not think your orders were so strong that you, a mortal man, could over-run the gods' unwritten and unfailing laws. Not now, nor yesterday's, they always live, and no one knows their origin in time." Consequently, natural law was a higher law, eternal and universal, and beyond the self-interest of the State, which ideally should act in conformity with it. Aristotle in *Politics* declared that what is "just by nature" is not necessarily just by the laws of men (Lauren, 2003: 12).

However, the high standards required by natural law could be far removed from reality. Lauren states: "What constituted these laws of nature was open to interpretation but invariably it meant the exclusion of the poor and powerless." For example equality did not extend to slaves, women, and resident foreigners. Consequently in Athens (508 B.C. to 322 B.C.), the "home" of democracy excluded the majority of the population from their form of direct democracy.

Similarly, later Roman civilization also failed to follow natural law (*ius naturale*) when it came to the "poor and the powerless." Micheline Ishay states: "Both Greek and Roman civilization were built on a fundamental distinction between the citizen and non-citizen, between the free and the unfree" (Ishay, 2004: 32).

Also in Rome was another body of law known as *ius gentium* which was concerned with custom and could be seen as a "half way house" between reality and the high ideals of natural law. Jeremy Waldron describes it as "a set of principles that had established itself as a sort of consensus among judges, jurists, and law makers around the world" (Waldron, 2005: 129, 134). Slavery was the custom throughout the then known world and while Waldron states that slavery was "always thought to be an affront to the law of nature" it was instead justified by *ius gentium* (while civil law, *ius civile*, was specific to an individual state) (Waldron, 2005: 134). With so few rights slaves were easily oppressed even when they made up the majority. They virtually only knew duty to the dominant elite. H. G. Wells describes the situation of the slaves in approximately AD 200: "The agricultural slaves were captives who spoke many different languages so that they could not understand each other, or they were born slaves, they had no solidarity to resist oppression, no tradition of rights, no knowledge, for they could not read or write. Although they came to form a majority of the country they never made a successful insurrection" (Wells, 1987: 85).

For Mahatma Gandhi, who regarded himself as "deeply traditional and orthodox Hindu" emphasized "the principle of non injury to others" (Lauren, 2003). For Gandhi "the true source of rights is duty" (Lauren, 2003: 10). And we have a "duty of citizenship to the world." In a letter to UNESCO in 1947 he stated: "I learnt from my illiterate but wise mother that all rights to be deserved and preserved came from duty well done. Thus the very right to live accrues to us only when we do the duty of citizenship to the world. From this one fundamental statement, perhaps it is easy enough to define the duties of Man and Woman and correlate every right to some corresponding duty to be first performed. Every other right can be shown to be a mere usurpation hardly worth fighting for (Gandhi, 1949: 18).

Paul Lauren describes how all the major religions—Hinduism, Christianity, Islam, Judaism, and Confucianism—emphasize duty. Lauren states: "All the major religions of the world seek in one way or another to speak to the issue of human responsibility to others" (Lauren, 2003: 5).

During the medieval period and the seventeenth century the Catholic religion despite scriptures, which placed considerable emphasis on compassion and duty to the poor, was far more concerned to ensure that duties to the monarch were fulfilled and consequently supported the highly unequal social structure. Later in the sixteenth century the Protestant religion, in preaching self-help and individual choice and later aligning itself with liberal rights, failed to recognize the abject servitude of the peasantry, nearly all semi-literate with minimal choices at their disposal. Rather because they were considered to have a choice the poor could be blamed for their predicament.

Lauren describes the importance attached to compassion and duty by Christian scriptures. He states: "During his ministry two thousand years ago, Jesus challenged the existing order of his day, taught about the value of all human beings in the sight of God, and spoke again and again about demonstrating love and compassion and of the need to give of one's self to others, of clothing the naked, of healing the sick, of feeding the hungry, of welcoming the stranger, of providing hope to the hopeless, and of caring for the oppressed of the world." Lauren adds that Jesus "demonstrated a level of respect for women, children, outcasts, and outsiders that many of his contemporaries found inappropriate. . . ." (Lauren, 2003: 7).

During the medieval period it was considered that many religious teachings could be regarded as natural law. Pennington describes how Gratian a twelfth century canon lawyer from Bologna saw the Golden Rule—the biblical injunction to do unto others what you would have them do unto you (Matthew 7.12)—as part of natural law, that is, "Each person is commanded to do to others what he wants done to himself," (Pennington). This Golden Rule finds expression in all of the major religions. It also reflects the biblical injunction "love thy neighbour as thyself" (Leviticus 19:18-33 Jerusalem Bible). In addition, from the duties of the Ten Commandments rights can be derived. For example from the injunction "thou shalt not steal" can be derived the right to property or "thou shalt not kill" can be derived the right to life (Pennington).

As a consequence Pennington states that "natural law became an integral part of medieval legal and theological thought." He states that "in private law the jurists used natural law in creative ways to justify and regulate particular legal institutions." And twelfth- and thirteenth-century jurists considered that "since natural law protected private property, they concluded that even the emperor, king or prince could not deprive a person of their property except for just and necessary reasons." Pennington added that "by the end of the twelfth century, the jurists included contractual rights under the provisions of natural law. A contract was concluded by oaths. Oaths were promises to God. Consequently, they concluded that private contracts were grounded in natural law. Even the prince was bound by the contracts that he might make with his subjects or with other princes. He may be sovereign but was not exempt from the precepts of natural law" (Pennington). In 1213 a dispute in England between King John and his nobles led to the signing of the Magna Carta which promised citizens "freedom from imprisonment, dispossession, prosecution or exile unless by 'lawful judgment.' It also guaranteed the right to a fair trial—'to none will we sell, deny or delay right of justice'" (Human Rights Commission, Celebrating The 50th Anniversary of the UDHR, 2). However, although ostensibly for everyone in the country it largely reflected the interests of the nobles. It was "simply a compromise on the distribution of power between King John and his nobles. . ." (Davidson, 1993: 2–3).

The social structure, particularly in medieval times, reflected the concept of the Great Chain of Being. This was a deep-seated belief that society was ordered in a hierarchical fashion by God for the good of humanity. There was a long list of gradations with God at the summit, followed by the pope (for Catholics), kings immediately beneath him, then—in descending order—the nobility and princes of the church, the knights and gentry, the legal and professional classes, merchants, and yeoman, and at the bottom the great mass of peasants. Any individual who attempted to rise above his station in life also challenged religion. Arthur Lovejoy has traced the development of the hierarchical ordering of being from early Greek thought such as Aristotle's Scala Natura (Ladder of Nature) to the Romantic Era (eighteenth to early nineteenth century). Lovejoy stated: "[the] conception of the plan and structure of the world which, through the Middle Ages and down to the late eighteenth century . . . most educated men were to accept without question—the conception of the universe as a 'Great Chain of Being,' composed of an immense, or . . . infinite, number of links ranging in hierarchical order from the meagerest kind of existents . . . through 'every possible' grade up to the ens perfectissu-mum" (Lovejoy, 1936: 20).

In the Great Chain of Being there were reciprocal duties, noblesse oblige, traditional collective property rights, and an institutional framework with the church providing charity for the poor. It was a feudal system with reciprocal duties between lord and vassal, with could involve the latter receiving land in return for military services, although "heaven" was unlikely to be on earth because the peasants were strictly controlled on class lines. However, it did provide the peasants with some meager security even though they could never hope to reach their full social potential. According to Brian, the old feudal restrictions, which had fixed peasants in place on the land and limited their income, had also guaranteed them a place in the world. He states: "They may not have prospered, but they were often able to fend off starvation and homelessness simply because they had been born onto estates from which they could not be removed against their wills" (Brian).

Later in the sixteenth century there was the Protestant Reformation with Martin Luther (1483–1546) "the first to formulate Protestant principles." While the Catholic Church interpreted the bible on behalf of the faithful, Protestantism allowed an individual interpretation of the bible. Ishay states: "By asserting individual responsibility in matters of salvation and in seeking happiness on earth, the Protestant influence helped advance a new credo relying on individual choice and rights" (Ishay, 2004: 70). Consequently, Protestantism, by allowing its adherents to act according to their conscience with their own interpretation of the bible, "privatized" religion thereby separating Church and State. This later legitimized the liberal "private sector" in the seventeenth century. Although the monarchy preferred Catholicism and according to Aylmer by the early seventeenth century in England "practicing Roman Catholics were now only a small minority in the country as a whole" (Aylmer, 1963).

The dissolution of the monasteries in 1536–1540 by King Henry VIII, who was head of the Church of England (Anglican), followed by the dissolution of religious guilds, fraternities, almshouses, and hospitals in 1545–1549, destroyed much of the institutional fabric which had provided charity for the poor in the past (Boyer,). In medieval Europe the church bore the responsibility for organizing and promoting poor relief, and it was not until the sixteenth century that the State began to take over this responsibility. Boyer states that the Elizabethan Poor Law of the sixteenth century was "adopted largely in response to a serious deterioration in economic circumstances, combined with a decline in more traditional forms of charitable assistance" (Boyer).

Harris Friedberg paints a picture of London during the sixteenth century—"from 1592 to 1594 London was gripped by a devastating outbreak of plague.

Upwards of 10 percent of the population died, and thousands more fled the terrified city. Famine followed pestilence; 1594 was the first of four successive bad harvests. The price of food, already high, doubled. Food riots broke out . . . . in the countryside, the practice of enclosure—throwing tenant farmers off the land to convert it to the more profitable use of pasturing sheep—forced more of the homeless into the city of London, increasing the overcrowding, the inflation, and the spread of contagion." The idea, spread by Protestantism and later Liberalism, that all people chose their lifestyle and were individually responsible also allowed blame to be leveled at those who did not conform. Friedberg adds: "The homeless—they were called vagabonds—were profoundly disturbing to the authorities and moralists, who tended to blame the victims for their state. Vagrants were considered idle by choice, men who "used to loiter and would not work." When they got to London, many of these "vagrants," "sturdy beggars," and "masterless men" gravitated toward the Liberties, those suburbs beyond the city walls and outside of the jurisdiction of the Lord Mayor and Corporation of London, and especially to the Liberty of Southwark, just across the Thames River" (Friedberg).

The Protestant Reformation led to religious wars throughout Europe in the sixteenth and seventeenth centuries—erupting in Germany, religious conflict soon spread to France, Holland, and Spain, and to England resulting in the Treaty of Westphalia in 1648 which, in giving greater recognition to the sovereignty of States and their ability to chose their own religion, undermined the global aspirations of the Catholic Church. According to Lauren the sovereign states "recognized no universal authority like that of an emperor or a pope from above, and no claims from feudal barons or subjects from below." In addition, Ishay states: "With the advance of the Reformation, from 1546 to the Treaty of Westphalia in 1648, the universalist message of the church had been severely compromised. While the separation of the Greek orthodox churches from Rome had provoked the first rupture in Christian unity the Protestant Reformation of the sixteenth and seventeenth centuries contributed decisively to its decline" (Ishay, 2004: 70). The Treaty of Westphalia led to the doctrine of national sovereignty whereby States had complete domestic jurisdiction, in other words, it was the States business how they treated their citizens. This included the principle of nonintervention of one State in the internal affairs of another State. Later respect for state sovereignty would be a basic requirement of the United Nations Charter although, as will be shown later, the development of international human rights law, after the Second World War, permitted interference in another state's affairs when there were gross violations of human rights.

The seventeenth century saw the development of liberalism based on natural rights benefiting largely the property holders in the dominant elite, particularly emerging middle-class commercial interests but these rights were to prove of little value to the great mass of peasants because of the grossly unequal social structure and because the natural rights, so conceived, failed to adequately reflect the interests of the peasants. Only when liberalism was forced, by the emergence of socialism in the nineteenth century, to adopt more socially responsible policies would the most disadvantaged see benefits such as the extension of manhood suffrage and improved welfare in some countries.

Lauren states that in the seventeenth century the decline of feudalism and the expansion of commerce, for example, gave economic and then political power to an emerging middle class anxious for individual freedom (Lauren, 2003: 13).

The seventeenth century was essentially a clash between two ideologies: the divine rights of the monarch and the emerging ideology of natural rights. Lauren states this involved "a struggle for supremacy between the higher classes in parliament, and the monarchy with the former gaining the ascendancy." Lauren adds: "From an emphasis on reciprocal duties under the Monarchy and the divine rights of the King developed an emphasis on individual rights with government under the rule of law" (Lauren, 1998).

The seventeenth century was also a time for major changes in a number of fields. Ideas and innovations possibly formerly suppressed by the conservative regime were unleashed by the emergence of liberalism with its emphasis on reason and the search for truth, at least within bounds of what was conceived as natural law and individual choice rather than mere obedience to the monarchy. These changes would eventually see the rise in the dominance of the bourgeoisie. These changes are described by Ishay who states: "The necessary conditions for the Enlightenment, which combined to bring an end to the Middle Ages in Europe, included the scientific revolution, the rise of mercantilism, the launching of maritime explorations of the globe, the consolidation of the nation-state, and the emergence of a middle class. These developments stimulated the expansion of Western power even as they created propitious prospects for the development of modern conceptions of human rights. They ultimately shattered feudalism and challenged the previously uncontested divine rights of kings" (Ishay, 2004: 7).

At this time democracy was only in its very formative stages. Aylmer states that "the franchise—that is the right to vote—varied very widely. In some boroughs most householders had it in others members of the governing body, or corporation' while the mass of peasants, well over half the population, 'had no share at all in public affairs . . .' and were said to be "outside of the political nation" (Aylmer, 1963: 46–47). Parliament reflected the lack of democratic representation. Aylmer states that "well over three-quarters of the members of any

House of Commons in this period were of gentry origin socially; they sat for the majority of the 'borough' as well as the fewer but more esteemed 'county' seats. However, many of them owed their seats to the patronage of peers, and commoners sitting as M.P.s were in fact sons and younger brothers of peers, some of whom would later succeed to peerages themselves" (Aylmer, 1963: 43).

The middle classes previously had not been politically active (Aylmer, 1963: 46). Increasingly throughout the middle ages there was an increasing expectation that acting in accordance to divine rights (known only to the king and God) was not enough and that the monarchy had a duty to natural law. By the early seventeenth century the monarchy came to be increasingly seen as failing in its duties to these natural laws. Lauren states:

". . . . the Renaissance and Reformation paved the way for the spiritual emancipation of the individual. In this context, resistance to political and economic bondage and to religious intolerance grew, criticisms that rulers had failed to meet their natural law obligations increased, and interest in freedom and individual expression expanded to unprecedented levels (Lauren, 2003: 13).

The ideological shift from an emphasis on duties to natural law to natural rights was to have profound effects around the world. Essentially, rather than exercising a duty to the monarch natural rights challenged the power of the monarchy and demanded that rights be respected. While this opened up a space of reason in society where old ideas were challenged and many new ideas could flourish it also resulted in increased individualism and the divesting of social responsibilities on the grounds that capitalism allowed people to help themselves, which was in fact far from the case for the great mass of semi-literate peasants. Lauren states: "For centuries most of these early philosophical theories of natural law—just like those of religious doctrine—focused on universal responsibilities and duties rather than what are now described as rights. But the modifications of theories and then the transformations of theory into practice always have been tied to particular political, economic, social, and intellectual upheavals throughout history. For concepts of natural rights to come to the fore, major changes in the beliefs and practices of society needed to take place. In this regard, movements of monumental proportions spread over a period of five hundred years began to take place in Europe" (Lauren, 2003: 13).

Liberalism meant that the rule of law, reflecting natural rights, would predominate and be protected by parliament. Everyone would be subject to the rule of law, even the monarchy. As a consequence sovereignty began to be increasingly transferred from the monarchy to Parliament. The ideological battle led to the English Civil Wars (1642–51) with Parliament becoming a revolutionary body and center of resistance to the king (Encyclopedia

Britannica, 2002). Following the revolution, the English Bill of Rights 1689 represented a social contract largely between the middle classes and the monarchy. Ishay states: "As the emerging liberal civil society confronted the absolutist state, tensions were inevitable. In the late seventeenth century, the English Bill of Rights, issued following the English Glorious Revolution, concluded with the reinstitution of the parliament and limitations on the executive power of the newly installed King William of Orange, demonstrating the capacity of the affluent bourgeoisie to extract concessions from the British monarchy" (Ishay, 2004: 328–329). The Bill of Rights ensured the supremacy of Parliament, the right to free elections, freedom of speech, the right to bail, freedom from cruel and unusual punishments and the right to trial by jury (Human Rights Commission, Celebrating the 50th Anniversary of the UDHR, 2). Aylmer also describes another important act – the Habeas Corpus Act of 1689 made it more difficult for the Crown to hold people indefinitely in prison for political reasons without being bought to trial. Also Aylmer describes increasing individual freedoms toward the end of the seventeenth century: after 1694–1695 there was no censorship of books, or newspapers before publication, and greater independence for the judiciary who gained "security of tenure and salary" (Aylmer, 1963: 228).

Natural rights led to the creation, within the Great Chain of Being, of a space for the private sector occupied by the middle classes and capitalism. The inclusion of the middle classes in the dominant elite would most likely have been seen by many peasants as yet another group to oppress them. Ishay states:

> This parceling of sixteenth- and seventeenth-century political and economic life created space for the development of relatively autonomous class, the bourgeoisie, which was concentrated in urban sites. Economically speaking, the bourgeoisie stood between the nobility and the clergy on one hand and the peasantry on the other hand. Its members earned their living by manufacturing, shop keeping, banking, trading—in general, by the various activities that have been stimulated by the expansion of commerce (Ishay, 2004: 72).

In the seventeenth century John Locke, described by Aylmer as "one of the greatest English Philosophers" was an Oxford don who produced a general argument justifying the Revolution of 1688 from the Whig (largely liberal) side (Aylmer, 1963: 228). This general argument was contained in his *Second Treatise on Government* described by Lauren as "one of the most influential political treatises of all time." Lauren states that Locke stressed that "every individual person in the state of nature' possessed certain 'natural rights' prior to the existence of any organized societies." These rights were universal and Lauren adds, "People are born, Locke declared, 'in a state of perfect equality, where naturally there is no superiority or jurisdiction of one over another'" (Lauren, 2003: 15).

Along with his contemporaries Locke was also a believer in the Great Chain of Being. Locke states: "And when we consider the infinite power and wisdom of the Maker, we have reason to think that it is suitable to the magnificent harmony of the universe, and the great design and infinite goodness of the Architect, that the species of creatures should also, by gentle degrees, ascend upward from us toward his infinite perfection, as we see they gradually descend from us downwards" (John Locke, 1690. 3, vi, 12). However, in his formulation of liberalism he made a radical departure from the hierarchical great chain. Unlike most of his contemporaries, Locke did not regard this hierarchy as existing within the human species, at least with respect to the natural rights chosen. He placed emphasis on these individual rights rather than duties to the monarch. All people were equal in these natural rights, and they consisted of the right to their property, life and liberty which, he conceived, originally existed in a (hypothetical) state of nature. These rights, by nature universal, transcended ordinary law which could be easily changed by the state. Rather these natural rights were constitutional in nature and a statement of the nation's "raison d'etre." Paul Lauren states: "John Locke helped to elevate these long-held notions of property rights to a higher philosophical plane by declaring that they were an integral part of 'natural rights' and absolutely essential to the pursuit of happiness" (Lauren, 2003: 26).

Because of the dangers inherent in the state of nature Locke considered that people entered into society to have these rights protected. Lauren states: "Indeed he argued that 'the great and chief end' of forming governments in the first place was 'the preservation of their property'" (Lauren, 2003: 26).

The relationship between government and people was in the form of a social contract. If the government failed to protect these rights people were entitled "to launch a revolution." Lauren states: "Any government that acted without limits imposed by the consent of the government, said Locke, thus dissolved the contract and gave people a right to resist" (Lauren, 2003: 15).

Locke proposed that to better protect these rights there should be a separation of powers between the monarchy, Parliament, and the judiciary rather than left to one section of government. Locke placed considerable emphasis on property because the rights to life and liberty were also part of the property a person had in themselves. Ishay states: ". . . Locke argued in 1689 that 'everyman has a property in his person; this nobody has a right to but himself. The labor of his body and the work of his hand, we may say, are properly his.'" (Ishay, 2004: 93).

However, Locke's rights to property, life, and liberty largely reflected the interests of the dominant elite, the middle class in particular. First, irrespective of Locke's view of their universality and equality, this view was unrealistic in a society dominated by the Great Chain of Being with the monarchy and aristocracy ensuring the hierarchy. So, these natural rights would largely only apply to the dominant elite. In other words, they would be very unlikely to be able to be implemented for all—so Locke's views lacked realism by ignoring the social hierarchy. For the great majority of the poor they may have been no more than aspirations. Secondly, Locke assumed that these rights were the only ones contained in "higher law" and did not consider that other rights, such as the right to education without which they could not access their natural rights, might be required before they could have relevance to the masses who were largely semi-literate and lived lives barely above subsistence level. So Locke's conception of the natural rights in the "state of nature" did not reflect the interests of the whole population. For instance, his rights to property, which were individualistic, did not protect the common land used by the peasants which was being converted to private ownership from the twelfth to nineteenth centuries in a process known as enclosure and which dispossessed many peasants. In fact, the individualistic rights of Locke may have contributed to the continuance of enclosure—whereas "official disapproval," under the monarchy, prevented most further enclosure movements in the sixteenth century under liberal influence "parliamentary enclosures" from 1760 to 1820s and involved government sanction (Early Modern History Encyclopedia of the Early Modern World, by an Answers Corp.com). Also, Locke's right to liberty did not extend to the poor whose few means of protest were to petition the king and to riot. These liberties were restricted during this period. Aylmer states that the exertion of popular pressure on Parliament was made more difficult by an act to restrict mass petitioning, which had been a marked feature of the 1640s (Aylmer, 1963: 168). Also the masses who "normally did not operate as a factor in politics," according to Aylmer, "every now and then they came on the scene." He describes major anti-enclosure riots in the east Midlands in 1607, in the West Country around 1630, and also anti-enclosure riots in several parts of the country in 1641 (Aylmer, 1963). However, Aylmer states in relation to the individual freedoms of the masses: "In matters of public order there was not much of a victory for the populace. Decisions as to when law and order were being infringed were put into the hands of local magistrates to an even greater extent than they had since 1660 (and) the operative statute comes a good deal later, the Riot Act (1715)" (Aylmer, 1963: 228).

During the English civil wars a peasant group called the Diggers received some prominence but their appeals for their natural rights were not heard. According to Ishay they were "animated by the vision of an agricultural communist society." They "conceived of the English civil wars as a struggle against the king and the great landowners" and asked for "the establishment of communal property" considering that "land should be made available for the very poor to cultivate." Ishay adds that they also called for further legal and political democracy and the rejection of the state church. Their increasing activities, however, alarmed the commonwealth government and triggered the hostility of local landowners. Harassed by legal actions and mob violence, they had dispersed by the end of March 1650 (Ishay, 2004: 92–93). Ishay concludes:

> The English civil war might have coincided with the development of fundamental rights (i.e., the right to life, freedom of opinion, and property), but those rights were not extended to everyone. The emergence of radical groups like the British agrarian communists the Diggers, who strove to be recognized as full-fledged citizens under the British sky, attested to the exclusive character of the revolution; their hopes for civil equality were soon thwarted by the political ascendancy of men of property (Ishay, 2004: 108).

However, the ideas of individual choice, individual responsibility, and self-help which stem from natural rights and the creation of a private sector had little relevance to the great mass of peasants who were only semi-literate, lived lives of sometimes extreme insecurity, and were "outside the political nation." Very few peasants would have been likely to be able to set up in business and, after being forced off their lands, would be used largely as cheap labor in factories owned by the bourgeoisie. For the poor the liberal revolution largely meant they owed more duties to more masters and extending the scope of rights to protect other groups from absolutism meant that the poor now also had duties to these groups.

Aylmer paints a picture of the conditions of the peasants in the early seventeenth century which indicate that education, an adequate economic security, and a democratic voice also reflected the needs of the peasants but these were not elevated to the status of natural law. Aylmer states: "These social classes [the masses], all of whom were normally outside of politics, and most of whom were on the borderline of subsistence level, are in the background to the political history of the century." He adds that these masses included the bulk of the poorer peasantry, almost all servants, most semi-literate, unskilled workers and a growing wage-earning class. Although there could be family support and peasants who owned some property, they lived at a level of subsistence. Aylmer states: "Many of the poorer classes depended on wages or casual earnings in the textile industry; so they were very easily affected by ups and downs in England's exports of cloth as by economic fluctuations at home. Increases in the price of grain could have a catastrophic affect on them pushing them over the borderline between poverty and destitution and in years of bad harvest there was always a danger of mass starvation" (Aylmer, 1963: 48).

The modern parliamentary system, as well as the principle of parliamentary sovereignty, quickly developed after the Revolution of 1688 (the Glorious Revolution). By the late seventeenth century, the power of the monarch had declined, and the relationship between the House of Lords and House of Commons had shifted in favor of the Commons (Encyclopedia Britannica, 2002).

The ideological struggle between liberalism and the divine right of kings continued into the eighteenth century with the American and French revolutions.

"The needs of the bourgeoisie, in the end, collided with monarchic interests, fueling the English, American, and French Revolutions" (Ishay, 2004).

Lauren states that the first successful challenge to absolutist authority came when the American colonists revolted against their British masters by firing those shots "heard around the world" due to their vast implications (Lauren, 2003: 17).

Major constitutional developments were spawned from the conflicts in the eighteenth century which greatly advanced the power of the bourgeoisie and the liberal ideology. In the United States there was the American Declaration of Independence 1776 and Constitution 1787 and in France there was the French Revolution and the Rights of Man and of Citizens 1791–1793. The focus of each of these documents was on freedom and liberty. Key rights sought to be protected were freedom of expression, thought, and religion and the right to a fair trial by the State. The rights are now termed civil and political. While claiming equal human rights, in reality a number of groups were discriminated against, including the most disadvantaged. Lauren states: "Despite the remarkable provisions of the new U.S. Bill of Rights, and the theories of natural law and inalienable rights that stood behind them, and the ringing words "We the people" in the Constitution's preamble, for example, actual practices denied equal rights to the majority comprising women, slaves, the unpropertied, indigenous peoples, and children" (Lauren, 2003).

While the U.S. Founding Fathers had dispensed with the Great Chain of Being (Walker), the social structure was dominated by men of property. Ishay describes Thomas Jefferson's concern about the "inequitable resolution of the American Revolution" when he complained in 1785 that "the property of this country is absolutely concentrated in very few hands" (Ishay, 2004: 108–109). The discriminations of the great chain, which was regarded as being created by God, was replaced by discrimination by those who controlled the human rights agenda and with natural law included in the Constitution there was now no means of appeal to a "higher law." Walker states in relation to the Constitution: "Who was discriminated against was determined by 'man' not fixed by God. Also as the temporal equivalent of divine justice had been determined by the 'civil rights' interpretation of natural law it was extremely difficult to appeal to the latter when faced with an injustice not covered by the Constitution. Consequently the precepts of Mahatma Gandhi and Martin Luther King that we owe a duty to a 'higher law' no longer applied" (Walker, 2001).

Alexis de Tocqueville, who wrote the book *Democracy in America* (1835), while overlooking the discriminated groups, was to state that in the United States "opportunity is widespread and the poor can, with luck and hard work, move up; wealth and poverty constitute possibly temporary situations, not permanent inequality." (Frederiksen). Frederiksen stated that: "There is little doubt that Tocqueville overestimated the equality of conditions in Jacksonian America, but in many ways compared to the aristocratic societies of Europe, America was indeed egalitarian (Frederiksen).

Lauren describes how "encouraged by this successful American experience, although pressed to breaking point by its own internal problems and pressures, France also exploded into violent revolutionary upheaval in 1789." He adds:

> The resulting French revolution not only destroyed a despotic monarch and the privileged elite of the old regime in France, but through its actions and its expressed ideology proved to be one of the most profound revolutions in history. The National Assembly proclaimed loudly and vehemently their own Declaration of Rights of Man and Citizen. Here they asserted that all men 'are born and remain free and equal in rights', that these rights were universal and 'natural and imprescriptible,' and they included liberty, property, security, and resistance to oppression (Lauren, 2003: 17–18).

However, as with the American constitution, various groups, including the most disadvantaged, were discriminated against: "The French Declaration was chiefly concerned with the rights of the middle class. The rights of women, people of different races and cultures and low-income people were usually overlooked or ignored" (Human Rights Commission, The 50th Anniversary of the Universal Declaration of Human Rights, 4). However, remarkably, the French Declaration was to include provisions which would eventually lead to the development of economic, social, and cultural rights. Lauren describes "one single, extraordinary year of 1791": "Additional provisions mandated public relief for the poor and free public education, items completely unknown in other constitutions of the time and ones that would come to inspire what eventually would come to be called social and economic rights" (Paul Lauren, *The Evolution of International Human Rights: Visions Seen*, (University of Pennsylvania Press, 2003), 18).

Ishay states that 'voting rights were restricted to owners of property, along the lines of the British and American example" (Ishay, 2004: 74).

Also Ishay states that as with the American Revolution there was "similar popular disillusionment over the consolidation of power by French propertied men." She states:

> Robespierre's proposal to limit the accumulation of wealth and grant every man the right to vote was rejected by the French National Assembly. Economically disadvantaged and political disempowered, members of the Fourth Estate—the peasantry and the sansculottes [members of the poorer classes]—were not able to bridge the growing economic gap between themselves and the wealthier. Though they were briefly in power, their radical agenda did not outlast Robespierre's revolutionary government and was superseded (in 1794) by Thermidorian reaction. The Thermidorians wanted to guarantee the social preeminence and political authority of the bourgeoisie within the liberal regime. With Thermidor, the progressive forces of the Enlightenment era were in retreat, challenged by the interests of a greedy commercial class (Ishay, 2004: 109).

At the same time in England, Thomas Paine published his famous *Rights of Man*. Drawing on the theory of natural law and natural rights, he introduced the specific expression "human rights" perhaps for the first time (Lauren, 2003: 20).

In 1972, Part Two of the Rights of Man was published with a welfare plan which was very radical for its day, particularly because Paine regarded such welfare as a human right rather than charity. This meant it was a state responsibility to provide adequate welfare because it was a right, social justice, and not just at the level of subsistence while blaming the poor for their predicament as with the poor laws. Also, it was not simply to be left to the private charities, the private sector, or the private consciences of individuals whose efforts could be grossly insufficient. Paul Hunt states:

> The crucial social chapter of Part Two envisages a graduated income tax to finance a benefit for newly-wedded couples; a maternity allowance; a benefit for poor families enabling them to raise and educate their children; public employment for those in need of work; a system of social security permitting workers to retire on a pension at age sixty; and a benefit for the decent burial for those who die in poverty (Hunt, 1996: 6).

Hunt adds: "Paine stated that he advocated 'not charity but a right, not bounty but justice'" (Hunt, 1996: 7). During the nineteenth century as a reaction to Classical Liberalism, the Industrial Revolution and its extreme hardships, there were popular rebellions and the development of the challenging ideas of socialism and economic, social, and cultural rights. Ishay states: "The route towards industrialization, however, created growing social hardships, as rural poor in search of work migrated en masse to industrial sites, worsening urban poverty. The widening gap between rich and poor ultimately sparked popular rebellions and prompted the revival of human rights discourses" (Ishay, 2004: 120–121).

As with present day Classical Liberalism in the nineteenth century a society was created where there was considerable inequality in terms of human rights. Ishay states: "The hope for a state predicated upon human rights was further challenged as the industrial revolution and global capitalism sharply divided mankind into an elite class enjoying security, liberty, and property and disenfranchised masses that did not enjoy any of those human rights" (Ishay, 2004: 286).

While Classical Liberalism and the middle classes gained considerable dominance over the old aristocratic order it led to unrestrained extreme oppression and exploitation. Brian states that "the Industrial Revolution had many profound effects on European civilization. It rendered much of the old aristocracy irrelevant, boosted the bourgeoisie to economic and political power, and drafted much of the old peasant class into its factories." He added that "the dissolution of this old order meant that workers could be hired and fired at will and had to sell their labor for whatever the going work cheaply enough to gain them an advantage in the job market." Furthermore, Brian states that this meant that "traditional rules and protections went by the board in the new factories, which often ran for twenty-four hours a day (two twelve-hour shifts), seven days a week under the most inhumane conditions." (Brian).

Lauren gives a vivid description of the working conditions of the time:

> Not all class divisions during the nineteenth century, of course, centered on hereditary serfs or peasants toiling the land in agriculture. In fact, with the emergence and the development of the Industrial Revolution, a rapid expansion in the numbers of exploited occurred among the working class of the urban proletariat. In the factories, textile mills, and mines throughout the industrializing world millions of men and—at the very bottom women and children, suffered in wretched squalor, thick smoke and soot, disease infested water, overcrowded slums, misery, and working conditions of oppression without any prospect of relief. Five-year-old boys chained around the waist hauled carts of coal in the mines, while girls of eight worked underground in complete darkness for twelve hours a day to open and close passage doors. Women stood on swollen feet for fifteen hours per day changing the thread on bobbins attached to power looms with no safety devices. Men labored under similar conditions, received pitiful payment for their efforts, remained at the mercy of those who owned the means of production, and suffered back-breaking hardships of almost unimaginable duration. Estimates place the average working week in Europe by mid-century at an appalling eighty-four hours. The exploitation of these urban workers with its

attendant starvation, poverty, crime, prostitution, epidemics, and family disloca-
tions became so tragic, in fact, it simply could not be hidden (Lauren, 2003: 54).

Because of these barbaric conditions, a consequence of Classical Liberalism, the meaning of human rights began to be questioned. Lauren states:
"Such obvious and severe misery endured by the working class ignited new
and profoundly serious questions about the meaning of human rights. What
good were civil rights such as the freedom of speech or political rights for
voting, asked those who suffered, to people like themselves who had no food,
no homes, no clothing, no medical care, or no prospect of an education" (Lauren, 2003: 54). Lauren adds: "It is out of this context of class exploitation that
we thus discover the significant emergence of a second generation on human
rights: namely, social and economic rights" (Lauren, 2003: 55).

The working class took on the role of being the major driving force behind
universal suffrage and economic rights against much opposition from the
aristocracy and the middle classes. Ishay states:

> A careful review of the nineteenth century, however, shows that for most so-
> cialists, the struggles for political and economic rights were closely linked.
> Their demands, however, were strongly opposed by aristocratic forces in the
> first decades after the Congress of Vienna [the redrawing of the continent's po-
> litical map in 1814 after the defeat of Napoleonic France] and were later resis-
> ted by the bourgeoisie wherever it had ascended to power (Ishay, 2004:
> 120–135).

The trade unions of the nineteenth century were much more likely to cham-
pion socialism than economic, social, and cultural rights. Given the desper-
ateness of the working class and the barbarity of the social system, class confrontation seems to have been necessary in self-defense and socialism, with
its avowed aims of nationalizing the means of production, revolution, and using class conflict to achieve the short-term aim of the dictatorship of the proletariat and long-term aim of a classless society, would best fulfill this role.
Often ardent adherents of Classical Liberalism claim that international trade
and liberal democracy ensures world peace but it must be seriously questioned when these societies descend to such ruthless exploitation in their own
country whether future international conflict is not being spawned. Economic
and social rights were still in their formative stages and were not captured by
the elite as they are in today's world but were driven by the trade unions with
an inclination to focus on the economic and social rights of the working class.
Ishay describes how Karl Marx inaugurated in 1864 the First International
with the aim to promote a broader alliance between socialist movements
("Workers of the world, unite!"). While the political agenda reflected some of

the common interests of the oppressed it overlooked some of the vital interests of the most disadvantaged, that is, the right to work, health, housing, and
welfare. The political agenda advocated universal suffrage, the abolition of
the right to property, a heavily progressive income tax, the abolition of the
right to inheritance, the reduction of working hours, the amelioration of
health and safety provisions in the workplace, the restriction of child labor,
the emancipation of women, and the abolition of slavery (Ishay, 2004:
332–333).

In the 1830s revolutions occurred resulting in "liberal victories against
conservative strongholds" in France, Spain, Belgium, and Greece. Revolution
was averted in England, where industrialization was most advanced and the
trade unions were strongest as there existed "the early development of a self-
conscious British working class." In 1832 British conservatives "fearing the
spread of the 1830s revolutions on the continent . . . reluctantly yielded" and
passed the First Reform Bill, which widened male suffrage (Ishay, 2004:
136–137). Other progressive legislation followed, mainly concerned with
workers rights: the 1833 Factory Act, which forbade employing children less
than nine years old in the textile mills, in 1842 the employment of women as
well as girls in coal mines was prohibited and the "greatest success" for the
working class arrived in 1847 with the Ten Hours Act, which limited the daily
work hours of women, children, and men (Ishay, 2004: 137–138). While a
new Poor Law (also known as the Speenhamland Law) was enacted in 1834,
resulting in an increase in spending for public relief "it was accompanied by
a policy that viewed pauperism among workers as a moral failing" (Ishay,
2004: 137).

Between 1848 and 1852, further revolutions occurred in most of western
and central Europe with exceptions such as the Netherlands, Belgium, and
Britain. Although the immediate cause was the economic hardship of 1846
and 1847 stemming from the failure of the potato and wheat crops throughout much of Europe as well as the spread of cholera they occurred where "a
state . . . continued to resist liberal and nationalist reforms" as "early industrialization strengthened the middle classes, who embraced liberalism and na-
tionalism" (Revolutions in Europe 1848–1852 (5), *The Encyclopedia of
World History, Sixth Edition*, Peter N. Stearns, General Editor, 2001).

The revolution in France in 1848 was led by Louis Blanc (1811–1882) who
advocated national communes for the poor as an example of the more altruistic
approach to economic and social rights that existed at the time. Ishay states:
"Blanc had hoped . . . that a newly constituted government would gradually
transform privately owned workplaces into social workshops designed to alleviate the lot of the needy." "The right to work, he further claimed, was an essential right that needed to be secured by the state. . . ." (Ishay, 2004: 120–140).

The economic hardships of the 1840s had left many people without employment. Workers and the socialists demanded that workers be guaranteed the right to work, the right to a minimum wage, and the right to be provided for in the case of illness and old age. The government recognized the right to work, the right to a living wage, and the right of workers to organize. National workshops were decreed to provide work or relief to all the unemployed (*The Encyclopedia of World History, Sixth Edition* Stearns, 2001).

However, in what was described as a "bourgeois betrayal," a socialist/liberal split occurred with "the French bourgeoisie who stole the political stage in 1848, marginalizing and executing the radicals [socialists] who helped them" (Ishay, 2004: 147). This led to the closing of the national workshops. Ishay states: "Guided by Louis Blanc's socialist vision, the city of Paris established national workshops to relieve the distress of the unemployed. Favoring an uncompromising liberal agenda, however, the newly formed Constituent Assembly soon dissolved these social projects and proclaimed martial law against any form of social resistance" (Ishay, 2004: 124). It was partly due to such divisions in the opposition which led to conservative regimes being restored throughout Europe.

Toward the end of the nineteenth century the liberal and conservative elites in a number of European governments were forced by the emergence of socialism to adopt more socially responsible policies. Ishay states: "Fear of communist rebellion now spurred reform. In 1883, at the zenith of German expansionist policies, German Chancellor Bismarck secured the passage of social legislation, including compulsory sickness insurance for workers, an accident insurance plan, and a comprehensive pension for the aged and disabled" (Ishay, 2004: 286).

However, apart from a small number of countries, "Europe and much of the rest of the world were based on the rule of law, individual liberty, private property and freedom of trade — 'classical liberalism,' as this set of beliefs was termed in the 19th century" (Ebeling).

The democratic process proved to be valuable as a means whereby groups such as liberals promoting civil and political rights, and the working class promoting socialism and economic, social, and cultural rights could increase their power vis-à-vis the aristocratic establishment by educating the people. For instance, Ishay states: "Social democratic parties, generally indebted to Marxist doctrine, sprang up in most of the countries of continental Europe" (Ishay, 2004: 126).

In 1867 in England a Second Reform Bill was passed. Ishay states that whereas the First Reform Bill added some 200,000 voters to the rolls, the Second Reform Act added nearly a million. She added that the United States underwent a similar battle to secure manhood suffrage (Ishay, 2004: 141). In addition Ishay states: "The near-end of slavery and the enfranchisement of propertyless male citizens can be recorded as the main nineteenth century achievements on behalf of human rights" (Ishay, 2004: 156).

The individual and economic freedoms promoted by liberalism were found to be unable to withstand the world wars in the twentieth century. With countries intent on mutual destruction, paranoia is rife and the interests of national security provide little room for civil rights while global instability seriously affects trade. Instead the dominant elite is concerned with getting the support of the people by increasing welfare programs while at the same time focusing on national security and repressing domestic dissent. Ishay states: "Historically, while it is true that freedom of expression and other civil rights were undermined in the West during the world wars, the Great Depression, and the cold war, conversely, during these same periods, liberal governments increased their attention to welfare rights programs. War and serious economic crises tend to create xenophobia, increase repression of all forms of domestic dissent, and encourage a political climate in which the rights to free speech and privacy are muted by patriotic fervor; these circumstances, however, also favor stronger governmental intervention in the economy" (Ishay, 2004: 282). For example, the rights of labor 'received significant attention during the Paris Peace Conference in 1919.' Lauren states: "Laborers had sacrificed much during World War I and, in order to maintain war production strength and "unity" on the "home front" governments had made many promises for the extension of social and economic rights once hostilities ceased" (Lauren, 2003: 94). Also, the Atlantic Charter signed by Churchill and Roosevelt during the Second World War, "declared that they sought the right to have 'improved labor standards, economic advancement and social security' in all nations, wanted people everywhere to be able to have the right to "live out their lives in freedom from want and fear," and desired "a wider and permanent system of general security" for the world (Lauren, 2003: 138–139).

Following the Bolshevik Revolution in Russia in 1917, the Declaration of Rights of the Working and Exploited Peoples of 1918 was incorporated into the Soviet constitution (Felice, 1996: 20). Lauren states: "The All-Russian Congress of Soviets, for example, adopted what it called the Declaration of Rights of the Toiling and Exploited Peoples, boldly pledging 'to suppress all exploitation of man by man, to abolish forever the division of society into classes, ruthlessly to suppress all exploitation, and to bring about the socialist organization of society in all countries' " (Lauren, 2003: 90). The Soviet constitution gave considerable prominence to economic, social, and cultural rights. The response of the liberal democracies was to adopt a more socially responsible international agenda with "the nearly simultaneous establishment of the League of Nations and the International Labour Organization, predicated upon progressive liberal notions of human rights" (Ishay, 2004: 177). Scott Davidson explains: "The International Labour Organisation, created by the Treaty of Versailles (1919), was a response to the Allied Powers' concerns about social justice and standards of treatment of industrial workers which had largely been prompted by the Bolshevik Revolution of 1917. The ILO, which became a specialised agency of the UN in 1946, may be seen as the precursor of systems for the protection of economic, social and cultural rights" (Davidson, 1993: 9). The focus of the International Labor Organization was on workers rights. Ishay states:

> The main thrust of this new organization (ILO) in relation to the League of Nations, was to enforce labor standards. . . . The new Labor Charter called for the establishment of a maximum working day and week, the provision of an adequate living wage, protection against sickness, disease, and injury arising out of a worker's employment, the protection of children, women, and immigrant workers, freedom of association, and so forth (Ishay, 2004: 207).

In addition, William Felice states that economic, social, and cultural rights were formulated in the Weimar constitution of Germany in 1919, the Constitution of the Spanish Republic of 1931, and the Constitution of Ireland of 1937 with the Mexican Constitution formulating them as early as 1917 (Felice, 1996: 20). These constitutions were inspired by socialism and religion. Ivo Duchacek states: "The economic and social articles found in national constitutions have been largely inspired either by Karl Marx's critique of nineteenth-century capitalism or the Roman Catholic papal encyclicals, Rerum Novarum (Leo XIII, 1891) and Quadragesimo Anno (Pius XI, 1931). Marx and the popes all condemned capitalist liberalism" (Duchacek, 1973: 108). Duchacek adds: "The Irish Constitution based its Directive Principles of State Policy on the social doctrine expounded in [the] two papal encyclicals. . . ." (Duchacek, 1973: 119).The Catholic Church, which has a tradition of occasionally speaking out on behalf of the poor, took an inclusive view of mankind. Lauren states: "Finally, in the face of overwhelming evidence of human deprivation and in the light of his own personal observations of the sufferings of the exploited poor across national borders, Pope Leo XIII issued his 1891 encyclical known as Rerum Novarum (Of New Things). He viewed society as a living whole whose members perform different functions and possess responsibilities, and where everyone has a right to procure what is necessary to live." (Lauren, 2003: 57). Lauren adds: "Such pronouncements contributed still further to developing and legitimizing international claims for social and economic rights" (Lauren, 2003: 57).

In line with Marx's class perspective the Soviet Union regarded civil and political rights as largely promoting the interests of the bourgeoisie. "The Soviet hostility to human rights, or at least of the first generation civil and political rights owed much to Marx's critique in On the Jewish Question" (Bowring, 1995: 107).

The Soviet Union nationalized the means of production and severely reduced the power of the "bourgeoisie." Ishay states: "In the Soviet Union not only were the means of production and consumption taken from the 'bourgeoisie' without any compensation, not only were they deprived of all political rights; they were at the same time victims of oppression and they alone were liable to do compulsory work!" (Ishay, 2004: 203).

As with the omission of economic, social, and cultural rights in domestic jurisdictions has resulted in extreme poverty on a massive scale, the omission of civil and political rights in the Soviet bloc resulted in atrocities on a massive scale. This indicates, in my opinion, the importance of the "equal status principle" and how excluding either set of rights can result in complete barbarity. Lauren describes the civil and political rights situation in the Stalin era. He states: "In the Soviet Union, despite the language of rights in the constitution, Joseph Stalin ruthlessly ruled his totalitarian state. He expelled thousands of opponents to the Siberian Gulag, condemned thousands to death during his public 'show trials,' and instituted state terrorism to persecute and execute even more who he considered disloyal. To compound this tragedy, Stalin forced the masses of peasants at gunpoint into collective farms under the control of the Communist Party, and then into deliberate famine. The sheer magnitude of this assault (described by writer Boris Pasternak as so horrendous as to 'not fit within the bounds of consciousness') is revealed by the fact that the state published the deaths of livestock but not people, and by estimates placing the total number of those who died at the staggering figure of more than twenty million human beings" (Lauren, 2003: 131).

However, while rejecting civil and political rights, the Soviet Union did provide economic, social, and cultural rights for its people. Cranston states: "Assuredly, the Communist governments could not seriously claim that they upheld the rights to liberty, property, or security from arbitrary arrest, secret trials, or forced labor: but they could fairly claim to provide universal education, social security, and 'periodic holidays with pay'" (Cranston, 1973: 54).

As the Soviet bloc provided employment, free health, free accommodation, and free education for most of its citizens, Western liberal democracies were pressured to do likewise as its citizens could turn to communism for hope of a better world. However, it took the Great War and the Great Depression in 1929 for liberal democracies to adopt more socially responsible policies in what came to be called Modern Liberalism such as Roosevelt's New Deal and economic bill of rights. Ishay states: "Nevertheless, the combination of the Great War together with the Great Depression had impelled European and America statesmen to seek popular legitimacy by introducing many of the economic and social safety-net policies that socialists had long promoted. Thanks to a corporate alliance of government, business, and workers, the welfare state was born" (Ishay, 2004: 208).

After each of the world wars, governments made numerous attempts to reconstruct a new world order to ensure global stability as well as to legitimize the dominant global elites, for whom irrespective of any ideological differences, wealth and power was still an interest in common. There have been the League of Nations and the United Nations. There have been regional defense pacts, like the North Atlantic Treaty Organization (NATO), and regional economic pacts, like the European Economic Community (EEC). There have been global economic pacts, like the General Agreement on Tariffs and Trade (GATT), the International Monetary Fund (IMF), and the World Bank.

However, following the horrors of the Second World War and the Holocaust, the capacity of global elites to rise above their self-interests was evident in the creation in 1948 of the Universal Declaration of Human Rights. Craven states: "Following the Second World War . . . the international human rights movement was born and the protection of human rights was declared to be one of the purposes of the United Nations (UN), and the UN Charter imposed certain obligations upon member States to that end" (see Art 1, 55 & 56: Arts 13, 62(2), and Chs XI and XII) (Craven, 1995: 6). The UDHR was adopted by 48 votes to 0 with eight abstentions (Byelorussia, Czechoslovakia, Poland, USSR, Saudi Arabia, Ukraine, South Africa, and Yugoslavia) (Craven, 1995: 17).

The declaration quickly became regarded as a document with considerable moral authority. Lauren states:

> Exactly as the advocates hoped, and as the critics feared, the Universal Declaration enormously accelerated the evolution of international human rights. Despite many efforts to present and portray the document as a "mere" statement of principle with no legally binding authority at all, the vision proclaimed struck a chord among the peoples of the world and rapidly began to take on a life of its own. It quickly came to assume, as we shall see, growing moral, political, and even legal force through customary law [usually dealing with serious violations such genocide, torture, state sanctioned racism etc]. This, in turn, inspired a veritable revolution in international, regional, and national actions on behalf of human rights. Indeed, it is precisely for this reason that the vision of the Universal Declaration of Human Rights is still described as 'the greatest achievement of the United Nations' and as 'one of the greatest steps forward in the process of global civilization' (Lauren, 2003: 232).

Former New Zealand prime minister Peter Fraser attended the Great Debate at the United Nations in 1948 and said on returning home, referring to the UN Charter, that "while the Charter certainly was not perfect and contained many defects. It nevertheless marked, he said, the best possible hope of realizing a vision of peace with human rights for millions of men, women and children of all nations around the world" (Lauren, 2003: 197).

Whereas previously States were largely considered responsible for their own citizens (State Sovereignty), the translation of the Universal Declaration of Human Rights into international human rights law made it a concern of all States how one of its member States treated its citizens. Craven states: "Prior to 1945, international law was generally not concerned with how states treated individuals within their own borders. Such matters were regarded as being within the domestic jurisdiction of each State. Exceptions did exist in the cases of slavery, humanitarian intervention, the treatment of aliens, minorities, and the laws of war but they were spasmodic, limited in scope, and largely political rather than idealistic in motivation" (Craven, 1995: 6). Henkin points out that 'the abiding and ineradicable memory of the Holocaust has made it impossible for any state to insist that, in principle, how it behaves towards its own people is no one else's business' (Henkin, 2000: 17).

The New Zealand delegation to the Great Debate at the United Nations was led by Fraser and put the New Zealand position. New Zealand supported not only civil and political rights, that is, traditional Western liberties, but to the consternation of its Western allies, also supported economic, social, and cultural rights. Professor Gordon Lauren of University of Montana, USA, who came to New Zealand in 1998 to research New Zealand's involvement in 1948, stated:

Prime Minister Peter Fraser and his colleagues Walter Nash and Carl Berendsen came to be convinced that the aftermath of the Second World War offered a unique opportunity to advance the cause of human rights. Together they pressed for traditional liberal values such as life, liberty, and freedom of speech in the form of civil and political rights favored by the West. At the same time, and to the frustration of a number of their Western colleagues, they successfully supported the inclusion of economic and social rights favored by the East [East European communist countries].

He added: "In launching this revolution, New Zealand was far out in front of other nations, though its role is not generally known and certainly not appreciated" (Lauren, *New Zealand Herald* 10/12/98).

New Zealand's address to the General Assembly was given by Colin Aikman (now Professor of Law at Victoria University):

My delegation . . . attaches equal importance to all the articles. . . . At the same time we regard with particular satisfaction the place which is given in the declaration to social and economic rights. Experience in New Zealand has taught us that the assertion of the right of personal freedom is incomplete unless it is related to the social and economic rights of the common man. There can be no difference of opinion as to the tyranny of privation and want. There is no dictator more terrible than hunger. And we have found in New Zealand that only with social security in its widest sense can the individual reach his full stature. Therefore it can be understood why we emphasize the right to work, the right to a standard of living adequate for health and well-being, and the right to security in the event of unemployment, sickness, disability, widowhood and old age. Also the fact that the common man is a social being requires that he should have the right to education, the right to rest and leisure, and the right to freely participate in the cultural life of the community (Aikman, 1999).

In addition, New Zealand played a prime role in having human rights included in the United Nations Charter. Former New Zealand foreign minister, Don McKinnon, now Commonwealth Secretary-General, states: "In the original Dumbarton Oaks draft of the UN Charter there was no mention of human rights, except for an insignificant sentence, right at the end of the draft. It is not as well-known as it should be that it was a New Zealand proposal to add, in the chapter on principles, the words:

"All members of the organisation undertake to preserve, protect and promote human rights and fundamental freedoms."

"This single sentence led in turn to the provision in the UN Charter which enshrined human rights as a legitimate concern between nations, so establishing a basis for the UN to concern itself with failures and abuses of human rights in individual member countries.

"With these words, which were carried through into the final text of the Universal Declaration, as Frank Corner (a former New Zealand Secretary of Foreign Affairs put it), 'New Zealand made an impact that helped to change the course of history'" (Bell, 1997).

However, instead of upholding the declaration as a whole, the member states of the United Nations separated into different ideological camps. Lauren states: "The complicating problem of international politics in the United Nations itself became particularly serious. The United States and its allies in the Cold War increasingly came to fear that the organization was falling under the radical influence of Communists interested in threatening the status quo by destroying colonial empires. The Soviet Union and its allies, on the other hand, came to believe that the United Nations was leaning in the direction of anti-Communist, imperialistic, and capitalist forces. . . ." (Lauren, 2003: 236).

As a consequence during the Cold War human rights was to become a political football with the liberal democracies championing civil and political rights and the East European communists advocating economic, social, and cultural rights. For example, Lauren states: "The Soviets repeatedly argued that political and civil rights represented nothing more than 'bourgeois' values, and thus served as little or no value for most of the world" (Lauren, 2003). As a consequence "an uneasy compromise was arranged whereby the commission would create drafts of two separate covenants, each focused of different kinds of rights" (Lauren, 2003: 238).

The liberal democracies considered that social responsibilities would be too restrictive on the individual—they preferred that such social responsibilities be essentially a private choice rather than a state concern. Arambulo states: "The States that were in favor of two separate Covenants, in particular the United States of America and other Western States opined that traditional principles derived from liberal theories, such as the primacy of the individual, would be infringed by placing economic and social rights on an equal footing with civil and political rights" (Arambulo, 1999: 17).

The result was two covenants—the International Covenant on Civil and Political Rights and the International Covenant on Economic, Social, and Cultural Rights—were created and were eventually adopted and opened for signature, ratification, and accession by the General Assembly on December 16, 1966. Regarding economic, social, and cultural rights Craven states:

> The International Covenant on Economic, Social and Cultural Rights entered into force on 3 January 1976 . . . . it took nearly twenty years to finalise the text of the Covenant. A further decade elapsed before the Covenant entered into force and yet another before the Covenant was provided with a supervisory body [the United Nations Committee on Economic, Social and Cultural Rights] that was worthy of the name (Craven, 1995: 1).

Apart from the Covenant itself, recognition of economic, social, and cultural rights may be found in the UDHR (Articles 22–8), the Convention on the Elimination of All Forms of Racial Discrimination (Article 5), the Convention on the Elimination of All Forms of Discrimination Against Women (Article 1), the Convention on the Rights of the Child, and the Convention on the Rights of Migrant Workers (Craven, 1995: 8).

The division of the Universal Declaration of Human Rights into two covenants allowed the global elite, disregarding the "equal status principle," to marginalize economic, social, and cultural rights at the international, regional, and domestic levels. Paul Hunt, New Zealand's independent expert on the United Nation's Committee on Economic, Social, and Cultural Rights, asserts that "one of the most striking features of contemporary human rights is the juridicial marginalization of social rights." He states:

> At the national level a variety of institutions, procedures, and constitutional arrangements—free and fair elections, bills of rights, habeas corpus, human rights commissions, Ombudsmen and so on—has evolved over generations to promote and protect civil and political rights. Although these devices remain inadequate and flawed, they are considerably more widespread and sophisticated than legal arrangements designed to implement social rights" (Hunt, 1996: 1).

Hunt adds that the same discrepancy between civil and political rights on the one hand and social rights on the other is also apparent at the international level (Paul Hunt, Reclaiming Social Rights, (Dartmouth Pub, 1996), 1). Guarantees for economic, social, and cultural rights are also found in agreements among countries in several regions: The Americas, the American Convention on Human Rights (1969); in Africa, the African Charter on Human and People's Rights (1982); and in Europe, the European Convention on Human Rights (1950) and the European Social Charter. However, Hunt describes the marginalization of economic, social, and cultural rights in these documents: "Although only in its infancy, international human rights law is evolving procedures which, in some circumstances, effectively protect civil and political rights. Consider, for example, the numerous cases heard by the UN Human Rights Committee, the European Court of Human Rights and within the American regional human rights system. By contrast, comparable international procedures for the legal protection of social rights are weak and unused. The African Charter on Human and People's Rights establishes what amounts to a complaints procedure in relation to social rights, yet ten years after the treaty entered into force no complaint alleging the violation of a social right had been submitted to its monitoring body" Hunt, 1996: 1).

While the bipolar world ensured that the West adopted socially responsible policies these, as well as security concerns, acted as a limitation on civil rights. Ishay states: "If socioeconomic rights were strengthened by the welfare state at the height of the cold war, civil liberties were simultaneously threatened. More broadly, it may be the case that war and economic depression tend to drive counties in the direction of social and economic justice at the expense of civil and political rights" (Ishay, 2004: 227).

In 1975 the Helsinki Final Act, involving thirty-three European nations as well as Canada and the United States, was signed. Lauren states that "it contained very explicit language recognizing 'the universal significance' of human rights and pledging the participating states to promote and encourage the effective exercise of civil, political, economic, social, and cultural rights" (Lauren, 2003: 260). According to Henkin, in signing the Helsinki Final Act the Soviet bloc "made a clear commitment to human rights. It did so at the price of détente and in exchange for commitments by the West not to seek to push back the postwar frontiers in Eastern and Central Europe (including the division of Germany)" (Henkin, 2000: 21). Lauren describes how the Helsinki Final Act played a substantial role in the collapse of the Soviet bloc and demonstrated the effects human rights can have when the populace is educated. He states that during the height of the Cold War "the Soviet Union joyously welcomed the surprise announcement that the United States would never sign any of the United Nations-sponsored covenants and conventions on human rights." He adds: "Such a decision allowed the Soviets suddenly to present themselves as the only superpower who defended the exploited and supported the right of self-determination for colonial peoples, cooperated in drafting new treaties, and then gave enormous publicity to their efforts in opposing apartheid." According to Lauren, the Soviets "seriously miscalculated." He states:

> By drawing so much ideological and political attention to their support for certain aspects of human rights, they unintentionally made the issue well known to their own people. Dissidents quickly invoked the principles of the Universal Declaration of Human Rights and the Helsinki Final Act as well as the International Covenant on Civil and Political Rights and the International Covenant on Economic, Social and Cultural Rights against their own government. By giving such prominence to human rights for other purposes, the Soviet authorities created an unexpected and powerful vehicle for change that helped to pull down their entire regime and empire (Lauren, 2003: 299–300).

At the time of the signing of the Helsinki Final Act in 1975, the number of liberal democracies in the world was thirty but by the time of the collapse of communism in Eastern Europe in 1989 the number of liberal democracies had approximately doubled (Fukuyama, 1992: 49–50).

In the late 1970s President Ronald Reagan in the United States and Prime Minister Margaret Thatcher in Britain introduced neoliberalism with its severe welfare cutbacks, unemployment, low wages, and assault on the trade unions. This is often attributed to an oil crisis but may also reflect the changing global balance of power in favor of liberal democracies as well as recognizing the vulnerability of the Soviet states whose ideology hinged on the provision of economic, social, and cultural rights. Ishay states: "The 1970s oil crisis, inflation and stagnating growth, hobbled liberal governments in England and the United States, and set the stage for a conservative backlash. With the victory of Margaret Thatcher, followed by that of Ronald Reagan in the United States, attacks were launched against trade unions and the welfare state." (Ishay, 2004: 251).

The introduction of neoliberalism, internal dissent in the Soviet bloc, with Solidarity, a Polish alliance between socialists, democrats, nationalists, and Catholics, leading the way as well as the global swing in the balance of power toward the liberal democracies, seem to be the main factors leading to the collapse of communism in Eastern Europe, which was based on the provision of economic, social, and cultural rights for their people. It is likely that these communist countries were not only losing the ideological battle, but could not compete economically when the West decided to lower the working conditions and welfare of their own people. Ishay states: "The forces of globalization proved sufficiently powerful to infiltrate the communist fortress and erode the Soviet empire. Outspent in its competitive war with the United States in every possible realm, and facing an inflexible, sclerotic, and steadily shrinking centralized economy, the USSR's only hope of retaining significant power was to undertake radical political and economic change" (Ishay, 2004: 252).

Following the collapse of the Soviet bloc, Russia underwent radical political and economic change—*uskorienniie* (acceleration), *glasnost* (openness), and *perestroika* (restructuring)—"new reforms that would soon unravel into popular discontent" (Ishay, 2004: 252).

It was sometimes said by Western intellectuals that the reason the Western democracies did not adopt economic, social, and cultural rights in domestic human rights law was due to the Cold War with each side adopting ideological positions. But the collapse of the Soviet bloc was to prove this view wrong. Instead, the West, ignoring the equal status principle and economic, social, and cultural rights, placed far greater emphasis on civil and political rights (freedom and democracy), which legitimized the West's global ideological and economic ambitions. David Beetham states that "although in theory the end of the Cold War could have provided an opportunity for ending the sterile opposition between the two sets of human rights, in practice it has reinforced the priorities of the United States, the country which has been most consistently opposed to the idea of economic and social rights. And the more general loss of credibility of socialism in any form has deprived the poor everywhere of an organizing ideology for political struggle and the politics of redistribution" (Beetham, 1995: 43).

There were no credible ideological alternatives. Ishay states: "With all boundaries removed, globalization no longer faced meaningful opposition anywhere in the world" (Ishay, 2004: 253).

The bipolar world meant that realpolitik (realism) rather than human rights dominated the relationships between states.

Responding to Soviet efforts to harness movements in Europe and the Third World, liberal notions of human rights soon collapsed into a foreign policy based on realpolitik. While the rhetorical commitment to universal liberal values continued, in practice, the United States soon dropped whichever elements of liberal human rights seemed incompatible with state power and the interests of private capital (Ishay, 2004: 226–227).

However, when the world became dominated by only one superpower, human rights came to the fore in foreign policy. Mullerson states:

> The end of the Cold War has increased the importance of human rights diplomacy. On the one hand, human rights seem to affect post-Cold War international relations more than before because there is no longer an overwhelming security threat; instead there are multifarious threats to international stability, many of which have their origin in the human rights situation of a particular country (Mullerson, 1997: 180).

Power et al. describe the increasing influence of human rights in American foreign policy:

> Though human rights has not become so central a feature that it overrides interest-based concerns, human rights advocates have managed to push the U.S. government from rhetoric and moral pressure in the 1970s, to economic sanctions in the 1980s, to military action in the 1990s. Indeed, it has become impossible for the Western powers to debate the cardinal issues of foreign policy, from trade to the use of force, without being reminded of their impact on human rights (Power, 2000: xiiv).

However, human rights has been used by the United States, with its own selective civil and political rights interpretation, to increase its global hegemony. Evans states:

> Promoting the American conception of human rights was part of a strategy intended to extend the U.S. sphere of influence over a much wider area, including gaining access to world markets. As self-proclaimed protector of universal human rights, the United States sought to legitimate its role as leader of the new world order and to justify intervention wherever and whenever it was necessary. Crucially, the success of the project rested upon gaining popular approval for a set of civil and political rights associated with liberalism, or more explicitly those rights already found in the Constitution of the United States of America (Evans, 1998: 7).

America has been determined to retain control of the human rights agenda (i.e., reflecting the U.S. constitution), thereby better enabling it to act unilaterally if necessary, as evidenced by its reluctance to accept the human rights interpretations of the United Nations or ratify human rights instruments. Evans states:

The end of the cold war has brought to a close the ideological struggle over human rights, leaving the USA as the unmatched superpower—Symbolic of this superiority is the USA's ratification of the International Covenant on Civil and Political Rights, following years of procrastination. At first sight this may suggest that the USA has lifted at least some of its historic objections to accepting human rights as developed at the UN, and there is now willingness to give hegemonic support to protect those rights. However, the US ratification includes many reservations, declarations and understandings, which suggest that little has changed (Evans, 1998: 11).

During the Cold War and afterwards New Zealand trade unions, and it also seems trade unions around the world, while some were prepared to promote socialism they would only deal with economic, social, and cultural rights at the elite level of the International Labour Organisation. This was even the case during the Cold War when "the influence of Soviet ideology at the time was significant" in New Zealand, particularly in the trade union movement. Fear of the communist influence in 1962 led New Zealand prime minister Keith Holyoake to expel two Soviet diplomats for spying while in 1980 New Zealand prime minister Rob Muldoon expelled the Soviet ambassador, allegedly for supplying funds to the Socialist Unity Party, which was prominent in the trade union movement (A. C. Wilson, 2004). However, after 1984 when the Lange government introduced neoliberal policies, the socialist influence in the trade union movement declined to the point that socialism virtually went underground. The collapse of communism in Eastern Europe seems to have seriously undermined socialism in the trade union movement worldwide. Ishay states that paralleling the trend in the United States, trade unions have also been severely weakened in Europe, as evidenced by the 1991 Maastricht agreement (Ishay, 2004: 345). Ishay adds: "The erosion of European labor rights policies became more apparent when, during the Maastricht talks, the British government opposed the Social Charter advocated by an economically integrated European Union, on the grounds that it provided too much prominence to trade unions" (Ishay, 2004: 263).

Bereft of an ideology and their numbers decimated, the trade unions joined the establishment, adopting the human rights agenda as defined by the dominant liberal elite and focusing on workers rights through the International Labour Organisation.

History shows that the most disadvantaged cannot rely on the elites to give them social justice. Whether it was the natural law of the ancient Greeks and Romans with the oppression of slaves, religion which emphasized duty to the monarchy in a highly unequal system, or liberalism in both its Classical and Modern forms for although the latter can be economically egalitarian the liberal elite retain control of the human rights agenda and discriminate against other ideologies. Also when the time is right, for example, the collapse of communism in Eastern Europe in 1989 has shown it will revert to Classical Liberalism. As the nineteenth century shows, liberalism had to be forced to become more socially responsible primarily by socialism. Both the Industrial Revolution, as well as the experience in the Soviet bloc and today's world where more than half of humanity lives in poverty, indicate the depths of barbarity to which humankind will sink when either civil and political rights or economic, social, and cultural rights are excluded. Although socialism is often associated with economic, social, and cultural rights, since Roosevelt's promotion of these rights they have nearly always only been dealt with at the elite level. Trade unions in the nineteenth century and during the Cold War, even when the trade unions were strong, preferred to promote socialism rather than economic, social, and cultural rights which would only be discussed at the level of the International Labour Organisation (Sibbel). The core obligations agenda deals with the most disadvantaged in terms of human rights. Typically Western societies view human rights as conditional on economic growth and as if they are luxuries like cell phones and computers—the needs of the middle classes are first addressed and later this will "trickle down" to the rest of the population. Human rights are dealt with in the same way—first the needs of the middle classes are addressed with the promise that one day the rest of the population will follow. However, human rights deal with vital needs not luxuries—surely those suffering the most serious violations should come first.

If history is to repeat itself then neoliberalism will be followed by an increase in authoritarian regimes and global conflict. There is a real need to provide people with ideas, different ideologies, and belief systems so if the world situation deteriorates further people will have a belief system to hold on to, some hope, and the promise of a better world. If peaceful belief systems are not available and people have not had time to think they may align themselves with a violent alternative.

Chapter Five

Lack of Will for Social Justice for the Most Disadvantaged at the UN

It is of considerable concern that the present draft Optional Protocol (OP, A/HRC/6/WG.4/2, 23/4/07, see Appendix V) to the International Covenant on Economic, Social, and Cultural Rights (ICESCR), a complaints procedure for those suffering social injustices, which has been discussed by open-ended working groups (OEWG) at the United Nations since 2004, is seriously flawed allowing States a broad "margin of appreciation" to give preference to the human rights, development, and, consequently, the lifestyles of the elite rather than addressing the much more serious human rights violations of the most disadvantaged. The broad "margin of appreciation" is described by Ms. Louise Arbour, United Nations High Commissioner for Human Rights, who states: "The Committee on Economic, Social and Cultural Rights has addressed this question head on in a Statement issued in May this year [2007]. Importantly, the Committee underlines that each State would enjoy a broad 'margin of appreciation' in determining the policies which it considers most suitable in its specific circumstances" (High Commissioner backs work on Mechanism to consider complaints of breaches of economic, social and cultural rights, United Nations Press Release, Geneva July 16, 2007).

Neoliberalism (and as probably would be the case with most ideologies) is concerned to reject any new ideas which pose a threat to its global dominance. The concept of core minimum obligations and their immediate fulfillment demand limitations to any ideological ends when the means involves inflicting extreme violence on people such as forcing them into extreme poverty and extreme powerlessness. In addition, by ensuring people remain ignorant of human rights they are prevented from thinking outside the "neoliberal square" which the human rights agenda, as defined by the United Nations and the domestic elite, supports. While it is likely that the addition of

ESC rights in domestic jurisdictions human rights rather than being an exclusive focus on the elite, as is presently the case, will be rather more democratic, extending protection and respect for the rights of the majority and so gaining broader support during these times of war and global terrorism. However, it seems inevitable, under the present draft OP, that human rights will not extend to the most disadvantaged and will fail them as miserably as previous human rights instruments included in domestic law in recent times. These instruments, under neoliberalism, failed to stem the rising numbers in the underclass and their increasing powerlessness in liberal democracies.

Article 4(1) of the draft OP states that the "Committee shall not consider a communication unless it has ascertained that available domestic remedies have been exhausted." Once States ratify the OP it is very likely that the Covenant on Economic, Social, and Cultural Rights, which the majority of States have ratified under international law, will be bought into domestic jurisdiction in some form, which so far few States have done. When New Zealand acceded to the OP for the International Covenant on Civil and Political Rights (ICCPR) in 1989 this was immediately followed by the New Zealand Bill of Rights Act (1990), the Human Rights Act 1993, plus a number of commissions to hear complaints. Previous United Nations human rights instruments—the Covenant and Conventions (see below)—have merely served to legitimize domestic elites who promptly "turn human rights on its head" emphasizing the interests of those at the top social levels while ignoring the effects of neoliberalism which created a large underclass. For instance, while much was made of equal pay between men and women on high salaries, concern for the voicelessness of the poor was virtually nonexistent. The spirit of the International Covenant on Economic, Social and Cultural Rights, which is essentially egalitarian, born in the Industrial Revolution of the nineteenth century and the Great Depression, would be utterly destroyed as well as the hopes and dreams of billions of people if these human rights are used simply to further elite interests, even if they involve some broader benefits to the majority.

It is expected that the final OP will be concluded in 2008 when there will be two one-week sessions of the open-ended working group (OEWG) on the OP for ICESCR at the United Nations Human Rights Council in January (14–18) and April (7–11). This OP, as its name implies, is optional so States do not have to ratify it if they do not wish to although I consider any failure to do so should be well publicized. As these instruments are almost set in cement once concluded it is likely to be the last chance for any instrument for those in most misery for a long time to come.

Unlike the International Covenant on Civil and Political Rights, whose rights are regarded as immediate and not limited by resource constraints, under the ICESCR the rights can only be progressively achieved due to limited resources. Article 8(4) of the draft OP states: "When examining communications under the present Protocol concerning article 2, paragraph 1 of the Covenant [ICESCR], the Committee will assess the reasonableness of the steps taken by the State Party, to the maximum of its available resources, with a view to achieving *progressively* the full realization of the rights recognized in the present Covenant by all appropriate means."

What I regard as the first major flaw of the draft OP is that the above article only refers to the progressive achievement of rights and allows States to defer addressing the serious violations experienced by the most disadvantaged by implementing a plan which is essentially open-ended as the State can always claim that they failed to meet their goals due to a lack of resources. Having any such progressive plan for the most disadvantaged can only be described as absurd given that it deals with the immediate needs of the hungry, homeless, seriously ill, the illiterate, the utterly powerless, and so forth (as well as the impossibility for such individuals to access their civil and political rights and consequently any ability to exert some influence over their situation such as using the democratic process and the media to make a plea to the ordinary people).

The draft OP needs to place an emphasis on the human rights of the most disadvantaged reflected in the immediate fulfillment requirement of the concept of "core minimum obligations" as described by the United Nations Committee on Economic, Social, and Cultural Rights (CESCR) (see General Comments No. 3 and No. 14, although the Committee uses the word "ensure" rather than "immediate" the former is the same language used in the ICCPR Article 2(1) which is almost universally interpreted as requiring "immediate" implementation). The CESCR has interpreted the obligation to take steps "to the maximum of its available resources" as requiring States parties to fulfill "a minimum core obligation to ensure the satisfaction of, at the very least, minimum essential levels of each of the rights." The obligation applies even in times of severe resource constraints, when the most vulnerable groups must continue to be protected (General Comment No. 3, para 12). In effect, the minimum core obligations are "non-derogable," unless it can be demonstrated that every effort has been made to use all resources that are at the disposal of the State Party (General Comment No. 14). In addition, according to the Committee it is a "prime facie" violation if a State fails to fulfill the core minimum; however, States can claim in their defense that they have limited resources. General Comment No. 3(10) states: "Thus, for example, a State party in which any significant number of individuals is deprived of essential foodstuffs, of essential primary health care, of basic shelter and housing, or of the most basic forms of education is, prima facie, failing to discharge its obligations under the Covenant. If the Covenant were to be read in such a way as not to establish such a minimum core obligation, it would be largely deprived of its raison d'etre. By the same token, it must be noted that any assessment as to whether a State has discharged its minimum core obligation must also take account of resource constraints applying within the country concerned." Ms. Louise Arbour, UN High Commissioner on Human Rights, states: ". . . the concept [of core minimum obligations] is seen to imply . . . . a duty immediately to satisfy, as a matter of priority, minimum essential levels of economic, social and cultural rights (core minimum obligations)[her brackets]" (Report of the United Nations High Commissioner for Human Rights, Economic & Social Council, June 25, 2007, item 14(g), E/2007/100, Part V (Concluding Remarks)). However, other statements have tended to fudge whether core minimum obligations are immediate or progressive (or both) allowing States to seize on the possibility that they are also progressive as are the higher levels of these rights. This is indicated in another comment by Ms. Arbour, which, in contrast to her previous statement, implies that core minimum obligations require benchmarks and consequently progressive achievement. She states:

> Arguably, core minimum levels of rights fulfillment are to some extent dependant on the specific situation of a given State. Thus the Commission on Human Rights, in a resolution adopted in 1994, invited States parties to the International Covenant on Economic, Social and Cultural Rights 'to identify specific national benchmarks designed to give effect to the minimum core obligation to ensure the satisfaction of the minimum essential levels of each of the rights' (Commission on Human Rights resolution 1994/20, para.11(22)).

However, surely, it is not so much a matter of whether core minimum obligations are dependent on the State's circumstances. It is a matter of taking responsibility for any violations—lack of economic resources can be a mitigating factor or even may constitute a diminished responsibility just as being hungry and homeless is a mitigating factor or involve diminished responsibility for a person who steals food. Furthermore, in its defense, the State and/or the Committee hearing the case can also point to the lack of cooperation of the international community, and its failure to assist, if it wishes but, in my view, this should be well publicized.

The above fudging regarding immediate/progressive realization amounts to another broad "margin of appreciation" for the State with the New Zealand Human Rights Commission (and other countries could likely follow suit), which is one of a small number of commissions around the world to have developed an action plan which includes economic, social, and cultural rights, has adopted the latter interpretation with respect to core minimums with "indicators" and "benchmarks" required, indicating the need for a plan required by progressive realization. The commission states: "The complexity of the economic, social and cultural rights can make it difficult to determine whether a State is meeting even its minimum commitments. For example, the right to health is not limited simply to appropriate healthcare but also covers the underlying determinants of health such as safe working conditions and adequate food and shelter. The Economic and Social Council (ECOSOC), which is responsible for monitoring the ICESCR, has endeavored to ensure a core minimum standard under each right by requiring that States establish indicators (yardsticks) and benchmarks (targets) against which their performance can be measured" (Human Rights in New Zealand Today, Human Rights Commission, 2004: 33). The OP for the ICESCR could clarify this confusion for once and for all.

But any notion that this concept of "core minimum obligations" is also progressive is not only absurd given the desperate needs of the most disadvantaged but is to regard ESC rights as being without a bottom line—or in the words of the Committee without a "raison d'etre"—yet without this bottom line there would be also be no bottom line to civil and political rights—how can you engage in any litigation regarding one's freedom of speech, discrimination, or a fair trial, and so forth when you are hungry and homeless! Louise Arbour, United Nations High Commissioner for Human Rights, states: "There is growing recognition of the vision that moved the drafters of the Universal Declaration, that it is impossible to enjoy one set of rights without the other" (Economic, social and cultural rights are human rights, *The Economist*, article, March 22, 2007, quoted on the Amnesty International site). Consequently, the ends of neoliberalism—global liberal democracy, expansion of the corporations, and consequent world domination by liberal, middle-class elites—can justify the means—the use of serious violence, through both neglect and oppression. Will the global liberal elites cease their use of extreme violence once they have reached their goal? If they have not been socially responsible to date will they be so when their dream is reached?

The second major flaw of the draft OP is the broad "margin of appreciation" in defining what constitutes "available resources" and allowing States, if they wish, to minimize human rights education and only target the elite. The two are closely linked. Typically "available resources" is viewed by the international human rights establishment as meaning "available economic resources" and overlook "human resources" and the value of a comprehensive human rights education to all people in maximizing "human resources" by allowing thinking, creativity, new ideas, the search for truth and meaning, and new development "outside the neo liberal square." One good idea, and only utilizing a minimum of available resources, can change the world, for example, micro loans to the poor have helped millions, and the loans are nearly always repaid. has defined resources to include human as well as economic resources stating that "the term not only refers to the financial capacity of a State, but also to other types of resources relevant to the realization of economic, social, and cultural rights, such as human, technological, and information resources" (Economic and Social Council, Item 14(g), E/2007/100, June 25, 2007). However, typically the international human rights establishment—the States, UN bureaucracy, and NGOs—discussing the OP for the ICESCR since 2004 have only regarded resources as economic resources (see the reports of the NGO Coalition for the OP for ICESCR and the Reports of the Working Groups Sessions for the OP for ICESCR, Office of the United Nations High Commission for Human Rights). In dismissing human resources and the value of maximizing human rights education ignores Article 1(3) of the UN Charter, which indicates that such education is a legal duty for States. The article requires: ". . . . promoting and encouraging respect for human rights and for fundamental freedoms for all. . . ." While it appears that the definition of resources is also within the broad "margin of appreciation of the States" so too is human rights education. The discretion of the States with respect to such education is described by Arbour who states:

> Equally, the Committee on Economic, Social and Cultural Rights and the Committee on the Rights of the Child have provided some general guidance in their recommendations to States parties and in their general comments. For example, the treaty bodies frequently call for educational measures as a means to promote economic, social, and cultural rights. However, in their recommendations to States parties the Committee on Economic, Social and Cultural Rights and the Committee on the Rights of the Child do not prescribe specific measures to be undertaken, in accordance with the margin of appreciation accorded to States parties. For example, concerning a specific problem of child labor in a given country, the treaty bodies would urge the State party concerned to take effective measures to address the problem, but leave it to the State to decide on the measures it deems to be the most appropriate in its specific circumstances (Report of the United Nations High Commissioner for Human Rights (32), Economic & Social Council, June 25, 2007, item 14(g), E/2007/100).

However, such education is virtually cost-free so falls within the range of "reasonableness" required by Article 8(4). Any costs, as with good ideas and new development, may be minimal while any significant costs could come from available economic resources—the apparatus of State control where, for instance, groups are kept divided, to maintain elite control, when they could share resources (see below). In addition, savings could be made with the mental health system and criminal justice system because by addressing core minimum obligations you are addressing the underlying causes of many social problems. Furthermore some of the costs of the military, and police force protecting largely elite property, could also be redirected to this purpose. In other words sharing resources between both prevention and social control rather than just focusing on the latter. Importantly, a comprehensive human rights education for all people is likely to assist greatly in the problem of progressive versus immediate implementation. Publicity regarding the serious violations of economic, social, and cultural rights will help ensure they are addressed immediately or, at least, they should be addressed as quickly as civil and political rights are. The Human Development Report 2000 states that "studies have shown some important causal links between such rights as freedom of participation and expression and freedom from discrimination and poverty." The report adds:

> There can be no better illustration of these links than the effect of the right of free expression and participation in political life on avoiding major social calamity. Amartya Sen pointed to this effect in his classic analysis, an examination of famines all over the world. His and other studies have shown that no famine continued unabated in modern times in any country—poor or rich—with a democratic government and a relatively free press. Loud popular demands, through political processes and the media, push governments to act to stop famine and other social calamities (Human Development Report 2000 chapter 4).

Consequently, if publicity is given to violations of core minimum obligations within a country it may also have the effect of putting pressure on government to fulfill these rights.

If the State is concerned that such human rights education it may consider would clash with the interests of the dominant ideology, for example, where ESC rights requires greater social responsibility rather than the individual responsibility required by neoliberalism the State (while being ultimately responsible), it could delegate such education to financially independent human rights NGOs which promote the equal status of both sets of rights. These NGOs could help create a space where intellectual debate is accepted and where people have sufficient acceptance to be creative, where intellectual freedom and the search for truth will not die, where new ideas and new development can flourish, thereby adding another domain of reason (in addition to civil and political rights) to place some limitation on the extremist neoliberal ideology. Hence, the ends of the latter will not justify the means. The delegation of the education function is similar to what the State has done when it has privatized some previously held State economic functions, and placed some social functions under the control of charitable organizations. NGOs could also research and report on the state of the most disadvantaged and

assist individuals to make claims domestically and internationally. Consequently, there is no excuse for States failing to maximize new ideas domestically
and internationally to address the needs of the 1.8 billion people living in extreme poverty and the majority of the world living in poverty. At present,
States usually only provide human rights education for the elite, with the
State deciding which rights to promote, while keeping the majority of the
population in darkness and in a state of abject powerlessness unable to use the
international human rights language to communicate with the elite or a belief
system to pursue social justice ("There's nothing you can do about it!" is the
often heard remark among the people reflecting their powerlessness) as mental illness soars and the state of the underclass worsens, and lives are short-
ened, yet all is largely invisible with much suffering within the individual and
among the underclass, with increasing violence within families, removed to
the outer suburbs only to come to public attention when some terrible crime
appears in the media.

In addition, failure to educate people in human rights transgresses the democratic principle that people have a right to important information so they can
make reasoned decisions at election time. The broad "margin of appreciation"
by allowing States to minimize human rights education, if they wish, perhaps
just focusing on the rights to property, contract and the rule of law, the major
concerns of the corporations, or just focus on individual freedoms (civil and
political rights) and economic freedoms for the liberal, middle-class, professional sector, they can manipulate the electorate. How can people have a free
choice at election time when they are kept ignorant of ESC rights? When the
media will ignore these rights as evidenced by the failure of the New Zealand
media to inform New Zealanders that the ESC rights was in the Human
Rights Commission's New Zealand Plan of Action for Human Rights in February 2005 (Index New Zealand, New Zealand Public Library, indicates no
newspaper, magazine, journal articles) and when none of the nine political
parties in New Zealand will publicly define social justice in human rights
terms (as evidenced by their web sites? While the Green Party has these rights
as policy they never get mentioned in the media). What chance would a new
political party, which promoted ESC rights, have? Our council stood candidates under the banner of the Human Rights Party, promoting the New
Zealand Plan of Action for Human Rights, in the past two elections, but apart
from a brief mention in two suburban newspapers we are almost completely
unheard of. The end result is evident in the New Zealand parliament with both
the party on the far left, the Greens, and the party on the far right, the Act
Party, both claiming to stand for liberal democracy although with a different
emphasis on social justice. To provide a different perspective—what if this
omission were to occur with respect to civil and political rights—what would

happen to "freedom and democracy"? Consequently, only those ideas receiving the support of the human rights agenda are acceptable—these perpetuate the status quo and the powerful interests that cling to it while many new ideas which could further the right to development for all are ignored as if they do not exist, for example, if people are ignorant of economic, social, and cultural rights then the people do not have the necessary authority and belief to struggle to defend the welfare state (such individual struggles by sometimes very vulnerable, isolated individuals would be much less necessary if ESC rights was in human rights law and defended by the courts). Consequently, so are many new ideas, seen as "too political" or "extremist," to further develop health, education, housing, and so forth, of the whole nation are excluded (It is really bizarre that those that do promote ESC rights are seen in this light given that it is actually the State which is "too political" and "extremist" in terms of the international human rights law that they have ratified and which their human rights acts in the preamble claim as their authority yet only incorporating civil and political rights in domestic law).

In my view, unless there is a comprehensive human rights education for all the people there is no defense for a State failing to immediately fulfill core minimum obligations—even if there is a lack of economic resources the State must take full responsibility for failing to fulfill core minimum obligations in the same way the most disadvantaged in society have to take complete responsibility for their actions despite often unbelievable pressures and extremely few choices. In other words, the State cannot keep people human rights illiterate, thereby limiting development, and then claim that it is maximizing resources to address serious violations. In addition, remarkably, the discussions relating to the OP for the ICESCR seems to have ignored the OEWG discussing the right to development, which has been occurring simultaneously at the United Nations. It requires that development takes place under the umbrella of both sets of rights which would ensure that all of society is entitled to this right. For instance Section 6(2) of the Declaration on the Right to Development (1988) states: "All human rights and fundamental freedoms are indivisible and interdependent [including both sets of rights]; equal attention and urgent consideration should be given to the implementation, promotion and protection of civil, political, economic, social and cultural rights." This is the third major flaw of the draft OP—namely the failure to include core minimum obligations with respect to the right to development. It is intuitively obvious that people should be able to use their talents and abilities and follow their dreams. This is reflected in the right to liberty (Article 9(1), ICCPR), the right to choice of employment (Article 6(1), ICESCR), "duties to the community" to enable "the free and full development of his [her] personality" (Article 29, UDHR) and the requirement that States "undertake to

respect the freedom indispensable for scientific research and creative activity" (Article 15(3), ICESCR). In addition is the nondiscrimination requirement contained in all the human rights instruments which imply that our prej-
udices should not prevent us from choosing a person on merit. However,
particular attention needs to be given to ensuring nondiscrimination on the
grounds of social origins, class, and caste and those who do not own property
because these grounds are presently excluded in domestic human rights law
(see Section 21, New Zealand Human Rights Act 1993) in New Zealand, and
this probably applies in most other liberal democracies. However, such
nondiscrimination is required in the international human rights instruments,
for example, Article 2(1) ICCPR. A meritocracy would seem essential to
maximize the talents and abilities of the nation. To help facilitate the right to
development the State should at the very least arrange for independent funding under the umbrella of both sets of rights and core minimum obligations
of human rights NGOs to ensure that whatever the prevailing dominant ideology that the independent spirit and talents are not entirely lost to the nation.

It would help civilize neoliberalism by recognizing that it may not possess
absolute truth and ensure that such neoliberal principles as the right to liberty
apply to all. From my long experience of attempting to get funding from both
the public and private sectors for our council, the Human Rights Council Inc.
(New Zealand), I have found that there is simply no funding unless you conform to the human rights agenda as defined by the domestic and global elites
which requires compatibility with neoliberalism.

In 1998 the Economic and Council set up OEWG to "monitor and review
progress made in the promotion and implementation of the right to development" and in 2004 established a high level task force on the implementation
of the right to development (Report of the Working Group on the Right to development, General Assembly, A/HRC/4/47, Feb 26—March 2, 2007, p. 3).

In the 1970s and 1980s the right to development (RTD) was introduced as
one of several rights belonging to a third "generation" of human rights.
Stephen Marks, who is presently Chairperson-Rapporteur of the High-Level
Task Force on the Implementation of the Right to Development, describes the
evolution, or various generations, of human rights: "According to this view,
the first generation consisted of civil and political rights conceived as freedom from State abuse. The second generation consisted of economic, social
and cultural rights, claims made against exploiters and oppressors. The third
generation consisted of solidarity rights belonging to peoples and covering
global concerns like development, environment, humanitarian assistance,
peace, communication, and common heritage" (Marks, Spring 2004: 138).
Marks adds: "The cataloguing of human rights into such neat generations is
appealing in its simplicity. A general priority has been given to guaranteeing

individual freedoms in eighteenth-century revolutionary struggles of Europe and North America, to advancing social justice in nineteenth- and twentieth-century struggles against economic exploitation, and to assigning rights and obligations to the principle agents able to advance public goods in the late twentieth century" Marks, Spring 2004: 138). However, Marks maintains that "on closer scrutiny, the basic aspirations at the root of the claims of all three 'generations' are not historically determined." He states: "People suffering repression and oppression have aspired to fair equitable treatment for millennia. Liberation from slavery and colonialism—based on premises similar to those of the so-called third generation rights—was expressed in terms later reflected in human rights language. Religious freedom was a human rights concern well before the mid-twentieth-century separation of civil and political rights from economic, social and cultural rights" (Marks, Spring 2004: 138). Marks states that the "formal articulation of the RTD in the form of texts using human rights terminology is a phenomenon of the late twentieth century, beginning in the early 1970s." Perhaps the real reason why the RTD has taken so long to gain recognition is the same reason that education in economic, social, and cultural rights has so rarely been implemented, namely because they are particularly empowering rights which may not depend on the dominant elite for their execution. Just as human rights education can empower people in making choices at election time, the right to development involving both sets of rights is an empowering belief system which allows the individual to persevere despite enormous odds. For example, microcredit has enabled many millions to pursue their dreams. The RTD also provides an all embracing human rights culture whose egalitarianism is found by many to be more appealing and supportive than the hierarchical approach, based on exclusion, which prevails. While remaining socially responsible the right to development allows you to do what you want "outside of the neoliberal square" while human rights education enables you to say what you want, including to "ordinary people," "outside of the neo liberal square." Because of the empowerment they give to the people these rights are particularly threatening to the global elites who rely on people remaining ignorant.

According to the Declaration on the Right to Development, both the individual and the state have a right to development (see Appendix 5). The OEWG on the right to development have focused on international rather than domestic development and are more concerned with the inequities of the international structure. In relation to domestic development, the right to development is largely only at the level of rhetoric rather than reality. Stephen Marks states: "At the national level, ministries of foreign affairs of most countries instruct their delegates to the Commission on Human Rights [now replaced by the Human Rights Council] and the General Assembly to vote for the RTD in these foreign policy positions, however, has little impact on national development policy and practice" (Marks, Spring 2004: 152). The major emphasis is on economic growth in the global rather than domestic market, that is, what is important is the global expansion of the corporations, each country specializing to its strengths and emphasizing efficiency often using the cheapest labor. The consequence of this approach with its cheap goods is a consumer society. New ideas, production, and the right to development of the rest of the population, and, consequently, the future are largely neglected especially if they do not further the interests of neoliberalism. This is a "growth first" approach which relegates many individuals and their right to development to the background of society while promising "trickle down" to alleviate the plight of the poor. However, "trickle down" has not occurred since neoliberalism gained global dominance in 1989 and the gap between rich and poor has grown while the voices and political influence of those lower on the social structure were drowned out in the former case and ignored in the latter case as conformity to the dominant ideology set in. In 1989 Jack Donnelly forecasted: "'Growth first' implies a capacity for redistribution afterwards, but such a strategy ignores the extremely strong and probably overwhelming resistance to ex post facto income redistribution." He adds: "But the needs and equality trade-offs imply major sacrifices by literally hundreds of millions of people. The conventional wisdom thus seems to border on culpable social science malpractice" (Donnelly, 1989: 179–180).

From my observation many people are aware that "trickle down" has not occurred but there is a sense that people feel they are on a "runaway train" and there is nothing that can be done about it so are prepared to go, albeit against their better instincts, blindly into the future not knowing what the end consequences will be. There is a need for statistical research on the numbers of people who have had to suppress their talents and dreams for the sake of survival in a neoliberal society. The latter essentially serves the interests of the middle-class, professional sector, in my view, obsessed with consumption, choices, services, and hostile to anything "new" and productivity in general. I strongly suspect that the results of such research would show that the numbers would be particularly significant and a number of these individuals would have ended up being major employers thereby directly alleviating poverty without the need for any reliance on "trickle down." Talents and dreams provide individuals with a purpose in life and adds to their happiness. This would not be the case if forced to pursue just money. When this becomes their only interest in life society becomes overly materialistic and consumer-oriented with obvious implications such as the current global concern with climate change that has attributed to the high levels of industrialization. Such research of people's human rights would also indicate the number of people who suffer violations, and this would indicate the level of fear that exists in society—a comparison can be made between the fear experienced by various socioeconomic groups and related to the emphasis placed on the right to development of these groups. For development to take place there is a need to eliminate fear, for example, a person, often, will not pursue their dream if the risk is such that he/she could drag their family down the "deep dark hole" that exists at the bottom of the social structure. The immediate fulfillment of core minimum obligation will alleviate such fear and represents an investment in the future. While such fulfillment is, in my view, incumbent on every State irrespective of the dominant ideology; however, if a State fails this social responsibility, say, claiming "limited resources," there can be no excuse for not allowing the independent funding of human rights NGOs (say, with loans financed by lotteries) concerned with promoting human rights in the mainstream media and the right to development. They can also be involved in human rights research. Also such NGOs can also be involved in supporting the holistic development of these individuals which is essential if one seeks longevity in one's purpose and achieving one's goals with social responsibility.

Even at the international level the right to development remains largely rhetorical and strongly influenced by America so such research is not carried out. Stephen Marks states: "The right to development has been part of the of the international debate on human rights for over thirty years but has not yet entered the practical realm of development planning and implementation. States tend to express rhetorical support for this right but neglect its basic precepts in development practice" (Marks, Spring 2004: 137). In addition, Stephen Marks states: "The U.S. government has tended to be behind the efforts to remove references to human rights at conferences and summits, like WSSD [World Summit on Sustainable Development], the Children's Summit, the General Assembly Special Session on HIV/AIDS and the Food Summit. . . . Similar observations can be made about the Specialized Agencies (WHO [World Health Organization], ILO, FAO [Food and Agriculture Organization], UNESCO, etc.) and UN funds and programs (UNDP [UN Development Program], UNIFEM, UNICEF, etc.), whose approaches to development cooperation rarely include human rights and almost never the RTD." Where such research could be done, that is, the Office of the High Commission for Human Rights, it is not financed. Marks states: "One part of the U.N. system where the RTD has an acknowledged place of prominence is the OHCHR, which includes a "Research and Right to Development Branch." When that office was created, the General Assembly required the High Commissioner to "recognize the importance of promoting a balanced and sustainable development for all people and of ensuring realization of the right to development, as established in the Declaration on the Right to Development" and included among the responsibilities of the Office "to promote and protect the realization of the right to development and to enhance support from relevant bodies of the United Nations system for this purpose. . . ." However, Marks states that this area, like many others falling within the responsibilities of the High Commissioner, is understaffed and underfunded. He adds that the United States has reminded the Commission that there are not enough resources to request a study on an aspect of RTD it would rather not have studied (Marks, Spring 2004: 155). Again because of the failure of the international system in this regard the onus falls back on the independent human rights NGOs to carry out such research.

Stephen Marks describes four groups reflecting the political positions of countries in the working groups on the RTD. One group, the Non-Aligned Movement (NAM), contains the "Like-Minded Group," which is described by Marks as the "most active members" of the NAM and consists of Algeria, Bangladesh, Bhutan, China, Cuba, Egypt, India, Indonesia, Iran, Malaysia, Myanmar, Nepal, Pakistan, the Philippines, Sri Lanka, Sudan, and Vietnam. Marks states that their interests are to use the RTD to reduce inequalities of international trade, the negative impacts of globalization, differential access to technology, the crushing debt burden, and similar factors they see as detrimental to the enjoyment of human rights and development (Marks, 2004: 141). For instance, sometimes they do not want to be limited by a narrow view of human rights and want international co operation as a legal requirement; for example, Cuba, speaking on behalf of NAM, in early 2007, called for international cooperation that is "not subject to conditionality, nor be treated as a matter of charity" (Report of the Working Group on the Right to development, General Assembly, A/HRC/4/47, February 26—March 2, 2007, 6). The second group, states Marks, consists of the more moderate developing countries that genuinely want to integrate human rights into their national policies and want to maintain a positive relationship with the donor community, the international development agencies, and financial institutions. A third group is made up of countries in transition and developed nations that tend to support the RTD as a vehicle to improve the dialogue between developed and developing countries and would like to see some progress made in implementing this right. This group, particularly the European Union, sometimes expresses skepticism and occasionally sees its role in the Commission (now replaced by the Human Rights Council) as damage-limitation. Marks states they will go along with a resolution if nothing particularly objectionable is inserted or will abstain. Marks states that the fourth group, in which the United States is almost always the key protagonist, votes against these resolutions. The other members of this group vary according to circumstances and have included Japan, Denmark, and Australia, along with smaller countries under the influence of the United States (Marks, Spring 2004: 141–142). Describing the United States opposition to the right to development Marks states:

> Especially under Republican administrations, but also under Democratic ones, the United States has expressed implicitly and at times openly the idea that the American experience is built on self-reliant, entrepreneurial efforts to create a great country out of the wilderness and that this hard-won success cannot be willed upon others through a Declaration (Marks, 2004: 143–144).

However, what the U.S. delegation overlooked is that in the past socialism forced the United States to be socially responsible and the right to development, although not described as such, was far more accessible to people as a whole especially in the American meritocracy. Today, without any credible ideological challenge with a socially responsible dimension, with a huge gap between rich and poor, and individual and economic liberties focused on the dominant elite many people do not have the right to development.

Vilfredo Pareto (1848–1923) made a distinction between "consolidators" and "innovators" within political society (Zetterberg, 1991: 9). The liberal forces were once regarded as innovators. They used civil rights to achieve almost complete domestic and international dominance. Now they have become the consolidators concerned with consolidating their wealth and power domestically and globally. Innovators, social and economic, or those with "new" ideas "outside of the neoliberal square" have been isolated and even the productive sector at the domestic level has been seriously diminished with truth, in my view, the major casualty of this largely "economic war." Economics professor Tim Hazeldine of Auckland University describes the detrimental effects on production: "When you wipe out one manufacturing job in three, as we did from 1986 to 1991, you should not realistically expect the survivors to shake off the shock and flourish—not soon, and perhaps not ever. We need to be more cautious, less dogmatic, more eclectic in our policy-making efforts" (Hazeldine, 1999). He adds: "We have been obsessed with free trade and getting the lowest prices, and have forgotten that before you can consume you have to produce. However cheap the goods and services, you still have to earn the wages and profits needed to pay for them." The consolidators, having the power, now are concerned with perpetuating the existing system. With no dream of a better world, apart from ideological conquest, their only concern becomes the money, and the budgeting mentality prevails focusing on efficiency and the old ideas represented by the corporations whose operations they hope will expand throughout the global market and so further consolidate their power. Pareto makes another distinction between "foxes" and "lions" within the consolidators with the "foxes" using "indirect and cunning means" of social control while the "lions" used "direct and more forceful means" (McLure, 2003: 16). The liberals or "foxes" are inclined to manipulate human rights law, for example, the present draft OP, to gain social control while the conservatives or "lions" prefer to uphold the status quo and rely on force, such as the War on Terror. What they both have in common is the desire to consolidate the wealth and power of the dominant elite, the prioritization of civil and political rights in domestic and international structures, and consequently the continued oppression and exploitation of the world's most disadvantaged. During the Cold War the Soviet States were subjected to strict ideological control by Moscow. In the case of the Western liberal democracies such strict ideological control by Washington is not so apparent because they are permitted to adopt a liberal or conservative position but outside of this framework they could be regarded as a renegade or authoritarian State. Consequently, most States adopt policies which would fall into either the liberal or conservative camps. It could be said that this flexibility of liberal democracy allowed it to adapt more readily to change than the communist countries of the Eastern bloc. Scott Davidson states: "These observations should not be seen, however, as a paean to the alleged triumph of capitalism, but it does suggest that the liberal-democratic State with its capacity for flexibility and adaptability is perhaps better suited to the satisfaction of not only first-generation [civil and political rights] but also second-generation [economic, social, and cultural rights]. The mixed economy with the potential for government intervention is perhaps better suited to the creation of conditions for the proper implementation of second-generation rights" (Davidson, 1993: 174). Core minimum obligations would ensure that there would be limitations placed on the liberal "foxes" and the conservative "lions" and their oppression and exploitation of the most disadvantaged and creative, intellectual and socially responsible entrepreneurs as well as offer the hope of a world where all the human rights in the declaration prevail.

However, where ignorance prevails Pareto observed that political elites taking turns in power are only too willing to be believed by desperate people. He states: "As usual, the new elite leaned on the poor and the humble; as usual, these believed in the promises made to them; as usual they were deceived, and the yoke weighed even heavier on their shoulder than before" (Pareto, 1991: 87)

States should be able to protect themselves from the pressures of the IMF and the World Bank to pursue neoliberal policies (see below) by having the core minimum obligations with respect to the right to development in the OP. Particularly, the underdeveloped countries should not be forced to consolidate when given their lack of international competitiveness they might be better off focusing on innovation—maximizing the ideas and development of the nation. They might not be able to compete well otherwise. Again, it seems it is not what is good for the nation as a whole but rather what is best for the domestic and international elites (see G8 loans below).

As the UN Committee on Economic, Social, and Cultural Rights states, the economic, social, and cultural rights are not "predicated on any particular ideology" (General Comment No. 3); hence, the State has the right to choose its ideology including neoliberalism (although because of the manipulation of the democratic process referred to above and described in another chapter it is, in my opinion, determined largely by global and domestic elites), so ESC rights (in addition to the civil and political rights in the domestic jurisdiction of most States) can be implemented, at least at the level of core minimum obligations, without clashing too much with the dominant ideology. The recent remarks of the Norwegian State Secretary Raymond Johansen reflect this view: "One solution could be to stress the importance of respecting a wide margin of appreciation for States as long as minimum standards have been ensured. The Covenant itself contains no reference to minimum standards, but the concept is elaborated in the General Comments of the Committee on Economic, Social and Cultural Rights" (An OP to the ICESCR: Norwegian Policies and Priorities, Oslo, Feb 8, 2006). Minimum core obligations would help civilize a society and avoid an absolutist mentality with respect to the chosen ideology as well as avoid likely overwhelming social control.

The draft OP could have provided an opportunity to rectify the miserable failures of previous human rights instruments—the Covenant and Conventions—to stem the rapid growth of an underclass under neoliberalism. At present according to Catarina de Albuquera, the chair of the OEWG, "the proposed text [of the draft OP for ICESCR] draws from existing communications procedures," which strongly suggests it will be as irrelevant to the most disadvantaged as the other instruments have been. In New Zealand recent international instruments which have been included in domestic law, such as the covenant on civil and political rights (including an OP), the conventions on antidiscrimination with respect to race (including a complaints procedure) and gender (including an OP). Since these UN instruments were introduced into New Zealand the voices of the underclass have been rarely heard, the number of women on the DPB has virtually doubled, and Maori unemployment increased dramatically averaging about 16 percent (the recent decline in unemployment is due largely, it seems, to the creation of a low waged economy) even though the international instruments were meant to protect them. Although according to the Social Report 2007, Ministry of Social Development, unemployment is only 3.8 percent; however, anecdotal evidence suggests that the low unemployment rate is to some extent due to Department of Work and Income pushing beneficiaries into a low wage economy.

The small number of complaints received by the UN complaints procedure (see below) and even State Reports have not stopped States ignoring the most disadvantaged in the past. State sovereignty is, in my view, not a valid excuse for the UN, international NGOs, and those involved in the OP for not taking full responsibility for the final outcome of their actions.

While the South African case of Grootbroom shows that domestic courts can consider core minimum obligations there was no domestic legal requirement for them to do so, and so few cases has little effect on the social conditions in the country. The case of South Africa demonstrates that despite having the rights of the UDHR in their constitution with ESC rights as justiciable rights (amenable to judicial determination), neoliberalism still dominates with its attendant mass misery (see the case of Alexandra, Western Cape, South Africa, with 60 percent unemployed). Fons Coomans considers that if such clarification is not determined at the international level it is unlikely to be done so at the national level. He states:

> As long as the majority of the provisions of the Covenant are not subject to detailed scrutiny at the international level by the Committee, it is not very likely that they will be subject to such scrutiny at the national level by a judicial body either. The main reason for this is that treaty provisions which are stated in very general terms are not likely to be applied directly or indirectly by judicial or administrative bodies, because of the lack of clarity about their implications for the domestic legal order (Coomans).

Besides core minimum obligations articulated by the Committee on Economic, Social, and Cultural Rights, there are some other obligations in the ICESCR that are immediate: nondiscrimination (Article 2(2), ICESCR), equality between men and women (Article 3, ICESCR), and other immediate obligations set out in General Comment No. 3 (para 5), including fair wages, equal remuneration for work of equal value, the right to form and join trade unions, special measures of protection for children, compulsory free primary education to all, and creative and scientific freedom. These parallel the "ensure and respect" (i.e., immediate) requirements of Article 2(1) of the ICCPR but without the concept of core minimum obligations many needs will still not be immediately addressed. Consequently, if core minimum obligations are seen as progressive rather than immediate there is very likely to be very little hope for the masses of homeless, long-term unemployed, those on minimal wages, the seriously ill, those living below the poverty line, and so forth.

The politics of the global elites in the OEWG indicates a move from elitism toward a global populism in line with the American foreign policy of promoting democracy. The draft OP by excluding the immediate implementation of the rights and their education allows states to continue to pursue neoliberalism. While civil and political rights continue to be prioritized at the international level, at the domestic level civil rights are being curbed. Now government is beginning to listen more to the people rather than the left wing liberals. The emphasis on democracy is likely to see a backlash against left wing liberalism with a more authoritarian approach in some respects with freedom fighters now regarded as terrorists, a harsher stance taken on crime and immigration. While the American camp played an obstructive role regarding the OP during the OEWG meetings they must have still been pleased with the outcome given the emphasis being placed on democracy. President George W. Bush, during his State of the Union address, discussed America's foreign policy of promoting democracy: "So we advance our own security interests by helping moderates and reformers and brave voices for democracy." He adds:

> In the last two years, we've seen the desire for liberty in the broader Middle East—and we have been sobered by the enemy's fierce reaction. In 2005, the world watched as the citizens of Lebanon raised the banner of the Cedar Revolution, they drove out the Syrian occupiers and chose new leaders in free elections. In 2005, the people of Afghanistan defied the terrorists and elected a democratic legislature. And in 2005, the Iraqi people held three national elections, choosing a transitional government, adopting the most progressive, democratic constitution in the Arab world, and then electing a government under that constitution. Despite endless threats from the killers in their midst, nearly 12 million Iraqi citizens came out to vote in a show of hope and solidarity that we should never forget (Bush, 2007).

While there were ideological differences in the OEWG the global elites shared a common interest in pursuing neoliberalism with its emphasis on social hierarchy and an increasing gap between rich and poor. Michael Freeman describes the global elite as a "club": "The UN is a club of States, represented by government leaders, and, not withstanding their conflicts of interest and ideology, they have a common interest in mutual accommodation" (Freeman, 2002: 54). This political shift towards global populism is designed to eliminate opposition to the expansion of liberal democracy—"freedom and democracy"—which has reached an impasse with a number of countries reverting to more authoritarian rule (see below). Consequently, a major concern is to quell the politicization of the population which occurs with global unrest. The two ideological camps at the OEWG were the American camp, prioritizing civil and political rights, and the less developed regions of Africa and South America, promoting the equal status of both sets of rights. But neither camp promoted the interests of the most oppressed and exploited, that is, neither promoted core minimum obligations which would provide the world's underclass with a belief system which could pose a serious challenge to neoliberalism. Rather the concern of both camps was global control and expansion of liberal democracy. The American camp, from the developed world, at the OEWG were concerned to maintain the status quo, consequently, their approach to the OP was more obstructive often promoting "no OP" as an option. The American camp often included such countries as Australia, the United Kingdom, Canada, Japan, Saudi Arabia, Sweden, Denmark, Switzerland, Poland, India, and Egypt. By contrast, the opposition, led by the developing regions of Africa and South America, wanted more emphasis on economic, social, and cultural rights, probably reflecting their greater need for unity in the face of the internal conflict they frequently experience domestically. The World Bank reports that during 1987–1997 more than 85 percent of all world conflicts were fought within national borders—fourteen were in Africa, fourteen in Asia, and one in Europe (Felice, 2003: 196). But the West, although more socially stable, also had good reason to provide a peaceful avenue for social justice as a number of those countries in the American camp had experienced major terrorist attacks in recent times—America, Australia (tourists in Bali), the United Kingdom, Saudi Arabia, and Egypt (see below). The continuance of the War on Terror seems to be in the interests of both camps.

The fundamental doctrine of international law is that of the sovereign equality of States (UN Charter Article 2(1)). Sovereign equality ensures political independence and nonintervention by other States as described by Christine Chinkin: "[Sovereign equality] assures States the prerogatives of territorial integrity and political independence. In legal terms these are upheld by the principle of non-intervention into matters of domestic jurisdiction, either by other States (Declaration on Principles of International Law) or by the institutions of the legal order, including the UN (UN Charter, Article 2)" (Chinkin, 1998: 106). However, there is a need to balance State sovereignty with human rights which are universal and concerned with individuals within States. Article 1(3) of the United Nations Charter states: "To achieve international co-operation in solving international problems of an economic, social, cultural, or humanitarian character, and in promoting and encouraging respect for human rights and for fundamental freedoms for all without distinction as to race, sex, language, or religion . . .". Ever since the Holocaust, in particular, the international community has been concerned about the human rights situation in any particular State but any intervention requires that the human rights violations are of such seriousness that they justify intervening in a States domestic affairs. But human rights has played a greater role since the collapse of the communist bloc with America and other liberal democracies wanting to impose its narrow view of human rights, which are most suited to the corporations, on the world. For example, a military coup took place in Fiji in December 2006. The military commander Commodore Frank Baini-marama, while stating there would be future democratic elections, would not commit to a date. The major liberal democracies in the region, Australia and New Zealand, decided that some intervention was justified because people had been deprived of their democratic rights. While Australia and New Zealand shied away from deploying armed military assistance to the elected Fiji government instead they applied a range of sanctions with New Zealand suspending Fiji from "special immigration access scheme and military training schemes in New Zealand," "Fijians will not be allowed to enter New Zealand for the purpose of sport," "new development and training assistance to Fiji is frozen and under review," and "the Fijian military will not be permitted to travel to New Zealand" (Hood and Manning, 2006).

Neoliberalism is now pursued by the "overwhelming majority of States" (Schwarb and Pollis, 2000: 214). Consequently, those at the OEWG meetings are making decisions regarding the OP when their governments are pursuing neoliberal policies. It is a case of ideology taking precedence over both the UDHR and the sovereignty of States many of whom were forced to adopt the structural adjustment programs of the IMF and the World Bank (see below).

Because liberal democracies marginalize economic, social, and cultural rights their judgment is often, in terms of the UDHR, severely skewed when it comes to foreign policy. This was the case in the debate in March 2006 regarding the new United Nations Human Rights Council to replace the United Nations Human Rights Commission. The U.S. Ambassador John Bolton, backed by a small minority of States, challenged the draft proposal, presented by the president of the General Assembly, Jan Eliasson. The proposal would (potentially) form the basis for the new UN Human Rights Council. The text dropped the requirement for election to the Council from a minimum two-thirds of UN Member States present and voting, to a simple majority of all Member States. However, the United States wanted to see greater power to exclude countries they consider to have poor human rights records. These could include such countries as Zimbabwe, Sudan, Libya, Cuba, and North Korea. To achieve this the Americans wanted members of the council to be elected by a two-thirds vote, not the "absolute majority" (96 votes in a 191-member General Assembly), to keep rights abusers out. However, in my view, it is not so much a matter of who is the human rights abuser but rather who is not. That one can get a completely skewed picture of life by seeing it through the lens of only one set of rights is evident in the 1999 report on Cuba, one of the so-called abusers, by Human Rights Watch, which is also only concerned with civil and political rights (see below for the political nature of many international NGOs). Teeple states that "conspicuously absent from the report is any mention of the whole range of social rights. Yet economic, social, and cultural rights are as much a part of the definition of human rights in the UDHR as are civil and political rights. And few countries in Latin America have matched Cuba's achievement in this area of rights." Teeple adds: "For that matter, even the United States has not matched Cuba's achievement on most measures of universal public health, literacy, housing, or basic education; but HRW, like most human rights advocacy groups, completely ignores this issue" (Teeple, 2004: 107).

Seen through a civil and political lens, States whose policies push people into extreme poverty are not regarded as human rights abusers. Yet, in his "Final Report" to the UN Commission on Human Rights, Special Rapporteur Leandro Despony cites the World Health Organization's characterizations of "extreme poverty" as "the world's most ruthless killer and the greatest cause of suffering on earth: 'No other disaster compared to the devastation of hunger which had caused more deaths in the past two years than were killed in the two World Wars together'" (Chomsky, 1998: 34).

Given that it is difficult to decide who is a human rights abuser rather than placing too much emphasis on exclusion it may be better, in terms of the UDHR, to set a good example. Those countries which promote the equal status of two sets of rights, at both the lower level of core minimum obligations and at the higher levels, should be regarded as peacemakers and given a special role to play on the Human Rights Council. This may encourage countries to take a more balanced view of human rights and encourage international cooperation.

The initial consideration of an OP for ICESCR occurred during the Commission on Human Rights (now replaced by the Human Rights Council) debates in 1954 on the drafting of the ICESCR, but was unsuccessful and two years later the first World Conference on Human Rights held in 1968 in Teheran called upon "all governments to focus their attention . . . on developing and perfecting legal procedures for prevention of violations and defense of "economic, social and cultural rights" (Lambert, 2005). The OP was not further pursued by the relevant UN bodies during the 1970s and 1980s. (Eibe Riedel, The Draft Optional Protocol to the International Covenant on Economic, Social and Cultural Rights "The Right to Development and Economic, Social and Cultural Rights" Prof. Dr. Eibe Riedel Universität Mannheim Wintersemester (1998/1999).

Following the collapse of communism in Eastern Europe in 1989, economic, social, and cultural rights became marginalized. The effect of the marginalization of ESC rights within the United Nations may be seen with the humanitarian disaster, which may not have occurred but for economic, social, and cultural rights losing its communist champions, that occurred following the imposition of comprehensive sanctions by the United Nations Security Council (Security Council Resolution 661 adopted in August 1990) on Iraq following its invasion of Kuwait in August 1990. It appears this led to the United Nations Committee on Economic, Social and Cultural Rights into formal discussions on an OP to ICESCR in its sixth session in 1991. Such an OP would increase the status of ESC rights at a time ESC rights were marginalized in the UN. Also it may be no coincidence that the United Nations Committee on Economic, Social and Cultural Rights provided its most authoritative interpretation of core minimum obligations in its fifth session (United Nations doc E/1991/23, 25 November—14 December 1990, General Comment No. 3) only a few months after the Security Council imposed the comprehensive sanctions on Iraq. This would be a recognition of the fact that the ends of sanctions (elimination of weapons of mass destruction which later Iraq was found not to have had) should not justify the means (violations of core minimum obligations). In 1997 this was followed by General Comment No 8 (41) (The relationship between economic sanctions and respect for economic, social, and cultural rights) which stated: "States parties should refrain at all times from imposing embargoes or similar measures restricting the supply of another State with adequate medicines and medical equipment. Restrictions on such goods should never be used as an instrument of political and economic pressure."

The humanitarian consequences of such comprehensive sanctions had been witnessed before. The Select Committee on Economic Affairs in the United Kingdom discussing Iraq stated that "comprehensive economic sanctions are those which seek to deny a target state all normal international financial, trade and service interactions except those exempted on humanitarian grounds." It adds that other cases since 1945 where they have been applied are the sanctions imposed on Rhodesia, Yugoslavia, South Africa, and Iraq (the country under discussion) (Select Committee on Economic Affairs Second Report, chapter 3: Comprehensive UN Sanctions—Iraq 1990–2003, The United Kingdom Parliament). The select committee, while not discounting its future use, states that the experience of comprehensive sanctions on Iraq has led many to argue that they should never be used again. For example, Mr. Carne Ross, First Secretary at the UK Permanent Mission to the UN from 1999 to 2003, stated: "I do not think that comprehensive economic sanctions should ever be imposed, on any country, ever again, because of what they did to the Iraqi people" (Select Committee on Economic Affairs Second Report, chapter 3: Comprehensive UN Sanctions—Iraq 1990–2003, The United Kingdom Parliament, 128).

In the year 2000 there were three high profile resignations because of the effects the U.N.'s embargo on Iraq was having on the civilian population. John Pilger cited these resignations: In 1998 Denis Holiday resigned as the

U.N.'s Coordinator of Humanitarian Relief to Iraq in protest against the effects of the embargo on the civilian population (Pilger, 2002: 55). Pilger quotes Denis Holiday: "The very provisions of the Charter of the United Nations and the Declaration of Human Rights are being set aside. We are waging a war, through the United Nations, on the children and people of Iraq. . . ." (Pilger, 2002: 56). In addition, Holiday describes a number of the basic economic, social, and cultural rights that needed to be addressed in Iraq: "Lifting sanctions is the only realistic way to end the human catastrophe in Iraq, rebuild the economy, get people back to work, and reestablish health care, education, electric power, clean water, sanitation, agriculture, oil production levels, and fix other sectors" (Cunniff, 2000). Also, on February 13, 2000, Hans Von Sponeck, who succeeded Holiday as Humanitarian Coordinator in Baghdad, also resigned. "How long," he asked, "should the civilian population of Iraq be exposed to such punishment for something they have never done?" (Pilger, 2002). Two days later, Jutta Burghardt, head of the World Food Program in Iraq, another UN agency, resigned, saying that she, too, could no longer tolerate what was being done to the Iraqi people (Pilger, 2002: 57). A Study by the United Nation's Children's Fund, UNICEF, found that between 1991 and 1998, there were 500,000 deaths above the anticipated rate among Iraqi children under five years of age (Pilger, 2002: 62). A Harvard University study team concluded that Iraq was heading for 'public health catastrophe,' with tens of thousands of deaths by the end of 1991 alone, the majority of them young children. The team of independent American professionals and academics estimated that, during the first eight months of sanctions when all shipments of food and medicines were blockaded, 47,000 children under the age of five had died (Pilger, 2002: 58–59).

Perhaps most illustrative of "the ends justifying the means" approach is the infamous interview in 1996 on the American current affairs program *"60 Minutes."* In the interview Madeleine Albright, then U.S. Ambassador to the United Nations, had been asked: "We have heard that half a million children have died . . . . is the price worth it?" Albright replied, "I think this is a very hard choice, but the price—we think the price is worth it" (Pilger, 2002: 64).

After 2004 interest in an OP, which previously States had shown little interest in, began to grow, perhaps reflecting the increase in global conflict and also the decline in the moral authority of the leading liberal democracies due mainly to the Iraq war. At the first session from February 23–March 5 2004, representatives of States, experts, United Nations specialized agencies, and nongovernmental organizations met "with a view to considering options regarding the elaboration of an optional protocol to the International Covenant on Economic, Social and Cultural Rights" (ECOSOC decision 2002/254 of July 25, 2002).

The Committee on Economic, Social, and Cultural Rights (formed in 1986) finalized a draft Optional Protocol that was presented for consideration to the Commission on Human Rights in 1997 (UN document E/CN.4/1997/105). In its decision 1997/104 of April 3, 1997, the Commission on Human Rights requested the Secretary-General to transmit the text of the draft optional to governments and intergovernmental and nongovernmental organizations for their comments for submission to the Commission on Human Rights. Only a handful of governments submitted their comments with the majority of States probably not very interested in the matter, as most member states never submitted any comments (Vandenhole).

ESCR-net, an NGO with consultative status with the UN, describing the first session (February 23–March 5, 2004, Geneva), was to report that while "there is a growing movement in favor of the adoption of an OP," there was "a very unsatisfactory ambiguity in the position of States on the adoption of the OP" with some government representatives attempting "to portray the debate as a North-South ideological confrontation" (developed versus developing countries) particularly over the issue of international cooperation with the less developed countries wanting such cooperation addressed in an OP while the developed nations were opposed. However ESCR-net pointed out that no simple division could be made (later it will be shown that States are best described as adopting a conservative or liberal approach). It states: "Despite the efforts of some government representatives to portray the debate as a North-South ideological confrontation, the reality showed a completely different scenario. In fact, diverse States such as Argentina, Venezuela, Finland and Portugal aligned in favor of an Optional Protocol while USA, Saudi Arabia, and India opposed it" (Calderhead, Khoza, and Sepulveda, 2004).

By the most recent session, July 16–July 18, 2007, the NGO Coalition was to report much greater support for the OP. It states: "There was widespread acknowledgement of and commitment to the principle of the indivisibility and interdependence of Human Rights and the equal status that ESC rights enjoy with civil and political rights. It was observed that there is a general consensus among State Parties that the current mandate of the working group is supported and the drafting an Optional Protocol to the Covenant is the objective" (NGO Coalition, Overview of Developments at the Open-Ended Working Group on an OP to the ICESCR).

One of the most contentious issues throughout the OEWG meetings was that of international cooperation and assistance (discussed in earlier chapters) and whether it was a moral or legal requirement of States to assist other States, particularly the less developed, in the achievement of economic, social, and cultural rights. The measures arrived at in the draft OP (Articles 13 and 14) seem rather timid and lacking in imagination considering the effects of the structural adjustment programs of the specialized agencies such as the IMF and the World Bank have had in creating underclasses in many States through welfare cuts. The measures arrived at in the draft OP are 1) where the United Nations Committee on Economic, Social, and Cultural Rights considers a case "indicates a need for technical advice and assistance" it will refer the matter to the UN Specialized Agencies and other competent bodies (Article 13) and, in addition, 2) set up a special fund to assist States "facing serious resource constraints in implementing the Committee's views and recommendations" (Article 14).

The importance of international assistance in achieving economic, social, and cultural rights is described by the UN Committee on Economic, Social, and Cultural Rights, which states: "A final element of article 2 (1) [ICESCR] to which attention must be drawn, is that the undertaking given by all States parties is "to take steps, individually and through international assistance and cooperation, especially economic and *technical* . . .". The Committee notes that the phrase "to the maximum of its available resources" was intended by the drafters of the Covenant to refer to both the resources existing within a State and those available from the international community through international cooperation and assistance. Moreover, the essential role of such cooperation in facilitating the full realization of the relevant rights is further underlined by the specific provisions contained in articles 11, 15, 22, and 23 (General Comment 3(13)). However, the Committee is silent on whether the State obligations are of a legal or moral nature. It states:

> The Committee wishes to emphasize that in accordance with Articles 55 and 56 of the Charter of the United Nations, with well-established principles of international law, and with the provisions of the Covenant itself, international cooperation for development and thus for the realization of economic, social and cultural rights is an obligation of all States. It is particularly incumbent upon those States which are in a position to assist others in this regard. The Committee notes in particular the importance of the Declaration on the Right to Development adopted by the General Assembly in its resolution 41/128 of 4 December 1986 and the need for States parties to take full account of all of the principles recognized therein. It emphasizes that, in the absence of an active program of international assistance and cooperation on the part of all those States that are in a position to undertake one, the full realization of economic, social and cultural rights will remain an unfulfilled aspiration in many countries (General Comment No 3(14)).

The Committee is more forthright with respect to core minimum obligations. General Comment 14 (45), on the right to health, states: "For the avoidance of any doubt, the Committee wishes to emphasize that it is particularly incumbent on States parties and other actors in a position to assist, to provide 'international assistance and cooperation, especially economic and technical' which enable developing countries to fulfill their core and other obligations . . . ". Louise Arbour, High Commissioner for Human Rights, regards both domestic and international measures as important in achieving economic, social, and cultural rights:

> I would like to point out that, obviously, an optional protocol—and legal protection more generally—is no panacea for the realization of economic, social, and cultural rights. The protection of these rights requires both the effective protection of other rights and a range of broader measures, including rights-based policies and programs and *international cooperation* [my emphasis]. Yet, a clearer recognition of economic, social, and cultural rights and a strengthened system of protection at the national and international levels are essential parts of any comprehensive strategy for the promotion and protection of these rights (Arbour, 2007).

According to Heidi Ost, the African Group insisted that the Covenant included a legal obligation to provide international assistance and wanted the OP to recognize this. For example the representative of the African Group from Ethiopia at the 2007 session of the OEWG said, in relation to international assistance, "States have a joint and an individual responsibility under the Covenant." The African Group got support from China, Belarus, and a few others, while "many European States did not welcome their suggestions. In fact, many of the 'so-called developed States strongly opposed the idea that there is a collective obligation arising from the Covenant' to provide international assistance." However, that it was not entirely a North versus South issue is indicated by the division in the Nordic countries. Heidi Ost states: "The Nordic region is clearly divided, with Finland and Norway broadly supportive of the elaboration of an OP and the proposed communications procedure, while Denmark and Sweden, somewhat surprisingly to many, are among the most reluctant and obstructive participants in the WG [OEWG]" (Heidi Ost).

Another significant omission of the draft OP is the failure to require that no retrogressive measures should be adopted by States especially with regard to core minimum obligations. If there was a requirement included in the OP it is likely States which were members of the IMF would have been a legally obliged to change the Articles of Agreement to ensure that States were not forced to violate these rights in return for loans. Francois Gianviti, General Counsel of the International Monetary Fund (IMF), states that the fund and the bank saw themselves as purely technical and financial organizations, whose Articles of Agreement enjoined them (explicitly in the case of the bank, implicitly in the case of the fund) from taking political considerations into account in their decisions. Their role as financial institutions was to provide economic assistance, not to dictate political changes (Gianviti, 2002). In addition, he states that "at the most general level, the Fund and the Bank [World Bank] saw themselves (and continue to see themselves) as international organizations separate from their members, governed by their respective charters" (Gianviti, 2002). This view is based on Article 24 of the ICE-SCR, which does not require the constitutions of the specialized agencies, such as the IMF, of which many of the States are members, and the World Bank, to conform to these human rights. The article states: "Nothing in the present Covenant shall be interpreted as impairing the provisions of the Charter of the United Nations and of the constitutions of the specialized agencies which define the respective responsibilities of the various organs of the United Nations and of the specialized agencies in regard to the matters dealt with in the present Covenant." Gianviti gave as an example the European Community which is not bound by the provisions of the European Convention on Human Rights, although its members are party to the Convention. However, States can include human rights in the Articles of Agreement. Gianviti states: "If the members of the Fund believe that it should adopt a more direct approach to the integration of human rights considerations in its decisions, they may of course propose an amendment to the Fund's Articles of Agreement" (Gianviti, 2002). Gianviti adds that "as was the case of the Bank, but unlike the United Nations, decision-making power in the Fund was vested in organs whose decisions were taken by weighted voting, rather than on a one-country, one-vote basis" (Gianviti, 2002). For example, the United States wields considerable power within the IMF. Sigrun Skogley states: "The voting power of the United States amounts to 17.56% of the total number of votes, effectively giving the country a veto power on all decisions that require the 85% majority" (Skogley, 2001: p. 80). Consequently, it is unlikely to be a coincidence that both America and the IMF promote neoliberalism.

Neoliberalism has overwhelming dominance globally. Peter Schwab et al. state: "Neo liberalism, with its doctrine of open borders and free markets, represents policies that are pursued by the overwhelming majority of States, either voluntarily or as imposed by the IMF and the World Bank" (Schwab and Pollis, 2000: 214). One of the main concerns of these international financial institutions was to minimize the size of the State which allow for large private sectors for the international corporations. Why couldn't governments buy certain corporations or big businesses especially those involving little risk and lease them out to the private sector where profits could then become social profits and returned to government? Both professionals and workers in these corporations could still be paid a competitive salary. The major difference would be that profits remain in the country rather than returned to the present corporation's country of origin. A number of these corporations are food outlets which could easily be replaced by domestic business. The reason the IMF has not required this to improve the State's financial situation seems to be political. For example, according to *Fortune Magazine* (2005), 405 of the top 500 companies come from America (162), Japan (126), France (42), Germany (41), and Britain (34), which are all liberal democracies. It is likely that it is in the interests of all liberal democracies to financially support the leading liberal democracies in their efforts to spread liberal democracy globally and it would be in the corporations interests to contribute financially toward this because where the liberal ideology goes they usually follow.

Paul Hunt, formerly a Rapporteur for the UN Committee on Economic, Social and Cultural Rights and presently Rapporteur for Health, describes how the ICESCR can be used as a "shield" by States, especially those from the economic South, against the pressures of the International Financial Institutions. He explains:

> It can also be used by the more vulnerable states to protect themselves from some of the policies and pressures of powerful global non-state actors. International financial institutions (IFIs)—the World Bank, IMF, Asian Development Bank and so on - wield a lot of power. In some ways, they have more power than numerous southern States which are desperate for loans, credits and other financial assistance. Numerous States have introduced IFI-sponsored structural adjustment programs (SAPs). In some cases, these SAPs have caused enormous hardship to the most vulnerable groups in society. Women have been disproportionately affected. Hospital clinics have been closed. Primary school fees have been introduced. Children's malnutrition has increased. Some SAPs have generated what, at first sight, appear to be widespread breaches of the Covenant.

In addition, Gianviti, General Counsel of the IMF, admits that as a consequence of the changes "there may be significant limits to the ability of a State party to devote resources to the promotion of the social rights set out in the Covenant, and some temporary regression in the achievement of these rights may be unavoidable." Hunt states: "Confronted with this type of scenario, it is open to a State to say to an International Financial Institution: 'We accept that our current economic arrangements are not sustainable. We know we have to reform our economy. We need your economic advice and financial assistance to make the necessary reforms. But these reforms must be both constructed and implemented in a way which is in conformity with our binding international obligations under the Covenant—especially our human rights obligations to our most vulnerable groups and individuals.'" The state might continue: "As a law-abiding international citizen, we are sure you would not encourage us to breach our binding international human rights obligations which we owe to all individuals in our jurisdiction." He adds that consequently, the Covenant has become a "shield" and "become a way of protecting a state from the worst excesses of ill-considered structural reform." He adds: "If used in this protective way the Covenant does not obstruct economic reforms. The re-structuring still occurs. But it does mean that the reforms are introduced in ways which minimize avoidable suffering, for instance by the introduction of safety nets for vulnerable groups—thereby contributing to the reform's long term sustainability" (Hunt, 2000). Consequently the draft OP should have clarified that it not acceptable to go in the opposite direction to the progressive realization of ESC rights, particularly with respect to core minimum obligations. If non-retrogression applied to all States it seems unlikely the IMF could require a State to take such measures. However, the OEWG on the OP for ICESCR ignored the General Comment No. 14 (32) of the United Nations Committee on Economic, Social and Cultural Rights, which considers that the ICESCR strongly imply that any retrogressive measures, especially with regard to core minimum obligations are not permitted, that is, pushing people into more extreme poverty and powerlessness. The Committee states:

> As with all other rights in the Covenant, there is a strong presumption that retrogressive measures taken in relation to the right to health are not permissible. If any deliberately retrogressive measures are taken, the State party has the burden of proving that they have been introduced after the most careful consideration of all alternatives and that they are duly justified by reference to the totality of the rights provided for in the Covenant in the context of the full use of the State party's maximum available resources.

The New Zealand government, anticipating the global neoliberal trend (and eagerly adopting it!) implemented a number of retrogressive measures since 1984, for example, there were the drastic benefit cuts of April 1991 and the introduction of market rentals for Housing New Zealand State tenants (1992) (both measures in violation of article 11(1) of the Covenant, the right to an adequate standard of living) and also the introduction of student fees and loans (1992) (in violation of Article 13(2)(c) requiring "the progressive introduction" of higher education) but these actions were rarely discussed in the media or political establishment in terms of human rights violations. Such retrogressive measures are only rarely taken by the New Zealand government but when they do they can have a profound effect, for example, the benefit cuts led to the use of food banks and begging on the streets, which are now commonplace in New Zealand cities. With both core minimum obligations and non-retrogression included in the OP couldn't the Special Fund be used to help fund independent human rights NGOs to make the public aware that these constitute human rights violations and seek domestic or international remedies? The developing countries could have also focused on the inclusion of non-retrogressive measures in the OEWG discussions but no such discussion was evident and, in my view, they were complicit in denying the most disadvantaged the empowering beliefs of core minimum obligations (see the reports of the NGO Coalition for the OP for ICESCR and the Reports of the Working Groups Sessions for the OP for ICESCR, Office of the United Nations High Commission for Húman Rights, Heidi Ost, Fourth Session of OEWG, 16—27.7.2007, Aland Islands Peace Institute and the Institute for Human Rights at Abo Akademi University, Internet).

Without such legal protections in the OP offers of international charity cannot be taken seriously. For instance, on June 11, 2005, the G8 finance ministers (a month prior to their summit in Gleneagles, Scotland) announced they would be writing off $40bn in debt owed by eighteen of the world's poorest countries, most of them in sub-Saharan Africa. However, without the legal protections of core minimum obligations, the right to development and non-retrogression, it is very unlikely that the poor will see any of the benefits of this debt relief as it is conditional on governments pursuing the same anti-poor, neoliberal policies, which brought them to their present desperate situation in the first place. John Pilger stated: "In summit after summit, not a single significant 'promise' of the G8 has been kept, and the 'victory for millions' is no different. It is a fraud— actually a setback to reducing poverty in Africa. Entirely conditional on vicious, discredited economic programs imposed by the World Bank and the IMF, the 'package' will ensure that the 'chosen' countries slip deeper into poverty." In fact, given the War on Terror and the high number of internal conflicts and increasing poverty in Africa, any benefits from the debt relief seems most likely to be redirected to increased spending on the apparatus of State control, that is, police and military condoned by the War on Terror rather than State welfare.

Another major issue considered by the OEWG is whether States should have a choice which rights and levels of obligation they are prepared to recognize. Some States wanted the OP to require a "comprehensive approach," others a "limited approach" and still others an "a la carte approach," as well as a number of variations of these. According to Annex II, Explanatory Memorandum, of the draft OP a "majority of delegates" favored a comprehensive approach which allowed for complaints for "communications under any of the rights of the Covenant." Some of the States which have expressed support for this approach have usually been the most supportive of an OP. These include the African Group, Angola, Argentina, Azerbaijan, Belgium, Brazil, Congo, Costa Rica, Croatia, Cuba, Ecuador, Egypt, Ethiopia, Finland, Italy,

Iran, Madagascar, Mexico, Morocco, Portugal, Senegal, Spain, South Africa, Switzerland, and Venezuela (Bolivarian Republic of). According to the State Positions Chart of the NGO Coalition, while by far the majority of the States are opting for a comprehensive approach a number of countries prefer an a la carte approach, including some of the leading liberal democracies. Some of these are Denmark, the Netherlands, Greece, Turkey, Switzerland, Australia, Japan, Poland, Sweden, Russia, New Zealand, and the United States. The "limited approach" largely meant excluding Part I of the ICESCR which contains the right to self-determination. Those countries concerned about internal minority aspirations to separate from the State favored this option, for example, Russia, China, Poland, Turkey, Sri Lanka. The "a la carte approach" involved a variety of approaches which allowed States to be selective as to which rights they would recognize for complaints to be made and/or which levels of obligation they would recognize. The latter are the duties of the States to respect, protect, and fulfill rights, for example, Switzerland wanted to "opt out" of the requirement to fulfill rights. Annex II of the draft OP gives the preferred "a la carte approach" as generally being an "opt out" approach which allowed a State party "to exclude the application of the communications procedure from one or several provisions contained in articles 2, paragraph 1, and articles 6 to 15 [of the ICESCR]." Some States wanted to limit the scope of the communications procedure to "core rights," "minimum contents," or serious violations of rights, for example, such proposals were made by Germany, Norway, Sweden, the United Kingdom, France, Greece, and the Republic of Korea. Although these proposals were only occasionally made during the OEWG it only referred to having "core rights" dealt with by the OP but would exclude any consideration of higher levels of these rights— such a suggestion could allow the State to having all beneficiaries as living at the level where they just had the core minimum obligations and no more. Hence the importance of non-retrogression to ensure existing levels of ESC rights are not removed and the necessity of human rights education to ensure people pressure government through the democratic process for a "continuous improvement of living conditions." The mere fact that nearly all States are so careful to keep their people ignorant of human rights indicates just how effective such pressure is likely to be if they were educated in these rights. To my knowledge no State or any of the most prominent NGOs suggested that both higher levels of ESC rights as well as the lower levels of core minimum obligations should be included with an emphasis on the latter.

To show how economic, social, and cultural rights can be manipulated to suit elite interests to the detriment of the most disadvantaged is the a la carte option given by Bernard Robertson in 1997 in his study for the New Zealand Business Roundtable entitled Economic, Social and Cultural Rights—Time for a Reappraisal. In the Executive Summary he states that "if the rights enumerated in the Covenant [ICESCR] are reappraised purely as negative rights [noninterference by government], the Covenant and the Committee set up to supervise its implementation have the opportunity to make a positive contribution to the welfare of citizens internationally." Robertson considers that economic, social, and cultural rights should be treated in the same way as civil and political rights, that is, there should be noninterference in both sets of rights. In other words, economic, social, and cultural rights should only be regarded as negative rights as are civil and political rights. In terms of the modern tripartite system of duties, negative rights would require the duties of the State to respect and protect an individual's rights but not to fulfill rights, which is positive, to groups of people such as the most disadvantaged as this would involve the provision of resources. Consequently, Robertson would only see a self-interested private sector as being involved in future development and no place for State investment in the greater good of society. But this would also mean that there would be no space travel, no conservation, no help in natural disasters because there is no money in it. Also, as shown in the chapter on the history during times of war, the State is eager to unite the people and gain the support of the most disadvantaged in the war effort. Robertson considers that as negative rights States would have to respect and protect free choice of employment (Article 6(1), ICESCR) and nondiscrimination (Article 2(2), ICESCR), which do not involve the provision of resources. Robertson considers that economic, social, and cultural rights as positive rights (i.e., the duty of the State to fulfill) involve the provision of resources which distorts the free market and infringes others' civil and political rights, for example, higher taxes would constrain the right to liberty, an individual's ability to choose how best to spend their own money and infringe that person's right to a "continuous improvement of living conditions" (Article 11(1) of ICESCR. Robertson states: "As a negative right, the right to continuous improvement in living conditions presumably means that the government should not take any decision deliberately aimed at reducing the living conditions of any group. This would entail not levying discriminatory taxation on any group even if the aim were redistributional since the rich are entitled to this right as anyone else" (Robertson, 1997: 27). However, Robertson agrees with the duty to respect and protect (e.g., nondiscrimination, etc.) because these are applied fairly whereas the duty to fulfill requires targeting certain groups, for example, the most disadvantaged. However, in my view, where private enterprise will not risk investment it makes good sense in terms of the right to development for the State to invest in certain individual business and social enterprises which could be of immediate benefit in reducing unemployment as well as a good long-term investment for the country. In addition,

Robertson continues showing how these rights can protect private enterprise: the right to choose one's employment would entail "governmental abstention from interfering with working relations" (although such relationships may be far from equal) and "avoidance of legislation which discourages individuals and businesses from making work available" such as legislation setting minimum wage rates (if there is no bottom line it is conceivable that many people might work for nothing, as many employers require experience, which is not very unusual in today's society), excessive levels of income tax which Robertson considers involves "preventing people from making work available" and the imposition of tariffs "which favor the jobs of some at the expense of others and which may well reduce employment overall" (Robertson, 1997: 39–40). Robertson makes the assumption that we live in a fair system where we all have a "fair go" and where no government intervention is required. Yet the reality of social hierarchy and extreme gaps between rich and poor totally belie this assumption. Robertson's a la carte approach seems only likely to provide certain protections for those who already have their ESC rights and will almost certainly make the situation of the most disadvantaged, who need their rights to be fulfilled immediately, much worse. What few opportunities they presently have are likely to be taken away from them.

Robertson points to a number of economic and social rights "which do not appear in the ICESCR." These include the right to property, "which would include a right not to have one's savings eroded by inflation, freedom of contract including the freedom to agree to the form of contract which best suits the mutual purposes of the parties making it, the right to obtain the best goods and services regardless of country of origin." He adds that "these rights can be protected in the same way as classical civil and political rights, by rules which instruct the government to abstain from activities such as interfering in contracts, inflationary spending, imposing tariffs and quotas, according privileges to particular groups and deficit budgeting" (Robertson, 1997: 59). These economic and social rights which were, as Robertson states, included in the UDHR but excluded from both covenants was due largely, in my view, to the Western tradition stemming from the seventeenth century of separating the private from the public, thereby keeping the economic function independent of government interference. In addition, the politics at the United Nations during the Cold War with the capitalists believing in private property while the communists believed in collective property may also contributed to exclusion of the right to property from the covenants. Consequently, at the international level these economic rights were kept separate, thereby avoiding interference by the United Nations. These "economic and social rights" were allocated to the specialized agencies, for example, the IMF and the World Bank, in order to avoid any clash between these rights and other rights in the covenant, as Robertson states, "the imposition of a positive right cancels out negative rights" (Robertson, 1997: 15). Both covenants (Article 24 ICESCR and Article ICCPR) separate out certain economic functions and rights from human rights. They state: "Nothing in the present Covenant shall be interpreted as impairing the provisions of the Charter of the United Nations and of the constitutions of the specialized agencies which define the respective responsibilities of the various organs of the United Nations and of the specialized agencies in regard to the matters dealt with in the present Covenant." In other words, human rights are not part of the Articles of Agreement of the IMF. Francois Gianviti, General Counsel of the IMF, also sees that "there exists a wider set of economic rights than those contained in the Covenant, and it involves economic considerations as well as legal ones." He adds that these rights "are essential for the achievement of the social rights set out in the Covenant. . . . For example, the right to property is stated in the Universal Declaration, but it is not included in any of the two covenants," and thus has remained outside the scope of the human rights monitoring system (Gianviti, 2002). In addition, he adds, that the rights to engage in economic activity and to trade are as important to the realization of the rights specified in the Covenant. He states: "These rights provide the very basic tools that all people, including the poor, can use to engage in economic activity and to improve their economic condition" (Gianviti, 2002). These economic freedoms or rights are those that in many cases have been forced on countries in the form of the structural adjustment programs. As most jurisdictions have civil and political rights in law, these individual freedoms were supplemented by the economic freedoms or economic rights imposed by the IMF. While Robertson and the IMF General Counsel have a particularly valid point and that the covenants should not exclude the right to property, however how this right is defined is another matter—it could be regarded, as is generally the case, as private property, just collective property, on the other hand it could be regarded as a mixture of private and collective property, or with private more akin to personal property perhaps extending to no more than one's dwelling or business or farm. The right to property could be defined to reflect the State conditions and the realities of the times—but however a State or the United Nations defines it, it should, in my view, be included in the covenants, especially as the Cold War has ended, and will likely no longer "be outside the scope of the human rights monitoring system" and, consequently, loans by the IMF will have to take into account all human rights.

The UN human rights treaty system, dealing with complaints of violations of the Covenant and Conventions, the Periodic Reports of States to the Committee on Economic, Social and Cultural Rights, and international human rights NGOs have failed to prevent the creation of large underclasses in most countries. Although it could be argued that many complaints are dealt with at the domestic level it seems more likely that it is the lack of human rights education which leads to the treaty system dealing with such few complaints. For example, Straight UN Facts reports, that in 2006 the treaty system registered less than 100 cases. This is despite the fact that 2.5 billion people live in States which permit formal complaints of rights violations to be made against them (Straight UN Facts, 2006). The report adds that those countries which are regarded as having the very worst human rights records are actually the subject of very few complaints. As such countries are also the most unlikely to provide domestic remedies this strongly suggests that the reason for the small number of complaints under the treaty system has more to do with lack of human rights education. For example, the largest number of States recognizing a right of complaint do so under the International Covenant on Civil and Political Rights (ICCPR) and its Optional Protocol. The subject matter covered by the ICCPR is very wide-ranging, including for example, the right to life, to vote, freedom of religion and expression, and nondiscrimination on any ground. According to the annual reports of the UN Human Rights Committee only 71 complaints was received in 2006, compared with 112 in 2005, 103 in 2004, 92 in 2003, and 103 in 2002. The number of people living in those States which grant a right to complain of violations of the ICCPR is 1.7 billion while the number of States permitting complaints that they have violated the ICCPR is 109. Current States party to the ICCPR having the highest number of registered complaints directed against them are Western countries where there is likely to be a greater awareness of these civil and political rights. In 2006 they were Canada (132); second highest number, Spain (105); third highest number, Australia (99). In 2005 the same countries were involved: Canada (123); Spain (98); and Australia (97). States parties to the ICCPR, where you would expect a large number of complaints, that have five or fewer complaints ever registered against them numbered sixty-two (56.9% of States Parties). Examples of these states include Angola, Burkina Faso, Central African Republic, Côte d'Ivoire, Equatorial Guinea, Nepal, Paraguay, Sierra Leone, Togo, and Turkmenistan. States where zero complaints have been registered under the ICCPR, again where you would expect a large number of complaints, include such states as Azerbaijan, Benin, Cape Verde, Chad, Congo, Djibouti, El Salvador, Gambia, Ghana, Guatemala, Guinea, Lesotho, Malawi, Niger, Somalia, and Uganda. Consequently, this indicates that unless there is education in human rights it is unlikely there will be many complaints irrespective of the number of violations within the country (Straight UN Facts, 2006).

Catarina Albuquera, chairperson of the open-ended working group discussing the OP for ICESCR, also described the small number of complaints received under the UN treaty system. She stated that "experience demonstrates" that the existence of an Optional Protocol does not lead to a proliferation of communications. She added: "For example, since the entry into force of the OP to CEDAW (Convention on the Elimination of Discrimination Against Women) in 2000, only two communications have been filed. Similarly, very few communications have been filed through the CERD (Convention on the Elimination of Racial Discrimination) procedure; moreover, provisions on the exhaustion of domestic remedies and admissibility will prevent vexatious communications" (Albuquera, 2004). So, obviously, the UN Treaty System, as it exists, does not hold out much hope for the poor.

To ensure that States Parties are complying with the ICESCR, the Committee on Economic, Social and Cultural Rights (CESCR) was established to monitor and review the activities of States Parties (the UN Human Rights Committee deals with reports on civil and political rights). The CESCR meets twice a year, and has eighteen independent experts, who are elected to the Committee by the States Parties to the ICESCR. Every five years, State Parties must submit a report to CESCR outlining their successes and challenges in implementing the ICESCR. Governments must present their reports to the Committee, and the experts have the opportunity of asking the government representatives a series of questions about their report and the implementation of ESC rights in their territory/ies. The CESCR then issues a series of observations, known as Concluding Comments. The Concluding Comments acknowledge both positive and negative measures and suggest actions which could improve implementation of the ICESCR or that would stop violations occurring. For example, in 2003 some of the Concluding Observations of the Committee regarding New Zealand (E/C.12/1/Add.88., 23/05/2003) under the heading "principle subjects of concern" were: 1/ The Committee notes with concern the relatively high unemployment rate among young people; 2/ The Committee is concerned about the relatively high suicide rate, especially among young people, in the State party; 3/ The Committee notes with concern that nearly one in four persons lives in poverty according to the measurement commonly used in the State party, and that clear indicators are lacking to assess the effectiveness of measures to combat poverty. However the CESCR's views are not legally binding. Also Audrey Chapman (Chapman and Robertson, 1999: 147) consider the Committee as overly diplomatic. In fact Chapman considers that these "concerns" should actually be regarded as human rights violations. Also Robertson states: "The United Nations system of 'State reporting' which obsessively avoids hurtful criticism, has been inadequate other than in helping to pinpoint priorities for the U.N.'s aid agencies, which cannot be seen to take issue with the political policies of member States which are assisted" (Robertson, 1999: 147). So, the system of State reports offers little assistance to the most disadvantaged.

Human rights NGOs, which often purport to being independent are, often part of the international and national human rights establishment and perpetuate the human rights agenda as defined by domestic and global elites. Gary Teeple states that "well over a thousand NGOs have consultative status at the UN, and an estimated 26,000 or more internationally recognized NGOs operate at the global level" (Teeple, 2004: 101). He considers that "the term nongovernmental organization itself is somewhat deceptive" as, he states that "many NGOs are funded by governments or state aid agencies, and/or by philanthropic foundations such as the Ford or Carnegie foundations and the Soros Open Society Institute." In these cases, he adds, "the agendas and operations of the NGOs almost certainly conform at least implicitly to the foreign policy goals of the sponsoring governments or foundations" (Teeple, 2004: 101). He adds that the enormous expansion of NGO numbers in the 1980s and 1990s most probably had much to do with the pervasive adoption of neoliberal policies (Teeple, 2004: 101). With the neoliberal emphasis on the minimal State social responsibility was marginalized. Much of what used to be in the domestic political domain was relegated to the international level. Domestic NGOs, usually always financed by government, were created to be nonpolitical and deal solely at the coal face of human need while NGOs dealing at the international level were able to be political but muzzled domestically. For instance while Amnesty International played a prominent role during the OEWG meetings promoting the OP and a comprehensive approach to ESC rights domestically, it says nothing about these rights. Similarly Franciscans International were also involved at the OEWG meetings but domestically the Catholic Church, apart from a small organization through Pax Christi, says nothing publicly. This despite the fact that the Vatican is one of the few States involved in the education of ESC rights. This is the same approach taken by the trade unions, who will express their social concerns through the International Labour Organisation, but say little publicly. Most of these human rights NGOs prioritize civil and political rights over economic, social, and cultural rights. Teeple states: "The NGOs that occupy themselves with human rights issues on the global level tend to ignore the issue of economic, social and cultural rights, or at least carefully select some of those issues for attention. Most of them prefer to focus their efforts almost exclusively on certain civil and political rights" (Teeple, 2004: 103).

Onuma Yasuaki states that "one of the most serious flaws in contemporary human rights discourse is the identification of civil and political rights with human rights in general." He adds: "Economic, social and cultural rights are referred to only in passing or as a supplement. . . . This bias is also evident in the discourse of many major human rights NGOs, the majority of whose operations depend on the support of people in the North. Their activities are widely reported, and their claims are generally regarded as more reliable than official governmental publications because of their independent status and their devotion to the course of human rights . . .". He adds that Amnesty International (while claiming the UDHR as its authority), Human Rights Watch, and Freedom in the World "deal almost exclusively" with civil and political rights (Yasuaki, 1999:113–114). Teeple states that "the names on the board of directors and advisory committees of Human Rights Watch, moreover, reads like a 'Who's Who' of past and present high officials in government, significant business figures, foundation people, and members of the U.S. academic elite, often based in so-called think tanks." (Teeple, 2004: p. 104). Similarly, "while Amnesty International purports to promote awareness and adherence to the UDHR—the most significant thrust of its practice is the focus on specific civil and political rights." Teeple states: "Given that Amnesty International is staffed, funded, and based in the West, this position should not be surprising. Like other human rights organizations, Amnesty International takes capitalism and its political form, liberal democracy, as unquestioned norms" (Teeple, 2004: 110).

The NGO Coalition for an OP to ICESCR, the most prominent NGO at the OEWG, opposed the Committee assessing "violations of only the core minimum obligations" which it described as "untenable." The NGO Coalition considers that admissibility requirements for core minimum obligations may differ between rich and poor States. It states: "Determinations as to what constitutes . . . . 'minimum core obligations' if made into determinations of admissibility of complaints, are fraught with difficulty and imprecision. Such restrictions would almost certainly have discriminatory consequences, and create arbitrary exclusions from the complaints process." For example, the Coalition adds, the poorer regions would be discriminated against. The Coalition states: "Complaints alleging violations in more affluent countries would be less likely to meet admissibility standards under . . . . a 'minimum core obligations' approach, simply because resources are more readily available to satisfy Covenant obligations. Many of the situations may be more readily achievable through available resources would thus be excluded, seriously undermining the effectiveness of the procedure." However, irrespective of whether the NGO Coalition's argument is a sound one as with some of the other States mentioned above, it did not seem to occur to the Coalition that higher levels of ESC rights should not be excluded; rather that serious violations (core minimum obligations) should get most attention. Even if the admissibility requirements for homelessness in Western countries could not be compared to States with a large numbers of slum dwellers the former could still be dealt with as a progressive requirement of the higher levels of ESC rights. Anyway, it is very dubious to imply that there is a major difference between poor and powerless individuals in rich and poor countries, or that an individual in the former is happier than an individual in the latter countries, despite the difference in numbers. Any measure of core minimum obligations requires a holistic interpretation considering the interdependence of all human rights. For instance, the poor in the West 'me' societies suffer extreme isolation whereas the poor in other 'we' countries, although with less material means, can belong to a strong family unit. Also Ted Honderich states: "Shall we be able to say that there is good reason for supposing that the very poor in the four African countries and others are no more short on freedom and power within their societies, and also on respect and self-respect than the very poor in the United States and the like" (Honderich, 2002: 23). But as already shown, the UN Treaty System actually only deals with very few complaints. By failing to emphasis serious violations it allows States to do likewise at the domestic level. And it is this latter situation that is most important because the inclusion of core minimum obligations will act as a policy guide for States. In fact, the Coalition's rejection of core minimum obligations allows States to overlook the underclass and continue with the pursuit of neoliberal policies. Also the NGO Coalition's view that "minimum core obligations if made into determinations of admissibility of complaints, are fraught with difficulty and imprecision" seems exaggerated. An experienced court could determine whether an individual's circumstances are life threatening or a major abuse of his/her dignity—such obvious situations as a homelessness, a serious case on the hospital waiting list, or benefits so low they necessitate people using food banks or begging on the streets. Apart from some cultural differences, such as the extended families of some poor countries, what is life threatening in one country is likely to be life threatening in another. And also there is also the guidance of the UN Committee on Economic, Social and Cultural Rights General Comments. Why couldn't a court direct (given that appropriate law is passed) the appropriate government agency to give those suffering serious violations priority treatment? For instance, in New Zealand there are waiting lists for hospital treatment, housing, as well as the long-term unemployed. It would be a matter of the court giving the individual priority on the list. Independently funded NGOs could assist these individuals to take the matter to court or to the commission. For example, in Auckland, New Zealand, is the Combined Beneficiaries Union which assists people who have difficulties with their benefit. It is a place where law students often get experience. The union helps ensure that people have their legal rights under the appropriate welfare act. First they will usually approach the welfare department to try to get the matter resolved and if unsuccessful may take the matter to court. If the matter were to be dealt with under human rights law welfare it would be not nearly as vulnerable to retrogressive measures (governments do not like to be seen as taking peoples' human rights away from them) and if claims could be taken to domestic human rights courts and ultimately the United Nations, such NGOs could carry considerable weight as they would be capable of embarrassing the government at an international level.

To assist the courts as to whether individuals are living well below the poverty line each country could determine a culturally appropriate national poverty threshold. Modern methods of poverty measurement such as the New Zealand Poverty Measurement Project make use of focus groups which take into account both relative (gap between rich and poor) and absolute (only meeting immediate needs) poverty (Stevens, Frater, and Waldegrave, 1984–1998). So the poverty threshold will based on essential needs, which are universal, but also be culturally relative, for example, in some countries families play a prominent role and benefits are not as necessary.

In the initial sessions of the OEWG in 2004 the issue of whether or not ESC rights were justiciable or not threatened to be a stumbling block to the OP to ICESCR. However, by July, 2007 the NGO Coalition was to report that while "there are still some States who query the justiciability of ESC rights . . . they are audibly in the minority" (NGO Coalition, Overview, Monday, July 16, 2007—Wednesday, July 18, 2007).

Justiciability describes whether a right is able to be dealt with by a court. Along with some leading liberal democracies New Zealand has also held to the view that ESC rights are not justiciable. In 2003, in the conclusions of the Committee on Economic, Social and Cultural Rights in its "principle subjects of concern" the Committee noted with regret "the view expressed by the State party's delegation [New Zealand] that economic, social and cultural rights are not necessarily justiciable." Consequently, during the OEWG (2004) New Zealand's position was "against drafting an OP" but "happy to continue with discussions" according to Maria Graterol, Programme Officer, of the International Women's Rights Action Watch Asia Pacific. Graterol added that she considered New Zealand as "light" opposition to the OP. Phil Goff, Minister of Foreign Affairs and Trade, on January 18, 2005, stated that New Zealand takes a cautious approach to treaties because even when they are "optional" New Zealand always tries to become a party to all international human rights treaties. He states: "Given the complex nature of the issues concerned, and the clear lack of international consensus on the way forward we consider that further discussion is warranted before any decision is taken to begin negotiations on a new instrument [consequently] New Zealand opposes immediate drafting of an OP" (personal correspondence January 18, 2005).

Vandenhole states that one of the main reasons given by the West who wanted the UDHR to be divided into two covenants was its argument that "ESC rights could not be placed on the same footing as civil and political rights, as ESC rights were not legally justiciable." He adds: "This ideological quarrel led to the adoption of two covenants" (Vandenhole). The major reason for its non-justiciability, according to the Western view, was that unlike civil and political rights, economic, social, and cultural rights are not justiciable because they usually have considerable resource implications, for example, they would say that a court cannot give a person a job whereas they can ensure that the State does not interfere in a person's individual liberties, such as, freedom of movement or freedom of the press. However, it is often pointed out that the right to a fair trial, a civil and political right, involves a considerable cost—the justice system, courts, police, and prisons. Also, the cost of the armed forces, which are necessary sometimes to protect people's physical security, is also a civil and political right. Also, there has been a growth in case law, which shows that these rights are justiciable. This case law has come from the African, European, and inter-American systems which all have either comprehensive, a la carte, or limited Optional Protocols for economic, social, and cultural rights. The African system is comprehensive, the European Social Charter adopts an a la carte approach while in the Inter-American system—the San Salvador Protocol (which the U.S. is not a party to)—allows for the submission of individual complaints to the Inter-American Commission and Inter-American Court with regard to trade union and association rights and the right to education. While the latter communications procedure is particularly limited, it "has provided for rich interventions on the justiciability of ESC rights." (Lambert, 2005). In addition, some States have included some economic, social, and cultural rights as justiciable rights in domestic human rights law. They are South Africa, Norway, Finland, and Russia.

Also the Committee maintains that all the rights in the covenant contain "some justiciable elements" and gives examples. General Comment No. 9 states: "While the general approach of each legal system needs to be taken into account, there is no Covenant right which could not, in the great majority of systems, be considered to possess at least some significant justiciable dimensions." In General Comment No. 3 (1990) it cited, by way of example, articles 3; 7, paragraph (a) (i); 8; 10, paragraph 3; 13, paragraph 2 (a); 13, paragraph 3; 13, paragraph 4; and 15; paragraph 3 (see Appendix III). According to Limburg Principle no. 8, "the application of some rights can be made justiciable immediately while other rights can become justiciable over time." Those elements which are more justiciable refer to the duties to respect and protect, which can be implemented immediately. The duty to fulfill as the draft OP stands is largely only seen as being addressed progressively, so it is not immediately justiciable although there are exceptions such as primary school education and the right to fair wages which are expected to be fulfilled immediately. However, if core minimum obligations were included in the draft OP then part of the duty to fulfill dealing with core minimum obligations would be immediately justiciable.

Often it is maintained by those who consider ESC rights as nonjusticiable that only the political system and not the court system should deal with matters involving significant resource implications. However, the Committee disputes this with General Comment No. 9 stating:

> It is sometimes suggested that matters involving the allocation of resources should be left to the political authorities rather than the courts. While the respective competences of the various branches of government must be respected, it is appropriate to acknowledge that courts are generally already involved in a considerable range of matters which have important resource implications. The adoption of a rigid classification of economic, social and cultural rights which puts them, by definition, beyond the reach of the courts would thus be arbitrary and incompatible with the principle that the two sets of human rights are indivisible and interdependent. It would also drastically curtail the capacity of the courts to protect the rights of the most vulnerable and disadvantaged groups in society.

Cecile Fabre describes the use of negative judicial review as a means the court can deal with economic, social, and cultural rights. He states:

> . . . giving the courts the power to tell the government to do x does not entail giving them the power to tell them how to do it: for the government to be under a duty to do x does not imply that the government is under a duty to do x in a certain way. If the constitution specifies that one has a constitutional right to, say, a reasonable standard of housing given the level of economic development and competing expenditures (and given what other needy people need), the judiciary will have to decide whether the income of the government allows for that level of provision, and whether the government is right to spend x amount of money on certain things. But if they find that the government can afford to provide people with housing, they can simply tell the government that the housing provision must be raised, by a certain date. They do not need to say how the standard of provision should be raised (Fabre, 2000: 149).

Recently Louise Arbour, UN High Commissioner for Human Rights, confirms that ESC rights are justiciable and that this is now the established view. She states:

> I am pleased to observe that the discussions in the Working Group have moved beyond the simple argument for or against the justiciability of economic, social and cultural rights. It is now widely recognized that there is nothing inherently

non-justiciable about economic, social and cultural rights, a fact which is amply
evidenced by the practice of domestic and regional courts all over the world. On
the contrary, access to legal or administrative remedies is increasingly playing a
role in the protection and enforcement of economic, social and cultural rights.
(Arbour, 16 July 2007).

It has taken fifty-seven years for the West to finally acknowledge that ESC
rights are justiciable. Now claims of nonjusticiability are seen as a political
stance, not one based on the facts.

The momentum gathered by the OEWG toward support for the OP for ICE-
SCR was probably due to a number of factors but none, in my view, really
pressing given that neoliberalism has no real challengers. But the concerns
were sufficient to increase the status of ESC rights on the UN agenda and emphasizing democracy because using force such as the War on Terror is not
likely to be as effective as regaining people's confidence in neoliberalism.
The worldwide antiglobalization demonstrations, the failure of trickle down,
the formation of regional groupings, the growth of global terrorism, the loss
moral legitimacy by the major liberal democracies, and the impasse in the
global growth of liberal democracy may have all played a part in gaining a
consensus for the OP. Between 1993 and 2003 there were twenty significant
terrorist acts, suspected of or inspired by Al Qaeda, whereas from 2004, the
first OEWG meeting, to 2007 there were thirteen such attacks (Information
Please, 2007). Also during the period of the OEWG discussions, there were
three major bombings targeting U.S. allies—the Madrid bombings in March
2004, killing 191 and injuring more than 1,500; the London bombings in July
2005, killing 52; and the Bali bombings in Indonesia, killing 22, mainly Australians. It would certainly seem that such terrorism is, in part, directed
against the American camp and neoliberalism.

In addition the global spread of liberal democracy has reached an impasse
with a number of countries reverting to authoritarian government. But probably the most significant factor is the decline in the moral authority of the
United States due to the Iraq war. Having the dominant ideology is not nearly
as effective if its prime advocate, the United States, has little moral authority.

Back in 1996, Steiner and Alston predicted that if neoliberalism fails the
world could see a reversion to authoritarian regimes. They state: "Democracy,
stability and peace cannot long survive in conditions of chronic poverty, dispossession and neglect. Political freedom, free markets and pluralism have
been embraced with enthusiasm by an ever increasing number of peoples in
recent years, in part because they have seen them as the best prospect of
achieving basic economic, social and cultural rights. If that quest proves futile
the pressures in many societies to revert to authoritarian alternatives will be
immense" (Steiner and Alston, 1996: 267).

In recent times, we have seen Russia, Venezuela, Iran, China, Belarus, Zimbabwe, and, most recently, Pakistan move toward authoritarian government. This seems to be a consequence of neoliberalism failing to deliver on economic, social, and cultural rights, leading to unrest and consequently the need for more coercive social control. Increasing the status of ESC rights represents a concession on the part of the elite, and is a way of quelling the politicization of the population. Zebra Arat, describing the situation in developing countries (which could also apply to developed countries) states:

> ...the decline in democracy and the transition to authoritarian rule in developing countries are attributable to policies that create an imbalance between the two groups of human rights, civil and political rights and socioeconomic rights, by ignoring the latter group. The increasing gap between the two groups of rights . . . . causes frustration and social unrest, which in turn is suppressed by coercive politics (Arat, 1991: 9).

According to the 2006 survey of Freedom House, as predicted by Steiner and Alston, a "reversion to authoritarian alternatives" is taking place. The survey states: ". . . the percentage of countries designated as Free has failed to increase for nearly a decade, suggesting an ongoing 'freedom stagnation'" and that the situation is actually deteriorating. The number of countries judged by Freedom in the World as Free in 2006 stood at 90, representing 47 percent of the global population. Fifty-eight countries qualified as Partly Free, with 30 percent of the world's population. The survey finds that 45 countries are Not Free, representing 23 percent of the world's inhabitants. About one-half of those living in Not Free conditions inhabit one country: China. Arch Puddington, director of research at Freedom House, noted the trend toward "authoritarianism." He states: "While the past year [2006] was not a good year for freedom, the trend over the past decade is even more disturbing. Not only have we failed to make significant breakthroughs, but we have seen the emergence of authoritarian regimes [see below] . . . that are aggressively hostile to democracy, are determined to crush all domestic advocates for freedom, and stand as models for democracy's adversaries everywhere" (Abrams, January 17, 2007).

Puddington states that "the most significant development was the decline in freedom in Asia and continued poor performance in Russia and the former Soviet Union." He describes the impasse: "Globally, many countries showed evidence of problems with press freedom, rule of law, and corruption." Freedom House also pointed to a growing "pushback" against democracy in such countries as Russia, Venezuela, Iran, China, Belarus, and Zimbabwe (also in November 2007 Pakistan was taken over by the military). Regimes used legalistic methods to smother independent media and marginalize nongovernmental organizations in a broad effort to eliminate sources of potential democratic ferment (Puddington, April 2007: 125–137).

In addition, as evidenced by the surveys, the moral authority of America is in decline, which makes it difficult for States to gain legitimacy if they are seen by their population as being directed by America. Gallup's Centre for Muslim Studies in New York carried out surveys of 10,000 Muslims in ten predominantly Muslim countries. The surveys were carried out in 2005 and 2006. Along with an earlier Gallup survey in nine other countries in 2001, they represent the views of more than 90 percent of the world's Muslims. Those that took an unfavorable view of the United States in 2005: Saudi Arabia, 79 percent, Jordan, 65 percent, Morocco, 49 percent, Iran, 52 percent, Pakistan, 65 percent (Gledhill, 2007). In addition, polls conducted by the Pew Research Center show a precipitous decline in positive attitudes about the United States since the year 2000 in eight of twelve countries for which multi-year comparisons can be made. According to the Pew polls, the proportion of the population feeling positively toward the United States has plummeted in Great Britain from 83 percent to 56, in France from 62 percent to 39, in Germany from 78 percent to 37, and in Spain from 50 percent to 23. Japan, too, has seen a decline. Similarly, polls by the German Marshall Fund and the Chicago Council on Global Affairs have found a significant and uniform decline in positive feelings toward the United States between 2002 and 2006 in the European countries they surveyed. Today, in France, Germany, Italy, Great Britain, the Netherlands, and Poland—all of them NATO allies— negative feelings about the United States are almost as frequent as positive ones. In Spain, negative sentiments predominate (Losing Hearts and Minds report, September, 2006).

The present draft OP is not necessarily the last word on the covenant on economic, social, and cultural rights. A future more enlightened international human rights establishment may well consider a Convention on the Rights of the Most Disadvantaged, and combine the two covenants into one covenant as was originally conceived in the early 1950s although this is likely to be a long way down the track, and the needs of the most disadvantaged are immediate. To derive core obligations with respect to the right to development is essential. There is far more dignity in being able to support oneself than to receive necessary benefits. What is most crippling to the individual is to be deprived of their right to development and then blamed for their poverty. But such is the desire of the dominant elite to consolidate its wealth and power they will deprive the individual and the world of such talents and abilities. Their "budgeting mentality" has no bottom line, in fact, in my view, the only answer of which they are capable, to the 1.8 billion people living in extreme poverty on $1 per day would be the provision of budgeting services (not uncommon in present-day liberal democracies) to stretch out the $1! Such a "budgeting mentality" has pervaded the thinking of the international human rights establishment involved in the OP for ICESCR (see the reports of the NGO Coalition for the OP for ICESCR and the Reports of the Working Groups Sessions for the OP for ICESCR, Office of the United Nations High Commission for Human Rights).

If the final OP for the ICESCR does not ensure that the most disadvantaged receive at the very least their core minimum obligations, the Committee should, in my view, resign en mass and so restore some credibility to the United Nations where neoliberalism is dominating both human rights and the sovereignty of States, even though this domination is likely to be tempered with an emphasis on democracy. The idea of having human rights principles is to keep to them irrespective of the dominant ideology. If human rights is not, at the very least, about those suffering the most misery then it is nothing but a fraudulent document used to further the interests of a global elite without the necessary will and understanding to address these major problems as evidenced by the poor progress of the Millennium Development Goals and the failure of the UN Decade of Human Rights Education (1995–2004).

Conclusion

The backlash against neoliberalism in the form of global demonstrations, global terrorism, and a global impasse to the expansion of liberal democracy, and so forth has led to the War on Terror intended, in my view, to subdue opposition to neoliberalism by redefining freedom fighters as terrorists or "friends of terrorists." Consequently, among the consolidators it is the more conservative forces which have gained considerable dominance over the left-wing liberals at the domestic level while the reverse is increasingly the case at the international level as evidenced by the OEWG discussions on the OP for ICESCR. This reflects the marginalization of social responsibility at the domestic level. This was also the case during the Cold War when economic, social, and cultural rights were recognized at the international level but not at the domestic level. Consequently, the State was able to compete with the Soviet empire in providing welfare without being ideologically committed. So domestically, welfare amounts to charity rather than a right. The left wing liberals are happy with structural violence but are concerned with the use of military force where it results in their own civil liberties being restricted to counter retaliation. So they are concerned at the increasing global conflict and often take the lead in the anti-globalization movements. But they see it as their role to uphold the status quo; their traditional freedoms are part of the dominant elite, so they remain consolidators not innovators. However, the use of force is an insufficient means of control. Its overuse can result in a loss of legitimacy. It is much safer to rule by consent than by military force. Edward Kannyo states:

> Whatever the philosophical justification for its existence, the state as an institution is, in the final analysis, based on the threat of the use of force to sustain itself and the prevailing socioeconomic order. However, while force is crucial no

stable state owes its survival solely to force. A far more important factor is the public acceptance of the legitimacy of the state and the socioeconomic and legal order expressed, promoted, and reinforced by its political, economic, social, and cultural institutions. Once this legitimacy is lost, tyranny, revolution, or anarchy must ensue (Kannyo, 1987: 386).

The change in emphasis from civil liberties to democracy seems to be an attempt to gain the consent of the global population. The curbing of civil liberties allows the state to subdue radical elements including some left-wing liberals who can disrupt elite unity. They played the major role in implementing neoliberal policies in the first place. In New Zealand it was the Labour government, strongly backed by the liberals, which first implemented neoliberal policies in 1984. In essence this left wing group, who aligned itself with structural violence and was part of the cause of the problem, reinvented itself as freedom fighters when its interests and civil liberties were threatened. While the War on Terror unites the global elites against those who would challenge their authority, economic, social, and cultural rights, or at least those rights chosen, is a means of uniting the global elite under a social agenda with the trade unions and the working class likely to gain greater prominence—a "cause celebre" to possibly replace the identity politics, women and race, which has dominated to date, that is, the "celebration of diversity" becomes the "celebration of unity" or patriotism. In human rights terms, far more gains would have been made if it was really the poor and oppressed women and racial groups that had been emphasized. However, human rights, as in the past, is likely to remain the preserve of the elite who now want to guard against the politicization of the people which is occurring due to the Iraq war and terrorism. In fact, not only does society, pivoting on civil and political rights, have a tendency to repeat the same mistakes but people, under neoliberalism, lose the capacity to think, they are "dumbed down" by the media and simply obey the prevailing orthodoxy, and, what is of considerable concern, avoid new truths "like the plague." Ted Honderich describes the situation that exists in Western democracies very well, in my view, when he states: "Self-deception is staying in a state of uncertainty about something, keeping a question open and unanswered. Better no answer than the one you may get. The way to do this is to keep away from places where you will get an answer, stay away from the evidence. We do this a lot. It is another part of the stupidity of our culture" (Honderich, 2002: 149). He adds: "Our societies as they are, if you will put up with some last plain speaking, are ignorant, stupid, selfish, managed and deceived for gain, self-deceived, and deadly" (Honderich, 2002: 147).

As the draft OP stands there is every indication that ESC rights, when introduced, will be more democratic, not simply focusing on the elite, as has been the case, but embracing a wider section of the population, for example, skilled workers. This group, by and large, are likely to gain greater respect and protection for their ESC rights but, as the draft OP stands, for those without rights most governments are very unlikely, in my view, to immediately fulfill their core minimum rights apart from offering the largely false hopes of future plans, and "moving expeditiously" toward benchmarks with indicators. In the West the likely future scenario then is a majority who could be somewhat better protected with respect to their rights but a minority underclass entombed in a social prison with fewer opportunities than before. If more "food" is delivered then it is likely to be at the expense of their "freedom." Whereas, from a holistic point of view, those that inflict these human rights crimes, often by omission and neglect, must take responsibility for their actions or inactions, and this severely limits their personal development, as they are trapped in their class-fearing isolation, and their ability to reach their full potential in their talents, that is, they are just as alienated as many of the poor in a "me," individualistic, Western world. I define alienation as a mind/heart imbalance which can be a consequence of a class system where people outside your class seem little more than distant objects as if they were members of some distant country. It is often not realized but the exclusion of the underclass causes violence to both the oppressed and the oppressor. While the former suffers a material poverty and a fear of economic insecurity the latter suffers a spiritual poverty with neoliberalism inducing considerable conformity, a lack of regard for truth, and a preoccupation with image. Both oppressors and oppressed often live in their own social prison fearing freedom, and, consequently neither can reach their maximum development personally or in their work. Although high status positions, wealth, consumer goods, and many choices help many to settle for a "comfortable mediocrity" but the oppressed, including those who wish to reach their full potential in life, particularly the poor, can have paltry choices, nearly always between bad and worse, and are often far from happy with this situation. The extreme obsession with consolidation destroys life's balance—between the "me" and the "we," between the "mind" and "heart," between the "spiritual and the material," between the "dreamer" and the "realist," between the "future" and "now," between "image" and "substance"—much can seem like illusion with, for example, the glossy brochures of the organization and State promising much but delivering little. A balance between material and spiritual well-being seems to be what is required. Is it surprising that Islamic Jihadists resist such an assault on spirituality by the materialistic West and instead seek their "heaven on earth"—a pan-Islamic Caliphate throughout the world. My own view based on my experience in a liberal democracy is that whereas direct immediate violence requires the use of violence in self-defense, structural violence is violence inflicted from a distance where the perpetrators are often unknown but it nearly always allows for some, however meager, choices with respect to how to defend oneself. I consider violence, as stated in the UDHR, should only be a last resort. Instead I consider using the truth as the best way of educating people rather than an enforced politicization by killing largely innocent people. Core minimum obligations and human rights can help redress life's balance and lead to a far more civilized future without discarding what is good in the present system.

In the bipolar world of the Cold War, socialism provided a challenge at the international level but also a bottom-up challenge in the domestic politics of the liberal democracies, for example, the New Zealand Labour Party used to have strong socialist links during this period. However, today there is no credible challenge to neoliberalism so the human rights agenda is determined almost completely from the top-down. To what extent the most disadvantaged get their human rights will be completely at the whim of the dominant elite because it is not promised in the OP for the ICESCR or in the other human rights instruments, rather, States are given a wide margin of discretion with respect to their implementation. In the New Zealand action plan core minimum obligations have been interpreted as requiring progressive achievement—so the most disadvantaged are likely to be offered largely false hopes. However, the differences between the covenants with respect to immediate and progressive implementation is now increasingly recognized as more of a political distinction than any intrinsic difference between the two sets of rights as is indicated by Henry Shue. He states: "It was the representatives of the United States, employing language about 'achieving progressively' the economic rights while saying nothing about achieving civil and political rights progressively, who led the efforts to split even the basic rights in the Universal Declaration into separately ratifiable International Covenants" (Shue, 1980: 158–159). He adds: "Instantaneous implementation has never been thought possible for the provision of either the International Covenant on Civil and Political Rights or the International Covenant on Economic, Social and Cultural Rights. The requirements of both covenants are being achieved at best only progressively, of course, and are not now fully satisfied in any country" (Shue, 1980: 158).

From Christmas Eve to New Year's Day 2004, members of our Council and Psychiatric Survivors Inc. protested against homelessness by sleeping overnight in a tent in a park in Cox's Bay Reserve, Grey Lynn, Auckland. At the time we stated: "It is a cause for real concern that the information kit of the New Zealand Plan of Action for Human Rights presently being conducted by the Human Rights Commission does not mention 'core' economic, social, and cultural rights obligations. For example, the provision of basic shelter is a 'core' obligation of housing, that is, it is the minimal requirement. The plan of action, which is due to be implemented in 2005, involves very important constitutional issues which are being buried by the media. It takes extreme action like ours to bring it to light. On Christmas eve we appeared on Television One News and will shortly be appearing in a half-hour interview with Triangle TV" (Ravlich, 2004).

As a result of our protest against homelessness, the Project Manager of the New Zealand Plan of Action for Human Rights, stated on February 29, 2004, about four weeks after our protest action, that the status report on the action plan due out in May 2004 "will include consideration of 'core obligations' in relation to economic and social rights, and in particular, the right to housing." Core minimum obligations were eventually included in the action plan but not as we would have liked, that is, it involved progressive rather than immediate implementation. However, anecdotal evidence suggests that Housing New Zealand made considerable improvements in the provision of housing New Zealand homes.

Also recently, Winston Peters, Minister of Foreign Affairs, in a speech in Sweden, announced New Zealand's candidacy for the UN Human Rights Council 2009–2012 and stressed the importance of countries fulfilling their core human rights obligations. Peters stated: "In recent years, developing countries have increasingly argued that Western states place too much emphasis on civil and political rights, and too little on economic, social and cultural rights, and the important developmental concerns these embody." He added: "We don't believe that any country should be excused from the full implementation of its core human rights obligations—although we understand the challenges faced by developing countries" (Peters,2007).

Members of the dominant elite can be influenced and may be sympathetic to your cause so it is always important to "keep an open door" rather than adopt a "them versus us" approach even though this has been usually the tactic of the dominant elite concerned with "tough love." The elite attracts authoritarian personalities sometimes called "control freaks." State oppression, even if it costs money in the short term, ensures people are kept too insecure to challenge their authority—a tactic also used by employers to undermine the trade unions even though a "happy" employee would make more money. Far more effective than educating the elite, although extremely difficult, is the education of the general public. However, it is worth remembering that while you are likely to elicit little response, in my experience, this is because speaking about human rights requires much study. However, a number are listening and understanding.

To what extent our council and Psychiatric Survivors Inc. played a part in the New Zealand government now promoting core minimum obligations will probably never be known but the Human Rights Development Report 2000 shows such human rights NGOs' actions as our own are taking place around the world. It describes "the strategic use of civil and political rights and legal instruments in empowering poor people." The report explains: "Civil action groups in all regions of the world are using civil and political rights—of participation, association, free speech and information—to enlarge the political space and press for economic and social rights." The report adds: "The strength of such action is growing locally and nationally, often with global support networks." The report gives a number of examples of such action such as "in India a group defending the interests of tribal peoples and forest workers is using the right to information to demand better budget allocations" and "in Thailand an NGO is using the right of assembly to draw attention to the human costs of dams, land and forest development, slum clearance and private investments" and also "in Russia a regional women's group is demanding action on the devastating health consequences of 50 years of nuclear mismanagement" (Human Development Report, 2000, chapter 4).

Since 1984 New Zealand has become as a country more reflective of a tribal society with social groups aligning themselves hierarchically in a "pecking order," united by a human rights agenda which is primarily in the interests of the dominant elite. In such a regimented, hostile situation groups becomes consumed with their own interests and do not get the opportunity to display a duty to the wider society or act altruistically for a better society in the future. Some of the groups involved in New Zealand are the elite (liberal, mainly the Labour Party and Green Parties, and conservative, mainly the National and Act Parties), the trade unions, Maori groups with their own political party, Pacific Island groups, other racial groups, women's groups, the churches, Grey Power, the gays, the family, etc. These groups can only consolidate their positions and perpetuate the status quo. In such a society the promotion of civil rights, designed particularly for the dominant elite, creates a "me" society in the same way as in a democracy people can just vote for themselves rather than the greater good. The "me" society keeps the more independent individuals at the bottom of the social structure isolated and divided. Erich Fromm states: "In any society the spirit of the whole culture is determined by the spirit of those groups that are the most powerful in that society" (Fromm, 1984: 97). In addition, he states:

". . . those groups have the power to control the education system, schools, church, press, theatre, and thereby to imbue the whole population with their own ideas; furthermore, these powerful groups carry so much prestige that the lower classes are more ready to accept and imitate their values and to identify themselves psychologically" (Fromm, 1984: 97).

Even where people who entered such groups did have hopes of benefiting New Zealand as a whole the realities of the group interests soon took hold. Mills observed the growth of these groups and employees in society and the decline of the independent individual. Mills states: "In 1800 about four fifths of the population of the United States were 'private enterprisers.' By 1950 only one fifth could be described this way, the bulk of the population having become employees (Mills, 1951). In addition, from my observation, there are extremely few truly independent human rights NGOs in society. Social control, in my view, is all pervasive. To avoid the complete elimination of the independent spirit a core minimum obligation with respect to the right to development needs to be ensured. Although a difficulty exists where the UDHR is divided into two covenants the right to development derives from both sets of rights. However, there is no reason why the UN Committee on Economic, Social and Cultural Rights and the Human Rights Council could not work together to arrive at such core minimum obligations with respect to the right to development.

The change in emphasis from civil rights to democracy has the potential to see a change in emphasis from particularism (group self-interest) to the more independent individual and perhaps small business enterprise and encouragement for the productive sector but, in my view, the inventiveness of the nation—when we proudly proclaimed to be able to use a "No. 8 Fencing Wire" for just about anything—has to a large extent been lost such were the tidal waves of hatred for anything different that came from the new "neoliberal" breed in 1984. So any attempt to rebuild the productive sector could take a very long time. Given the emphasis on globalization and the corporations it seems more likely that the emphasis on democracy will only give some greater power to the trade unions.

Also, it may not be surprising if there is some backlash to what was started by the liberals in 1984, and we are seeing more populist, authoritarian approaches, for example, with respect to immigration, crime, different political opinions, that is, those who are not moderates, and more conservative stances on women and race. But the whole trend of society since 1984 toward particularism and consolidation has, in my view, resulted in a profoundly conformist society, an unthinking people, with society representing more of a social army intent on crushing unacceptable truths.

An example of the democratic emphasis likely to be taken by governments toward the most disadvantaged is New Zealand's In Work Payment (April, 2006) as part of the government's Working for Families package which provides assistance to mid- to low-income working-class families; however, the children in benefit families were excluded. Dr. Susan St. John of the Child Poverty Action Group stated: "Child poverty can only deepen for those families left out. Children's needs do not change because their parents do not work. The all-or-nothing In Work Payment will create double jeopardy. When incomes fall as a result of job losses or reduced work hours, the child-based In Work Payment will also disappear." She adds: "Families with children make up the majority of food bank clients, and the need for food assistance continues to grow. Hungry children are not inevitable, they are a symptom of our continued lack of support for low-income families" (St. John, 2006).

Also an example of how human rights can be manipulated from the top-down is the exclusion of the right to fair wages in the New Zealand Plan of Action for Human Rights. The right to fair wages (Article 7(a)(i), ICESCR) is one right that is meant to be "ensured," that is, applied immediately. This exclusion is very convenient at a time when a low wage economy has been created in New Zealand. It is possible to have very low unemployment but still many living in poverty due to the low wages.

On November 26, 2007, the Paediatric Society of New Zealand released "a damning report into the health of New Zealand children" (*New Zealand Herald*, November 27, 2007, A3). For example, the report states that New Zealand's hospital admission rates for childhood skin infections have increased to double those in Australia and the United States—serious skin infections for children under fourteen have more than trebled, admission rates were much higher for those living in the most deprived New Zealand households, vaccine-preventable diseases such as whooping cough continue to occur at rates higher than other developed countries, and hospital admissions for under twenty-five-year-olds have almost doubled since 1990. Dr. Nikki Turner, speaking on behalf of the child health coalition Kia Mataara Well Health, said that the overwhelming message from the reports was that the strongest risk factor for getting sick was being poor. And yet in the article, which is nearly always the case, there was no mention that poverty is a human rights issue. Independent human rights NGOs have an important role in getting this message across to the general public. International and domestic problems can be translated in human rights terms to inform the people. An extensive survey conducted by the Disability Rights Commission, in July 2007 in Britain, demonstrates just how ignorant of human rights the populations in liberal democracies are. The survey showed that "seventy per cent of the British population cannot name any of their human rights." Bert Massie, chairperson of the DRC stated: "The poll makes it clear that we are in a state of ignorance about our human rights, which is detrimental to the people who need it most . . . ." (Massey, 2006).

It is also important to be aware that left wing liberal organizations will sometimes use the plight of the poor to further their own interpretation of human rights (not that of the UDHR) and, therefore, largely their own interests.

They use the system to gain benefits for people, but do not deal with the underlying causes of social problems. Consequently, they perpetuate the status quo. For instance, in 2006 in Los Angeles, the U.S. 9th Circuit Court of Appeals decided in favor of six homeless people who were arrested for violating a municipal ordinance which states that "no person shall sit, lie or sleep in or upon any street, sidewalk or public way." It was considered that this violates the constitutional prohibition against cruel and unusual punishment. The case was filed by the American Civil Liberties Union (Southern California) and the National Lawyers Guild (Victory in Homeless Rights Case, ACLU, April 14, 2006). But there was no concern regarding their homelessness. So now the homeless have the freedom to sleep on the very dangerous streets of Los Angeles irrespective of the weather conditions.

Also, there were recently a number of trade union strikes in Auckland, New Zealand, involving youth rates at McDonalds, Kentucky Fried Chicken, Burger King, Wendy's, Starbucks, and so forth as part of the "SupersizeMy Pay.com" campaign by the Unite Union. But the union only sought higher wages. They did not fight for the ESC rights in the action plan, the right to a reasonable standard of living, or to have the right to fair wages included in the action plan but confined itself to what the system permitted, that is, the right to nondiscrimination on the ground of age (civil rights) and increasing the minimum wage. The National Secretary of the Unite Union stated that the union's focus now would be on the government to make sure it moved a minimum rate and to get rid of youth rates. "Next year we will work through all employers who have young people to try to lift their wages up" (Thompson, 2006). The young and idealistic need to be made aware of such organizations and realize that although they can provide some short-term benefits, essentially they largely only prop up the system and do not prevent the same problems from being repeated. For example, the small monetary gains made by the trade union protest could be soon offset by oil price increases leading to further strike action and much self-sacrifice on the part of workers. However, having the right to fair wages or an adequate standard of living in law will mean that lower salaries could be monitored by focus groups "ensuring a decent living for themselves and their families" (Article 7(ii), ICESCR). This could be overseen by a Lower Salaries Commission paralleling the existing Higher Salaries Commission. Ultimately, with ESC rights included in the New Zealand Bill of Rights Act 1990, any legislation that could result in human rights infringements could be corrected at that stage in the same way that present legislation is tested for consistency with civil rights. This would mean that there would be less need for individuals to make sometimes enormous personal sacrifices to get social justice. Another group which gives the impression of being radical and for the oppressed are those left-wing liberals who sometimes portray themselves as socialist. They are anti-corporation, anti-globalization, anti-war, and pro-trade unions. They are usually acceptable to the establishment because they promote high standards of civil liberties to ideologically support capitalism. However, their claims to support the most disadvantaged must be regarded as very dubious because, at the domestic level, they usually do not promote economic, social, and cultural rights and core minimum obligations.

One approach our Council used to get the human rights message across was the use of the debate on human rights in the broader sense. Representatives from various parties, the trade unions and the Human Rights Commission, were invited to debate economic, social, and cultural rights on Triangle Television, which bordered on the mainstream at the time and is now considered mainstream. It proved very successful. Also early in 2007 Iranian president Mahmoud Ahmadinejad said that the government is ready to host a conference on "human rights" between Islamic and European thinkers in the presence of the Western media (IranMania, January 2, 2007). To my knowledge the West did not take up the offer but this would seem to be the best way of educating people in human rights. In my experience, having contacted a number of the world's top human rights intellectuals, they would be more than willing to take part in such debates (a possible television station could be Al Jazeera).

The United States, by taking an extremist view of human rights, should not be surprised when there is an extremist response. However, the United States itself, could adopt the plan set out in this book by considering minimum core obligations as necessary to being able to access the civil and political rights in the Constitution. There is the well-known case of *Airey* v. *Ireland* which has been frequently cited as a precedent for demonstrating there are economic and social rights dimensions within civil and political rights and that States may have positive obligations (duties to fulfill) with respect to civil and political rights. In addition, the case has formed an important precedent for arguing that the right to legal aid is an integral part of human rights (ESCR-net, *Airey* v. *Ireland*, 32 Eur Ct HR Ser A (1979): [1979] 2 E.H.R.R. 305). In addition, the UN Human Rights Committee (which deals with civil and political rights) General Comment No. 6 (1982), while interpreting the right to life of the International Covenant on Civil and Political Rights, clearly stated that the Article imposes a duty on State Parties to reduce infant mortality and to increase life expectancy, especially through adopting measures to eliminate malnutrition and epidemics. This, therefore, means that the right to life (civil and political rights) goes hand in hand with the right to food (economic, social, and cultural rights) (Nakayi, 2007). The U.S. government need make no mention of ESC rights but merely recognize what is obvious, that you need at least core minimum obligations to be able to access your human rights. This would mean eliminating homelessness, the use of food banks, begging on the streets, those urgently requiring medical treatment, and so forth. When you are at that level the chance you have of improving your lifestyle is virtually nil and the same applies to your human rights.

America seems to have largely opposed the right to development at the UN because of the ESC rights component but they may be prepared to accept the concept of core minimum obligations with respect to the right to development of which a meritocracy would certainly be a part and something the United States has probably provided in the past better than any other country. In other words, in my view, paradoxically perhaps, the United States could actually take a world lead in social justice. However, given the present emphasis on democracy, it seems that the United States considers they only need to appeal to the majority to pursue neoliberalism and are prepared to endure any rise in trade union activity that might result from such an emphasis as well as any further terrorism—the result of such organizations as Al Qaeda recruiting among increasingly disaffected unemployed youth. However, it is possible. Prior to its "about face" after the Second World War, America played a major role in having ESC rights included in the UDHR and the welfare state in the United States, however inadequate, has become embedded. Steiner and Alston state: "The welfare system and other rights granted by legislation (for example, laws against racial discrimination) are so deeply embedded as to have near-constitutional sturdiness. . . . And Americans have begun to think and speak of social security and other benefits as matters of entitlement and right" (Steiner and Alston, 1996: 272). It is also possible for the above approach to be adopted by New Zealand and many other countries. New Zealand, in particular, is committed to the role of peacemaker. The New Zealand Nuclear Free Zone, Disarmament, and Arms Control Act is a New Zealand law passed by the Labour government in 1987 "to establish in New Zealand a Nuclear Free Zone, to promote and encourage an active and effective contribution by New Zealand to the essential process of disarmament and international arms control." As a consequence the United States suspended its ANZUS (defense alliance) obligations to New Zealand.

There is a strong possibility that New Zealand, along with Australia, could be involved in an East Asian regional bloc, comparable to the European Union and the Americas grouping. A regional bloc was a major area of discussion at the East Asian Summit, which concluded in Kuala Lumpur, Malaysia, on December 14, 2006. It was attended by Prime Minister Helen Clark, Minister of Foreign Affairs, Winston Peters, and leaders from the ten Association of Southeast Asia Nation (ASEAN) countries, ASEAN+3 (China, Japan, and the Republic of Korea) and Australia, New Zealand, and

India. Prime Minister Helen Clark stated: "If there's going to be three big regions, we've got to be linked somewhere. We just can't afford to be excluded from developments in the region" (Clark, 2005). This East Asian regional grouping represents about half the world's population and a fifth of global trade. While New Zealand has the support of other liberal democracies such as Japan (a close ally of the United States and taking a leadership role), South Korea, India, and Australia, other countries, such as Vietnam, Malaysia, and Singapore, may well support the emerging power, China, a communist country. Historically, these latter countries have, at times, promoted Asian values with its emphasis on economic, social, and cultural rights, that is, "food over freedom" (Anthony Ravlich, New Zealand could lead in Human Rights in the proposed East Asia Regional Bloc). But New Zealand, given its "peacemaker role," would not want to become embroiled in any ideological controversy—we have no military or economic power, largely, we only have the force of our truth. Consequently, New Zealand, takes the present liberal stance internationally, and promotes the equal status of both sets of rights at the international level and, more recently, promoting core minimum obligations. The latter allows for flexibility with respect to human rights and removes much of the politics from the equation. To a certain extent you can agree with both sides—sometimes it is necessary to curb civil rights because of terrorism or curb economic, social, and cultural rights to focus on growth, however core minimum obligations and their immediate implementation constitute a rigid bottom line, no compromise. In other words there is, at least, a need for "some food and some freedom." However, if you fail to live up to your beliefs at the domestic level you are open to the charge of hypocrisy and deception and, consequently, not taken seriously. It is in New Zealand's interests to ensure core minimum obligations on the domestic front and address the problem of the underclass, and so forth.

Some countries may use their broad "margin of appreciation" to address these serious violations. However, because there is no ideological commitment to do so, such as the inclusion of core minimum obligations in the draft OP for ICESCR, these countries can withdraw benefits, and so forth, at a future date. This is what happened with the collapse of the Soviet empire, the West was able to cut benefits without being prevented from doing so by human rights law. Even when a liberal democracy provides an economically egalitarian society as during the Cold War, civil rights will always be prioritized and, consequently, the power will always be in the hands of the dominant elite. And this is very likely to be the case when States ratify the OP for ICESCR—as with other human rights instruments the focus of education will very likely largely be at the elite level, and there is very little likelihood of their inclusion in the New Zealand Bill of Rights Act 1990.

It was Henry Shue in his book *Basic Rights* who considered that the right to security and subsistence were essential to the enjoyment of the other rights. He called this "the morality of the depths" as "they specify the line beneath which no one is to allowed to sink." He states: "Deficiencies in the means of subsistence can be just as fatal, incapacitating, or painful as violations of physical security." He adds: "Basic rights are everyone's reasonable demands upon the rest of humanity" (Shue, 1980: 18–24). The United Nations Committee on Economic, Social and Cultural Rights expanded on this in its General Comment No. 3 in 1990. According to this view all human rights were seen as being of equal status but all have a core content (similar to Shue's basic rights), and this constitutes the core minimum obligation of the State. However, these core minimum obligations, such as the right to shelter or primary health are largely bestowed. They do not empower people to seek them themselves. Consequently, the empowering right of human rights education should also be regarded as a core minimum obligation so the democratic process can be used to achieve ESC rights. In addition, core minimum obligations with respect to the right to development, another empowering right, should be devised. Microcredit has proven very successful in helping the poor achieve their dreams. Further, it envisages such core minimum obligations should also be applied to civil and political rights (the UN Human Rights Committee has not yet done so) with the strict requirement that both sets of rights have equal status at the level of core minimum obligations, and these require immediate implementation. Higher levels of such rights, while the equal status principle still applies, would only require progressive realization. Given the present reality it is likely to take a very long time before ESC rights gains equal status with CP rights at the higher human rights levels. But such an approach would considerably help to eliminate the politicization of human rights whereby one set of rights can be prioritized over another, and where higher, less serious, levels of human rights can be prioritized over the more serious violations, the core minimum obligations. It is also considered that any retrogressive measures should require a high democratic standard. The present global human rights debate needs to be considerably broadened—beyond civil and political rights, even beyond economic, social, and cultural rights and the right to development. It is necessary to discuss the immediate implementation of core minimum obligations, particularly the empowerment rights. Human rights need to come from the "bottom-up" rather than the "top-down" simply because a liberal oligarchy only concerned with the consolidation of its power may not reflect the democratic will of the people if all options are made available to them. What human rights are included in any constitution should be for the people to decide using the democratic process. It is they who may have to die for it and it is their children who will have to live with it. The necessary education could take a long time given the present state of human rights ignorance but most people can read and understand the UDHR and have a sense of what is right and wrong. Human rights NGOs could do much to educate people in social problems such as crime, gambling, unemployment, homelessness, terrorism, and discuss the underlying causes from a human rights point of view.

Our Council formed the Human Rights Party which promotes the Human Rights Commission's New Zealand Plan of Action for Human Rights. This contains both sets of rights, with the aim to have economic, social, and cultural rights and core minimum obligations also included in human rights law. We maintain a very close relationship with Psychiatric Survivors Inc., so are closely in touch with what is happening to the most disadvantaged. In addition our Council provides support for a number of talented, creative, holistic people, who otherwise would gain little acceptance in this society. Our members also come from different classes in society — middle class, lower-middle class, and the underclass. It is egalitarian, rather than the hierarchical nature of society and many NGOs. This egalitarianism reflects a growing bohemian, artistic sector in society. Independently funded human rights NGOs could not only ensure people were educated in human rights but could also be involved in providing financial assistance to ensure the right to development under the umbrella of both sets of rights. This is important for those who fall outside the "neoliberal square" who the State will not fund. It is hoped that a similar approach to ours will be adopted in New Zealand and other parts of the world. While it is necessary to challenge the neoliberals to publicly debate their policies, something they are very reluctant to do, the focus should, in our view, be on creating the world we want through the democratic process. Although it is necessary to point out the human rights hypocrisy and deception of the dominant elite thereby undermining their legitimacy, it is more important to be positive and give people some hope of a better future. It is important not to adopt the same 'them versus us' approach of the dominant elite, a number of whom may be just waiting for a credible alternative plan of action to support.

The inclusion of economic, social, and cultural rights, and core minimum obligations, particularly relevant to the economically oppressed and exploited, is likely to give more people meaning in life, and they may take a greater interest in human rights in general as well as providing them with a nonviolent way of achieving social justice. With the addition of meaning in one's life, the consumer lifestyle is less important, and this may also have beneficial effects in addressing global warming. People might become more altruistic and prepared to do voluntary work, which would considerably lower the costs in addressing the core minimum obligations. In addition, such a belief system helps to ensure an independence of mind, less vulnerable to the manipulation of the national and international systems, and also enables a person to think outside the "neoliberal square," be more inventive, and have the necessary perseverance to pursue his or her dream and keep struggling for a world which is for everyone not just global elites. I consider that such a cause is most suited to young, idealistic, "masterless" men, especially given that the struggle can be a long, hard one requiring a strong focus. In my experience, many women are reluctant to mix with the underclass without sufficient security and as this cause involves forging a new path the social structures are not yet in place. Also, as many men seem to lack a purpose, given they are no longer the sole 'bread winner,' they might be best suited to such a cause. This could help fulfill this need, and they can take the leading role in socially responsible businesses or community organizations, perhaps focusing on a particular human right, for example, the right to health, housing, and so forth although, because of the hostility that exists in neoliberal societies, I would very seriously advise having the necessary support structures in place. Although our Council has managed to survive without funding there are great personal costs, which, quite frankly, I would not expect of anyone. Also, its not size, that is, organization or State, rather it is the truth content of the ideas that really count. These ideas could just as well apply to an individual, organization, country, or the world. This is how neoliberalism can reach into "every nook and cranny of society" and how control seems so overwhelming. It is a matter of changing attitudes. It is also a belief system which may be attractive to many intellectuals concerned with the most disadvantaged, in particular.

Just as in history slavery was permitted by the human rights agenda of the day, extreme poverty and powerlessness is also accommodated by the human rights agenda, as defined by domestic and global elites, today. The abolition of these extreme violations may be just as difficult as it was to abolish slavery. The biggest losers in society are the underclass, which is almost completely dominated by individuals who are not only materially poor and spiritually poor, and subjected to severe discrimination. In my view, they have extremely little hope without intervention. It is individuals from this group who are given to violent outbursts, and this is likely to increase. Even with the best will in the world it could take a long time for them to rehabilitate, but a good start would be to be proactive and give them something to do with decent remuneration which, in my view, will slowly build up their self-esteem to a point where they can help themselves, which gives a person much more dignity. Since I began promoting human rights in 1991, I have never seen any human rights statistical research done on the underclass. The World Bank's Voices of the Poor study, discussed earlier in the book, was not conducted from a human rights perspective. The lack of such research is a glaring omission and another example of keeping people ignorant of human rights and that "freedom and democracy" on applies to those higher on the social structure. In my view, such research would show that the underclass is treated as sub-human, and many will say they have no human rights.

The global elites are largely consumed with consolidating their power, therefore change must come from the "bottom-up," from socially responsible people everywhere, even from amongst the global elites themselves, led by the independent human rights NGOs. The 'sky rocketing food prices' occurring in many countries of the world in recent times, leading to food riots across the African continent, gives added urgency to implementing core minimum obligations in order to curb the excesses of the market (Karon, 2008).

I hope this book has shown people who are concerned about the direction their country and world is taking that there is something that can be done about it. If you agree with the above vision of the future you could become actively involved with NGOs, which promote it, be a supporter, or simply hang up a copy of the UDHR at work or at home or give a copy to a friend. Also some personal development—self-education, reading national and world affairs, and/or furthering holistic development—is within the ability of most people.

A belief system embracing human rights, which ensures the core minimum obligations will, in my view, provide people with the best chance of freedom from their social prisons.

Appendices

Appendix I

Universal Declaration of Human Rights

Preamble

Whereas recognition of the inherent dignity and of the equal and inalienable rights of all members of the human family is the foundation of freedom, justice and peace in the world,

Whereas disregard and contempt for human rights have resulted in barbarous acts which have outraged the conscience of mankind, and the advent of a world in which human beings shall enjoy freedom of speech and belief and freedom from fear and want has been proclaimed as the highest aspiration of the common people,

Whereas it is essential, if man is not to be compelled to have recourse, as a last resort, to rebellion against tyranny and oppression, that human rights should be protected by the rule of law,

Whereas it is essential to promote the development of friendly relations between nations,

Whereas the peoples of the United Nations have in the Charter reaffirmed their faith in fundamental human rights, in the dignity and worth of the human person and in the equal rights of men and women and have determined to promote social progress and better standards of life in larger freedom,

Whereas Member States have pledged themselves to achieve, in cooperation with the United Nations, the promotion of universal respect for and observance of human rights and fundamental freedoms,

Whereas a common understanding of these rights and freedoms is of the greatest importance for the full realization of this pledge,

Now, therefore,

The General Assembly,

Proclaims this Universal Declaration of Human Rights as a common standard of achievement for all peoples and all nations, to the end that every individual and every organ of society, keeping this Declaration constantly in mind, shall strive by teaching and education to promote respect for these rights and freedoms and by progressive measures, national and international, to secure their universal and effective recognition and observance, both among the peoples of Member States themselves and among the peoples of territories under their jurisdiction.

Article 1

All human beings are born free and equal in dignity and rights. They are endowed with reason and conscience and should act towards one another in a spirit of brotherhood.

Article 2

Everyone is entitled to all the rights and freedoms set forth in this Declaration, without distinction of any kind, such as race, colour, sex, language, religion, political or other opinion, national or social origin, property, birth or other status.

Furthermore, no distinction shall be made on the basis of the political, jurisdictional or international status of the country or territory to which a person belongs, whether it be independent, trust, non-self-governing or under any other limitation of sovereignty.

Article 3

Everyone has the right to life, liberty and security of person.

Article 4

No one shall be held in slavery or servitude; slavery and the slave trade shall be prohibited in all their forms.

Article 5

No one shall be subjected to torture or to cruel, inhuman or degrading treatment or punishment.

Article 6

Everyone has the right to recognition everywhere as a person before the law.

Article 7

All are equal before the law and are entitled without any discrimination to equal protection of the law. All are entitled to equal protection against any discrimination in violation of this Declaration and against any incitement to such discrimination.

Article 8

Everyone has the right to an effective remedy by the competent national tribunals for acts violating the fundamental rights granted him by the constitution or by law.

Article 9

No one shall be subjected to arbitrary arrest, detention or exile.

Article 10

Everyone is entitled in full equality to a fair and public hearing by an independent and impartial tribunal, in the determination of his rights and obligations and of any criminal charge against him.

Article 11

1. Everyone charged with a penal offence has the right to be presumed innocent until proved guilty according to law in a public trial at which he has had all the guarantees necessary for his defence.

2. No one shall be held guilty of any penal offence on account of any act or omission which did not constitute a penal offence, under national or international law, at the time when it was committed. Nor shall a heavier penalty be imposed than the one that was applicable at the time the penal offence was committed.

Article 12

No one shall be subjected to arbitrary interference with his privacy, family, home or correspondence, nor to attacks upon his honour and reputation. Everyone has the right to the protection of the law against such interference or attacks.

Article 13

1. Everyone has the right to freedom of movement and residence within the borders of each State.

2. Everyone has the right to leave any country, including his own, and to return to his country.

Article 14

1. Everyone has the right to seek and to enjoy in other countries asylum from persecution.

2. This right may not be invoked in the case of prosecutions genuinely arising from non-political crimes or from acts contrary to the purposes and principles of the United Nations.

Article 15

1. Everyone has the right to a nationality.

2. No one shall be arbitrarily deprived of his nationality nor denied the right to change his nationality.

Article 16

1. Men and women of full age, without any limitation due to race, nationality or religion, have the right to marry and to found a family. They are entitled to equal rights as to marriage, during marriage and at its dissolution.

2. Marriage shall be entered into only with the free and full consent of the intending spouses.

3. The family is the natural and fundamental group unit of society and is entitled to protection by society and the State.

Article 17

1. Everyone has the right to own property alone as well as in association with others.

2. No one shall be arbitrarily deprived of his property.

Article 18

Everyone has the right to freedom of thought, conscience and religion; this right includes freedom to change his religion or belief, and freedom, either alone or in community with others and in public or private, to manifest his religion or belief in teaching, practice, worship and observance.

Article 19

Everyone has the right to freedom of opinion and expression; this right includes freedom to hold opinions without interference and to seek, receive and impart information and ideas through any media and regardless of frontiers.

Article 20

1. Everyone has the right to freedom of peaceful assembly and association.

2. No one may be compelled to belong to an association.

Article 21

1. Everyone has the right to take part in the government of his country, directly or through freely chosen representatives.

2. Everyone has the right to equal access to public service in his country.

3. The will of the people shall be the basis of the authority of government; this will shall be expressed in periodic and genuine elections which shall be

by universal and equal suffrage and shall be held by secret vote or by equivalent free voting procedures.

Article 22

Everyone, as a member of society, has the right to social security and is entitled to realization, through national effort and international co-operation and in accordance with the organization and resources of each State, of the economic, social and cultural rights indispensable for his dignity and the free development of his personality.

Article 23

1. Everyone has the right to work, to free choice of employment, to just and favourable conditions of work and to protection against unemployment.

2. Everyone, without any discrimination, has the right to equal pay for equal work.

3. Everyone who works has the right to just and favourable remuneration ensuring for himself and his family an existence worthy of human dignity, and supplemented, if necessary, by other means of social protection.

4. Everyone has the right to form and to join trade unions for the protection of his interests.

Article 24

Everyone has the right to rest and leisure, including reasonable limitation of working hours and periodic holidays with pay.

Article 25

1. Everyone has the right to a standard of living adequate for the health and well-being of himself and of his family, including food, clothing, housing and medical care and necessary social services, and the right to security in the event of unemployment, sickness, disability, widowhood, old age or other lack of livelihood in circumstances beyond his control.

2. Motherhood and childhood are entitled to special care and assistance. All children, whether born in or out of wedlock, shall enjoy the same social protection.

Article 26

1. Everyone has the right to education. Education shall be free, at least in the elementary and fundamental stages. Elementary education shall be compulsory. Technical and professional education shall be made generally available and higher education shall be equally accessible to all on the basis of merit.

2. Education shall be directed to the full development of the human personality and to the strengthening of respect for human rights and fundamental freedoms. It shall promote understanding, tolerance and friendship among all nations, racial or religious groups, and shall further the activities of the United Nations for the maintenance of peace.

3. Parents have a prior right to choose the kind of education that shall be given to their children.

Article 27

1. Everyone has the right freely to participate in the cultural life of the community, to enjoy the arts and to share in scientific advancement and its benefits.

2. Everyone has the right to the protection of the moral and material interests resulting from any scientific, literary or artistic production of which he is the author.

Article 28

Everyone is entitled to a social and international order in which the rights and freedoms set forth in this Declaration can be fully realized.

Article 29

1. Everyone has duties to the community in which alone the free and full development of his personality is possible.

2. In the exercise of his rights and freedoms, everyone shall be subject only to such limitations as are determined by law solely for the purpose of securing due recognition and respect for the rights and freedoms of others and of meeting the just requirements of morality, public order and the general welfare in a democratic society.

3. These rights and freedoms may in no case be exercised contrary to the purposes and principles of the United Nations.

Article 30

Nothing in this Declaration may be interpreted as implying for any State, group or person any right to engage in any activity or to perform any act aimed at the destruction of any of the rights and freedoms set forth herein.

Appendix II

International Covenant on Civil and Political Rights

Adopted and opened for signature, ratification and accession by General Assembly resolution 2200A (XXI) of 16 December 1966 entry into force 23 March 1976, in accordance with Article 49

Preamble

The States Parties to the present Covenant,

Considering that, in accordance with the principles proclaimed in the Charter of the United Nations, recognition of the inherent dignity and of the equal and inalienable rights of all members of the human family is the foundation of freedom, justice and peace in the world,

Recognizing that these rights derive from the inherent dignity of the human person,

Recognizing that, in accordance with the Universal Declaration of Human Rights, the ideal of free human beings enjoying civil and political freedom and freedom from fear and want can only be achieved if conditions are created whereby everyone may enjoy his civil and political rights, as well as his economic, social and cultural rights,

Considering the obligation of States under the Charter of the United Nations to promote universal respect for, and observance of, human rights and freedoms,

Realizing that the individual, having duties to other individuals and to the community to which he belongs, is under a responsibility to strive for the promotion and observance of the rights recognized in the present Covenant,

Agree upon the following articles:

PART I

Article 1

1. All peoples have the right of self-determination. By virtue of that right they freely determine their political status and freely pursue their economic, social and cultural development.

2. All peoples may, for their own ends, freely dispose of their natural wealth and resources without prejudice to any obligations arising out of international economic co-operation, based upon the principle of mutual benefit, and international law. In no case may a people be deprived of its own means of subsistence.

3. The States Parties to the present Covenant, including those having responsibility for the administration of Non-Self-Governing and Trust Territories, shall promote the realization of the right of self-determination, and shall respect that right, in conformity with the provisions of the Charter of the United Nations.

PART II

Article 2

1. Each State Party to the present Covenant undertakes to respect and to ensure to all individuals within its territory and subject to its jurisdiction the rights recognized in the present Covenant, without distinction of any kind, such as race, colour, sex, language, religion, political or other opinion, national or social origin, property, birth or other status.

2. Where not already provided for by existing legislative or other measures, each State Party to the present Covenant undertakes to take the necessary steps, in accordance with its constitutional processes and with the provisions of the present Covenant, to adopt such laws or other measures as may be necessary to give effect to the rights recognized in the present Covenant.

3. Each State Party to the present Covenant undertakes:

(a) To ensure that any person whose rights or freedoms as herein recognized are violated shall have an effective remedy, notwithstanding that the violation has been committed by persons acting in an official capacity;

(b) To ensure that any person claiming such a remedy shall have his right thereto determined by competent judicial, administrative or legislative authorities, or by any other competent authority provided for by the legal system of the State, and to develop the possibilities of judicial remedy;

(c) To ensure that the competent authorities shall enforce such remedies when granted.

Article 3

The States Parties to the present Covenant undertake to ensure the equal right of men and women to the enjoyment of all civil and political rights set forth in the present Covenant.

Article 4

1. In time of public emergency which threatens the life of the nation and the existence of which is officially proclaimed, the States Parties to the present Covenant may take measures derogating from their obligations under the present Covenant to the extent strictly required by the exigencies of the situation, provided that such measures are not inconsistent with their other obligations under international law and do not involve discrimination solely on the ground of race, colour, sex, language, religion or social origin.

2. No derogation from articles 6, 7, 8 (paragraphs I and 2), 11, 15, 16 and 18 may be made under this provision.

3. Any State Party to the present Covenant availing itself of the right of derogation shall immediately inform the other States Parties to the present Covenant, through the intermediary of the Secretary-General of the United Nations, of the provisions from which it has derogated and of the reasons by which it was actuated. A further communication shall be made, through the same intermediary, on the date on which it terminates such derogation.

Article 5

1. Nothing in the present Covenant may be interpreted as implying for any State, group or person any right to engage in any activity or perform any act aimed at the destruction of any of the rights and freedoms recognized herein or at their limitation to a greater extent than is provided for in the present Covenant.

2. There shall be no restriction upon or derogation from any of the fundamental human rights recognized or existing in any State Party to the present Covenant pursuant to law, conventions, regulations or custom on the pretext that the present Covenant does not recognize such rights or that it recognizes them to a lesser extent.

PART III

Article 6

1. Every human being has the inherent right to life. This right shall be protected by law. No one shall be arbitrarily deprived of his life.

2. In countries which have not abolished the death penalty, sentence of death may be imposed only for the most serious crimes in accordance with the law in force at the time of the commission of the crime and not contrary to the provisions of the present Covenant and to the Convention on the Prevention and Punishment of the Crime of Genocide. This penalty can only be carried out pursuant to a final judgement rendered by a competent court.

3. When deprivation of life constitutes the crime of genocide, it is understood that nothing in this article shall authorize any State Party to the present Covenant to derogate in any way from any obligation assumed under the provisions of the Convention on the Prevention and Punishment of the Crime of Genocide.

4. Anyone sentenced to death shall have the right to seek pardon or commutation of the sentence. Amnesty, pardon or commutation of the sentence of death may be granted in all cases.

5. Sentence of death shall not be imposed for crimes committed by persons below eighteen years of age and shall not be carried out on pregnant women.

6. Nothing in this article shall be invoked to delay or to prevent the abolition of capital punishment by any State Party to the present Covenant.

Article 7

No one shall be subjected to torture or to cruel, inhuman or degrading treatment or punishment. In particular, no one shall be subjected without his free consent to medical or scientific experimentation.

Article 8

1. No one shall be held in slavery; slavery and the slave-trade in all their forms shall be prohibited.

2. No one shall be held in servitude.

3.

(a) No one shall be required to perform forced or compulsory labour;

(b) Paragraph 3 (a) shall not be held to preclude, in countries where imprisonment with hard labour may be imposed as a punishment for a crime, the performance of hard labour in pursuance of a sentence to such punishment by a competent court;

(c) For the purpose of this paragraph the term "forced or compulsory labour" shall not include:

(i) Any work or service, not referred to in subparagraph (b), normally required of a person who is under detention in consequence of a lawful order of a court, o r of a person during conditional release from such detention;

(ii) Any service of a military character and, in countries where conscientious objection is recognized, any national service required by law of conscientious objectors;

(iii) Any service exacted in cases of emergency or calamity threatening the life or well-being of the community;

(iv) Any work or service which forms part of normal civil obligations.

Article 9

1. Everyone has the right to liberty and security of person. No one shall be subjected to arbitrary arrest or detention. No one shall be deprived of his liberty except on such grounds and in accordance with such procedure as are established by law.

2. Anyone who is arrested shall be informed, at the time of arrest, of the reasons for his arrest and shall be promptly informed of any charges against him.

3. Anyone arrested or detained on a criminal charge shall be brought promptly before a judge or other officer authorized by law to exercise judicial power and shall be entitled to trial within a reasonable time or to release. It shall not be the general rule that persons awaiting trial shall be detained in custody, but release may be subject to guarantees to appear for trial, at any other stage of the judicial proceedings, and, should occasion arise, for execution of the judgement.

4. Anyone who is deprived of his liberty by arrest or detention shall be entitled to take proceedings before a court, in order that that court may decide without delay on the lawfulness of his detention and order his release if the detention is not lawful.

5. Anyone who has been the victim of unlawful arrest or detention shall have an enforceable right to compensation.

Article 10

1. All persons deprived of their liberty shall be treated with humanity and with respect for the inherent dignity of the human person.

2.

(a) Accused persons shall, save in exceptional circumstances, be segregated from convicted persons and shall be subject to separate treatment appropriate to their status as unconvicted persons;

(b) Accused juvenile persons shall be separated from adults and brought as speedily as possible for adjudication.

3. The penitentiary system shall comprise treatment of prisoners the essential aim of which shall be their reformation and social rehabilitation. Juvenile

offenders shall be segregated from adults and be accorded treatment appropriate to their age and legal status.

Article 11

No one shall be imprisoned merely on the ground of inability to fulfil a contractual obligation.

Article 12

1. Everyone lawfully within the territory of a State shall, within that territory, have the right to liberty of movement and freedom to choose his residence.

2. Everyone shall be free to leave any country, including his own.

3. The above-mentioned rights shall not be subject to any restrictions except those which are provided by law, are necessary to protect national security, public order (ordre public), public health or morals or the rights and freedoms of others, and are consistent with the other rights recognized in the present Covenant.

4. No one shall be arbitrarily deprived of the right to enter his own country.

Article 13

An alien lawfully in the territory of a State Party to the present Covenant may be expelled therefrom only in pursuance of a decision reached in accordance with law and shall, except where compelling reasons of national security otherwise require, be allowed to submit the reasons against his expulsion and to have his case reviewed by, and be represented for the purpose before, the competent authority or a person or persons especially designated by the competent authority.

Article 14

1. All persons shall be equal before the courts and tribunals. In the determination of any criminal charge against him, or of his rights and obligations in a suit at law, everyone shall be entitled to a fair and public hearing by a competent, independent and impartial tribunal established by law. The press and the public may be excluded from all or part of a trial for reasons of morals, public order (ordre public) or national security in a democratic society, or

when the interest of the private lives of the parties so requires, or to the extent strictly necessary in the opinion of the court in special circumstances where publicity would prejudice the interests of justice; but any judgement rendered in a criminal case or in a suit at law shall be made public except where the interest of juvenile persons otherwise requires or the proceedings concern matrimonial disputes or the guardianship of children.

2. Everyone charged with a criminal offence shall have the right to be presumed innocent until proved guilty according to law.

3. In the determination of any criminal charge against him, everyone shall be entitled to the following minimum guarantees, in full equality:

(a) To be informed promptly and in detail in a language which he understands of the nature and cause of the charge against him;

(b) To have adequate time and facilities for the preparation of his defence and to communicate with counsel of his own choosing;

(c) To be tried without undue delay;

(d) To be tried in his presence, and to defend himself in person or through legal assistance of his own choosing; to be informed, if he does not have legal assistance, of this right; and to have legal assistance assigned to him, in any case where the interests of justice so require, and without payment by him in any such case if he does not have sufficient means to pay for it;

(e) To examine, or have examined, the witnesses against him and to obtain the attendance and examination of witnesses on his behalf under the same conditions as witnesses against him;

(f) To have the free assistance of an interpreter if he cannot understand or speak the language used in court;

(g) Not to be compelled to testify against himself or to confess guilt.

4. In the case of juvenile persons, the procedure shall be such as will take account of their age and the desirability of promoting their rehabilitation.

5. Everyone convicted of a crime shall have the right to his conviction and sentence being reviewed by a higher tribunal according to law.

6. When a person has by a final decision been convicted of a criminal offence and when subsequently his conviction has been reversed or he has been pardoned on the ground that a new or newly discovered fact shows conclusively that there has been a miscarriage of justice, the person who has suffered punishment as a result of such conviction shall be compensated according to law, unless it is proved that the non-disclosure of the unknown fact in time is wholly or partly attributable to him.

7. No one shall be liable to be tried or punished again for an offence for which he has already been finally convicted or acquitted in accordance with the law and penal procedure of each country.

Article 15

1. No one shall be held guilty of any criminal offence on account of any act or omission which did not constitute a criminal offence, under national or international law, at the time when it was committed. Nor shall a heavier penalty be imposed than the one that was applicable at the time when the criminal offence was committed. If, subsequent to the commission of the offence, provision is made by law for the imposition of the lighter penalty, the offender shall benefit thereby.

2. Nothing in this article shall prejudice the trial and punishment of any person for any act or omission which, at the time when it was committed, was criminal according to the general principles of law recognized by the community of nations.

Article 16

Everyone shall have the right to recognition everywhere as a person before the law.

Article 17

1. No one shall be subjected to arbitrary or unlawful interference with his privacy, family, home or correspondence, nor to unlawful attacks on his honour and reputation.

2. Everyone has the right to the protection of the law against such interference or attacks.

Article 18

1. Everyone shall have the right to freedom of thought, conscience and religion. This right shall include freedom to have or to adopt a religion or belief of his choice, and freedom, either individually or in community with others and in public or private, to manifest his religion or belief in worship, observance, practice and teaching.

2. No one shall be subject to coercion which would impair his freedom to have or to adopt a religion or belief of his choice.

3. Freedom to manifest one's religion or beliefs may be subject only to such limitations as are prescribed by law and are necessary to protect public safety, order, health, or morals or the fundamental rights and freedoms of others.

4. The States Parties to the present Covenant undertake to have respect for the liberty of parents and, when applicable, legal guardians to ensure the religious and moral education of their children in conformity with their own convictions.

Article 19

1. Everyone shall have the right to hold opinions without interference.

2. Everyone shall have the right to freedom of expression; this right shall include freedom to seek, receive and impart information and ideas of all kinds, regardless of frontiers, either orally, in writing or in print, in the form of art, or through any other media of his choice.

3. The exercise of the rights provided for in paragraph 2 of this article carries with it special duties and responsibilities. It may therefore be subject to certain restrictions, but these shall only be such as are provided by law and are necessary:

   (a) For respect of the rights or reputations of others;

   (b) For the protection of national security or of public order (ordre public), or of public health or morals.

Article 20

1. Any propaganda for war shall be prohibited by law.

2. Any advocacy of national, racial or religious hatred that constitutes incitement to discrimination, hostility or violence shall be prohibited by law.

Article 21

The right of peaceful assembly shall be recognized. No restrictions may be placed on the exercise of this right other than those imposed in conformity with the law and which are necessary in a democratic society in the interests of national security or public safety, public order (ordre public), the protection of public health or morals or the protection of the rights and freedoms of others.

Article 22

1. Everyone shall have the right to freedom of association with others, including the right to form and join trade unions for the protection of his interests.

2. No restrictions may be placed on the exercise of this right other than those which are prescribed by law and which are necessary in a democratic society in the interests of national security or public safety, public order (ordre public), the protection of public health or morals or the protection of the rights and freedoms of others. This article shall not prevent the imposition of lawful restrictions on members of the armed forces and of the police in their exercise of this right.

3. Nothing in this article shall authorize States Parties to the International Labour Organisation Convention of 1948 concerning Freedom of Association and Protection of the Right to Organize to take legislative measures which would prejudice, or to apply the law in such a manner as to prejudice, the guarantees provided for in that Convention.

Article 23

1. The family is the natural and fundamental group unit of society and is entitled to protection by society and the State.

2. The right of men and women of marriageable age to marry and to found a family shall be recognized.

3. No marriage shall be entered into without the free and full consent of the intending spouses.

4. States Parties to the present Covenant shall take appropriate steps to ensure equality of rights and responsibilities of spouses as to marriage, during marriage and at its dissolution. In the case of dissolution, provision shall be made for the necessary protection of any children.

Article 24

1. Every child shall have, without any discrimination as to race, colour, sex, language, religion, national or social origin, property or birth, the right to such measures of protection as are required by his status as a minor, on the part of his family, society and the State.

2. Every child shall be registered immediately after birth and shall have a name.

3. Every child has the right to acquire a nationality.

Article 25

Every citizen shall have the right and the opportunity, without any of the distinctions mentioned in article 2 and without unreasonable restrictions:

(a) To take part in the conduct of public affairs, directly or through freely chosen representatives;

(b) To vote and to be elected at genuine periodic elections which shall be by universal and equal suffrage and shall be held by secret ballot, guaranteeing the free expression of the will of the electors;

(c) To have access, on general terms of equality, to public service in his country.

Article 26

All persons are equal before the law and are entitled without any discrimination to the equal protection of the law. In this respect, the law shall prohibit any discrimination and guarantee to all persons equal and effective protection against discrimination on any ground such as race, colour, sex, language, religion, political or other opinion, national or social origin, property, birth or other status.

Article 27

In those States in which ethnic, religious or linguistic minorities exist, persons belonging to such minorities shall not be denied the right, in community with the other members of their group, to enjoy their own culture, to profess and practise their own religion, or to use their own language.

PART IV

Article 28

1. There shall be established a Human Rights Committee (hereafter referred to in the present Covenant as the Committee). It shall consist of eighteen members and shall carry out the functions hereinafter provided.

2. The Committee shall be composed of nationals of the States Parties to the present Covenant who shall be persons of high moral character and recognized competence in the field of human rights, consideration being given to the usefulness of the participation of some persons having legal experience.

3. The members of the Committee shall be elected and shall serve in their personal capacity.

Article 29

1. The members of the Committee shall be elected by secret ballot from a list of persons possessing the qualifications prescribed in article 28 and nominated for the purpose by the States Parties to the present Covenant.

2. Each State Party to the present Covenant may nominate not more than two persons. These persons shall be nationals of the nominating State.

3. A person shall be eligible for renomination.

Article 30

1. The initial election shall be held no later than six months after the date of the entry into force of the present Covenant.

2. At least four months before the date of each election to the Committee, other than an election to fill a vacancy declared in accordance with article 34, the Secretary-General of the United Nations shall address a written in-

vitation to the States Parties to the present Covenant to submit their nominations for membership of the Committee within three months.

3. The Secretary-General of the United Nations shall prepare a list in alphabetical order of all the persons thus nominated, with an indication of the States Parties which have nominated them, and shall submit it to the States Parties to the present Covenant no later than one month before the date of each election.

4. Elections of the members of the Committee shall be held at a meeting of the States Parties to the present Covenant convened by the Secretary General of the United Nations at the Headquarters of the United Nations. At that meeting, for which two thirds of the States Parties to the present Covenant shall constitute a quorum, the persons elected to the Committee shall be those nominees who obtain the largest number of votes and an absolute majority of the votes of the representatives of States Parties present and voting.

Article 31

1. The Committee may not include more than one national of the same State.

2. In the election of the Committee, consideration shall be given to equitable geographical distribution of membership and to the representation of the different forms of civilization and of the principal legal systems.

Article 32

1. The members of the Committee shall be elected for a term of four years. They shall be eligible for re-election if renominated. However, the terms of nine of the members elected at the first election shall expire at the end of two years; immediately after the first election, the names of these nine members shall be chosen by lot by the Chairman of the meeting referred to in article 30, paragraph 4.

2. Elections at the expiry of office shall be held in accordance with the preceding articles of this part of the present Covenant.

Article 33

1. If, in the unanimous opinion of the other members, a member of the Committee has ceased to carry out his functions for any cause other than absence

of a temporary character, the Chairman of the Committee shall notify the Secretary-General of the United Nations, who shall then declare the seat of that member to be vacant.

2. In the event of the death or the resignation of a member of the Committee, the Chairman shall immediately notify the Secretary-General of the United Nations, who shall declare the seat vacant from the date of death or the date on which the resignation takes effect.

Article 34

1. When a vacancy is declared in accordance with article 33 and if the term of office of the member to be replaced does not expire within six months of the declaration of the vacancy, the Secretary-General of the United Nations shall notify each of the States Parties to the present Covenant, which may within two months submit nominations in accordance with article 29 for the purpose of filling the vacancy.

2. The Secretary-General of the United Nations shall prepare a list in alphabetical order of the persons thus nominated and shall submit it to the States Parties to the present Covenant. The election to fill the vacancy shall then take place in accordance with the relevant provisions of this part of the present Covenant.

3. A member of the Committee elected to fill a vacancy declared in accordance with article 33 shall hold office for the remainder of the term of the member who vacated the seat on the Committee under the provisions of that article.

Article 35

The members of the Committee shall, with the approval of the General Assembly of the United Nations, receive emoluments from United Nations resources on such terms and conditions as the General Assembly may decide, having regard to the importance of the Committee's responsibilities.

Article 36

The Secretary-General of the United Nations shall provide the necessary staff and facilities for the effective performance of the functions of the Committee under the present Covenant.

Article 37

1. The Secretary-General of the United Nations shall convene the initial meeting of the Committee at the Headquarters of the United Nations.

2. After its initial meeting, the Committee shall meet at such times as shall be provided in its rules of procedure.

3. The Committee shall normally meet at the Headquarters of the United Nations or at the United Nations Office at Geneva.

Article 38

Every member of the Committee shall, before taking up his duties, make a solemn declaration in open committee that he will perform his functions impartially and conscientiously.

Article 39

1. The Committee shall elect its officers for a term of two years. They may be re-elected.

2. The Committee shall establish its own rules of procedure, but these rules shall provide, inter alia, that:

(a) Twelve members shall constitute a quorum;

(b) Decisions of the Committee shall be made by a majority vote of the members present.

Article 40

1. The States Parties to the present Covenant undertake to submit reports on the measures they have adopted which give effect to the rights recognized herein and on the progress made in the enjoyment of those rights:

(a) Within one year of the entry into force of the present Covenant for the States Parties concerned;

(b) Thereafter whenever the Committee so requests.

2. All reports shall be submitted to the Secretary-General of the United Nations, who shall transmit them to the Committee for consideration. Reports shall indicate the factors and difficulties, if any, affecting the implementation of the present Covenant.

3. The Secretary-General of the United Nations may, after consultation with the Committee, transmit to the specialized agencies concerned copies of such parts of the reports as may fall within their field of competence.

4. The Committee shall study the reports submitted by the States Parties to the present Covenant. It shall transmit its reports, and such general comments as it may consider appropriate, to the States Parties. The Committee may also transmit to the Economic and Social Council these comments along with the copies of the reports it has received from States Parties to the present Covenant.

5. The States Parties to the present Covenant may submit to the Committee observations on any comments that may be made in accordance with paragraph 4 of this article.

Article 41

1. A State Party to the present Covenant may at any time declare under this article that it recognizes the competence of the Committee to receive and consider communications to the effect that a State Party claims that another State Party is not fulfilling its obligations under the present Covenant. Communications under this article may be received and considered only if submitted by a State Party which has made a declaration recognizing in regard to itself the competence of the Committee. No communication shall be received by the Committee if it concerns a State Party which has not made such a declaration. Communications received under this article shall be dealt with in accordance with the following procedure:

(a) If a State Party to the present Covenant considers that another State Party is not giving effect to the provisions of the present Covenant, it may, by written communication, bring the matter to the attention of that State Party. Within three months after the receipt of the communication the receiving State shall afford the State which sent the communication an explanation, or any other statement in writing clarifying the matter which should include, to the extent possible and pertinent, reference to domestic procedures and remedies taken, pending, or available in the matter;

(b) If the matter is not adjusted to the satisfaction of both States Parties concerned within six months after the receipt by the receiving State of the initial communication, either State shall have the right to refer the matter to the Committee, by notice given to the Committee and to the other State;

(c) The Committee shall deal with a matter referred to it only after it has ascertained that all available domestic remedies have been invoked and exhausted in the matter, in conformity with the generally recognized principles of international law. This shall not be the rule where the application of the remedies is unreasonably prolonged;

(d) The Committee shall hold closed meetings when examining communications under this article;

(e) Subject to the provisions of subparagraph (c), the Committee shall make available its good offices to the States Parties concerned with a view to a friendly solution of the matter on the basis of respect for human rights and fundamental freedoms as recognized in the present Covenant;

(f) In any matter referred to it, the Committee may call upon the States Parties concerned, referred to in subparagraph (b), to supply any relevant information;

(g) The States Parties concerned, referred to in subparagraph (b), shall have the right to be represented when the matter is being considered in the Committee and to make submissions orally and/or in writing;

(h) The Committee shall, within twelve months after the date of receipt of notice under subparagraph (b), submit a report:

(i) If a solution within the terms of subparagraph (e) is reached, the Committee shall confine its report to a brief statement of the facts and of the solution reached;

(ii) If a solution within the terms of subparagraph (e) is not reached, the Committee shall confine its report to a brief statement of the facts; the written submissions and record of the oral submissions made by the States Parties concerned shall be attached to the report. In every matter, the report shall be communicated to the States Parties concerned.

2. The provisions of this article shall come into force when ten States Parties to the present Covenant have made declarations under paragraph 1 of this article. Such declarations shall be deposited by the States Parties with the Secretary-General of the United Nations, who shall transmit copies thereof to the other States Parties. A declaration may be withdrawn at any time by notification to the Secretary-General. Such a withdrawal shall not prejudice the consideration of any matter which is the subject of a communication already transmitted under this article; no further communication by any State Party shall be received after the notification of withdrawal of the declaration has been received by the Secretary-General, unless the State Party concerned has made a new declaration.

Article 42

1.

(a) If a matter referred to the Committee in accordance with article 41 is not resolved to the satisfaction of the States Parties concerned, the Committee may, with the prior consent of the States Parties concerned, appoint an ad hoc Conciliation Commission (hereinafter referred to as the Commission). The good offices of the Commission shall be made available to the States Parties concerned with a view to an amicable solution of the matter on the basis of respect for the present Covenant;

(b) The Commission shall consist of five persons acceptable to the States Parties concerned. If the States Parties concerned fail to reach agreement within three months on all or part of the composition of the Commission, the members of the Commission concerning whom no agreement has been reached shall be elected by secret ballot by a two-thirds majority vote of the Committee from among its members.

2. The members of the Commission shall serve in their personal capacity. They shall not be nationals of the States Parties concerned, or of a State not Party to the present Covenant, or of a State Party which has not made a declaration under article 41.

3. The Commission shall elect its own Chairman and adopt its own rules of procedure.

4. The meetings of the Commission shall normally be held at the Headquarters of the United Nations or at the United Nations Office at Geneva. However, they may be held at such other convenient places as the Commission

may determine in consultation with the Secretary-General of the United Nations and the States Parties concerned.

5. The secretariat provided in accordance with article 36 shall also service the commissions appointed under this article.

6. The information received and collated by the Committee shall be made available to the Commission and the Commission may call upon the States Parties concerned to supply any other relevant information.

7. When the Commission has fully considered the matter, but in any event not later than twelve months after having been seized of the matter, it shall submit to the Chairman of the Committee a report for communication to the States Parties concerned:

(a) If the Commission is unable to complete its consideration of the matter within twelve months, it shall confine its report to a brief statement of the status of its consideration of the matter;

(b) If an amicable solution to the matter on tie basis of respect for human rights as recognized in the present Covenant is reached, the Commission shall confine its report to a brief statement of the facts and of the solution reached;

(c) If a solution within the terms of subparagraph (b) is not reached, the Commission's report shall embody its findings on all questions of fact relevant to the issues between the States Parties concerned, and its views on the possibilities of an amicable solution of the matter. This report shall also contain the written submissions and a record of the oral submissions made by the States Parties concerned;

(d) If the Commission's report is submitted under subparagraph (c), the States Parties concerned shall, within three months of the receipt of the report, notify the Chairman of the Committee whether or not they accept the contents of the report of the Commission.

8. The provisions of this article are without prejudice to the responsibilities of the Committee under article 41.

9. The States Parties concerned shall share equally all the expenses of the members of the Commission in accordance with estimates to be provided by the Secretary-General of the United Nations.

10. The Secretary-General of the United Nations shall be empowered to pay the expenses of the members of the Commission, if necessary, before reimbursement by the States Parties concerned, in accordance with paragraph 9 of this article.

Article 43

The members of the Committee, and of the ad hoc conciliation commissions which may be appointed under article 42, shall be entitled to the facilities, privileges and immunities of experts on mission for the United Nations as laid down in the relevant sections of the Convention on the Privileges and Immunities of the United Nations.

Article 44

The provisions for the implementation of the present Covenant shall apply without prejudice to the procedures prescribed in the field of human rights by or under the constituent instruments and the conventions of the United Nations and of the specialized agencies and shall not prevent the States Parties to the present Covenant from having recourse to other procedures for settling a dispute in accordance with general or special international agreements in force between them.

Article 45

The Committee shall submit to the General Assembly of the United Nations, through the Economic and Social Council, an annual report on its activities.

PART V

Article 46

Nothing in the present Covenant shall be interpreted as impairing the provisions of the Charter of the United Nations and of the constitutions of the specialized agencies which define the respective responsibilities of the various organs of the United Nations and of the specialized agencies in regard to the matters dealt with in the present Covenant.

Article 47

Nothing in the present Covenant shall be interpreted as impairing the inherent right of all peoples to enjoy and utilize fully and freely their natural wealth and resources.

PART VI

Article 48

1. The present Covenant is open for signature by any State Member of the United Nations or member of any of its specialized agencies, by any State Party to the Statute of the International Court of Justice, and by any other State which has been invited by the General Assembly of the United Nations to become a Party to the present Covenant.

2. The present Covenant is subject to ratification. Instruments of ratification shall be deposited with the Secretary-General of the United Nations.

3. The present Covenant shall be open to accession by any State referred to in paragraph 1 of this article.

4. Accession shall be effected by the deposit of an instrument of accession with the Secretary-General of the United Nations.

5. The Secretary-General of the United Nations shall inform all States which have signed this Covenant or acceded to it of the deposit of each instrument of ratification or accession.

Article 49

1. The present Covenant shall enter into force three months after the date of the deposit with the Secretary-General of the United Nations of the thirty-fifth instrument of ratification or instrument of accession.

2. For each State ratifying the present Covenant or acceding to it after the deposit of the thirty-fifth instrument of ratification or instrument of accession, the present Covenant shall enter into force three months after the date of the deposit of its own instrument of ratification or instrument of accession.

Article 50

The provisions of the present Covenant shall extend to all parts of federal States without any limitations or exceptions.

Article 51

1. Any State Party to the present Covenant may propose an amendment and file it with the Secretary-General of the United Nations. The Secretary-General

of the United Nations shall thereupon communicate any proposed amendments to the States Parties to the present Covenant with a request that they notify him whether they favour a conference of States Parties for the purpose of considering and voting upon the proposals. In the event that at least one third of the States Parties favours such a conference, the Secretary-General shall convene the conference under the auspices of the United Nations. Any amendment adopted by a majority of the States Parties present and voting at the conference shall be submitted to the General Assembly of the United Nations for approval.

2. Amendments shall come into force when they have been approved by the General Assembly of the United Nations and accepted by a two-thirds majority of the States Parties to the Covenant in accordance with their respective constitutional processes. 3. present When amendments come into force, they shall be binding on those States Parties which have accepted them, other States Parties still being bound by the provisions of the present Covenant and any earlier amendment which they have accepted.

Article 52

1. Irrespective of the notifications made under article 48, paragraph 5, the Secretary-General of the United Nations shall inform all States referred to in paragraph I of the same article of the following particulars:

(a) Signatures, ratifications and accessions under article 48;

(b) The date of the entry into force of the present Covenant under article 49 and the date of the entry into force of any amendments under article 51.

Article 53

1. The present Covenant, of which the Chinese, English, French, Russian and Spanish texts are equally authentic, shall be deposited in the archives of the United Nations.

2. The Secretary-General of the United Nations shall transmit certified copies of the present Covenant to all States referred to in artic

Appendix III

International Covenant on Economic, Social and Cultural Rights
Adopted and opened for signature, ratification and accession by General Assembly resolution 2200A (XXI) of 16 December 1966 entry into force 3 January 1976, in accordance with article 27

Preamble

The States Parties to the present Covenant,

Considering that, in accordance with the principles proclaimed in the Charter of the United Nations, recognition of the inherent dignity and of the equal and inalienable rights of all members of the human family is the foundation of freedom, justice and peace in the world,

Recognizing that these rights derive from the inherent dignity of the human person,

Recognizing that, in accordance with the Universal Declaration of Human Rights, the ideal of free human beings enjoying freedom from fear and want can only be achieved if conditions are created whereby everyone may enjoy his economic, social and cultural rights, as well as his civil and political rights,

Considering the obligation of States under the Charter of the United Nations to promote universal respect for, and observance of, human rights and freedoms,

Realizing that the individual, having duties to other individuals and to the community to which he belongs, is under a responsibility to strive for the promotion and observance of the rights recognized in the present Covenant,

Agree upon the following articles:

PART I

Article 1

1. All peoples have the right of self-determination. By virtue of that right they freely determine their political status and freely pursue their economic, social and cultural development.

2. All peoples may, for their own ends, freely dispose of their natural wealth and resources without prejudice to any obligations arising out of international economic co-operation, based upon the principle of mutual benefit, and international law. In no case may a people be deprived of its own means of subsistence.

3. The States Parties to the present Covenant, including those having responsibility for the administration of Non-Self-Governing and Trust Territories, shall

promote the realization of the right of self-determination, and shall respect that right, in conformity with the provisions of the Charter of the United Nations.

PART II

Article 2

1. Each State Party to the present Covenant undertakes to take steps, individually and through international assistance and co-operation, especially economic and technical, to the maximum of its available resources, with a view to achieving progressively the full realization of the rights recognized in the present Covenant by all appropriate means, including particularly the adoption of legislative measures.

2. The States Parties to the present Covenant undertake to guarantee that the rights enunciated in the present Covenant will be exercised without discrimination of any kind as to race, colour, sex, language, religion, political or other opinion, national or social origin, property, birth or other status.

3. Developing countries, with due regard to human rights and their national economy, may determine to what extent they would guarantee the economic rights recognized in the present Covenant to non-nationals.

Article 3

The States Parties to the present Covenant undertake to ensure the equal right of men and women to the enjoyment of all economic, social and cultural rights set forth in the present Covenant.

Article 4

The States Parties to the present Covenant recognize that, in the enjoyment of those rights provided by the State in conformity with the present Covenant, the State may subject such rights only to such limitations as are determined by law only in so far as this may be compatible with the nature of these rights and solely for the purpose of promoting the general welfare in a democratic society.

Article 5

1. Nothing in the present Covenant may be interpreted as implying for any State, group or person any right to engage in any activity or to perform any

act aimed at the destruction of any of the rights or freedoms recognized herein, or at their limitation to a greater extent than is provided for in the present Covenant.

2. No restriction upon or derogation from any of the fundamental human rights recognized or existing in any country in virtue of law, conventions, regulations or custom shall be admitted on the pretext that the present Covenant does not recognize such rights or that it recognizes them to a lesser extent.

PART III

Article 6

1. The States Parties to the present Covenant recognize the right to work, which includes the right of everyone to the opportunity to gain his living by work which he freely chooses or accepts, and will take appropriate steps to safeguard this right.

2. The steps to be taken by a State Party to the present Covenant to achieve the full realization of this right shall include technical and vocational guidance and training programmes, policies and techniques to achieve steady economic, social and cultural development and full and productive employment under conditions safeguarding fundamental political and economic freedoms to the individual.

Article 7

The States Parties to the present Covenant recognize the right of everyone to the enjoyment of just and favourable conditions of work which ensure, in particular:

(a) Remuneration which provides all workers, as a minimum, with:

(i) Fair wages and equal remuneration for work of equal value without distinction of any kind, in particular women being guaranteed conditions of work not inferior to those enjoyed by men, with equal pay for equal work;

(ii) A decent living for themselves and their families in accordance with the provisions of the present Covenant;

(b) Safe and healthy working conditions;

(c) Equal opportunity for everyone to be promoted in his employment to an appropriate higher level, subject to no considerations other than those of seniority and competence;

(d) Rest, leisure and reasonable limitation of working hours and periodic holidays with pay, as well as remuneration for public holidays.

Article 8

1. The States Parties to the present Covenant undertake to ensure:

(a) The right of everyone to form trade unions and join the trade union of his choice, subject only to the rules of the organization concerned, for the promotion and protection of his economic and social interests. No restrictions may be placed on the exercise of this right other than those prescribed by law and which are necessary in a democratic society in the interests of national security or public order or for the protection of the rights and freedoms of others;

(b) The right of trade unions to establish national federations or confederations and the right of the latter to form or join international trade-union organizations;

(c) The right of trade unions to function freely subject to no limitations other than those prescribed by law and which are necessary in a democratic society in the interests of national security or public order or for the protection of the rights and freedoms of others;

(d) The right to strike, provided that it is exercised in conformity with the laws of the particular country.

2. This article shall not prevent the imposition of lawful restrictions on the exercise of these rights by members of the armed forces or of the police or of the administration of the State.

3. Nothing in this article shall authorize States Parties to the International Labour Organisation Convention of 1948 concerning Freedom of Association and Protection of the Right to Organize to take legislative measures which would prejudice, or apply the law in such a manner as would prejudice, the guarantees provided for in that Convention.

Article 9

The States Parties to the present Covenant recognize the right of everyone to social security, including social insurance.

Article 10

The States Parties to the present Covenant recognize that:

1. The widest possible protection and assistance should be accorded to the family, which is the natural and fundamental group unit of society, particularly for its establishment and while it is responsible for the care and education of dependent children. Marriage must be entered into with the free consent of the intending spouses.

2. Special protection should be accorded to mothers during a reasonable period before and after childbirth. During such period working mothers should be accorded paid leave or leave with adequate social security benefits.

3. Special measures of protection and assistance should be taken on behalf of all children and young persons without any discrimination for reasons of parentage or other conditions. Children and young persons should be protected from economic and social exploitation. Their employment in work harmful to their morals or health or dangerous to life or likely to hamper their normal development should be punishable by law. States should also set age limits below which the paid employment of child labour should be prohibited and punishable by law.

Article 11

1. The States Parties to the present Covenant recognize the right of everyone to an adequate standard of living for himself and his family, including adequate food, clothing and housing, and to the continuous improvement of living conditions. The States Parties will take appropriate steps to ensure the realization of this right, recognizing to this effect the essential importance of international co-operation based on free consent.

2. The States Parties to the present Covenant, recognizing the fundamental right of everyone to be free from hunger, shall take, individually and through international co-operation, the measures, including specific programmes, which are needed:

(a) To improve methods of production, conservation and distribution of food by making full use of technical and scientific knowledge, by disseminating knowledge of the principles of nutrition and by developing or reforming agrarian systems in such a way as to achieve the most efficient development and utilization of natural resources;

(b) Taking into account the problems of both food-importing and food-exporting countries, to ensure an equitable distribution of world food supplies in relation to need.

Article 12

1. The States Parties to the present Covenant recognize the right of everyone to the enjoyment of the highest attainable standard of physical and mental health.

2. The steps to be taken by the States Parties to the present Covenant to achieve the full realization of this right shall include those necessary for:

(a) The provision for the reduction of the stillbirth-rate and of infant mortality and for the healthy development of the child;

(b) The improvement of all aspects of environmental and industrial hygiene;

(c) The prevention, treatment and control of epidemic, endemic, occupational and other diseases;

(d) The creation of conditions which would assure to all medical service and medical attention in the event of sickness.

Article 13

1. The States Parties to the present Covenant recognize the right of everyone to education. They agree that education shall be directed to the full development of the human personality and the sense of its dignity, and shall strengthen the respect for human rights and fundamental freedoms. They further agree that education shall enable all persons to participate effectively in a free society, promote understanding, tolerance and friendship among all nations and all racial, ethnic or religious groups, and further the activities of the United Nations for the maintenance of peace.

2. The States Parties to the present Covenant recognize that, with a view to achieving the full realization of this right:

(a) Primary education shall be compulsory and available free to all;

(b) Secondary education in its different forms, including technical and vocational secondary education, shall be made generally available and accessible to all by every appropriate means, and in particular by the progressive introduction of free education;

(c) Higher education shall be made equally accessible to all, on the basis of capacity, by every appropriate means, and in particular by the progressive introduction of free education;

(d) Fundamental education shall be encouraged or intensified as far as possible for those persons who have not received or completed the whole period of their primary education;

(e) The development of a system of schools at all levels shall be actively pursued, an adequate fellowship system shall be established, and the material conditions of teaching staff shall be continuously improved.

3. The States Parties to the present Covenant undertake to have respect for the liberty of parents and, when applicable, legal guardians to choose for their children schools, other than those established by the public authorities, which conform to such minimum educational standards as may be laid down or approved by the State and to ensure the religious and moral education of their children in conformity with their own convictions.

4. No part of this article shall be construed so as to interfere with the liberty of individuals and bodies to establish and direct educational institutions, subject always to the observance of the principles set forth in paragraph I of this article and to the requirement that the education given in such institutions shall conform to such minimum standards as may be laid down by the State.

Article 14

Each State Party to the present Covenant which, at the time of becoming a Party, has not been able to secure in its metropolitan territory or other territories under its jurisdiction compulsory primary education, free of charge, undertakes, within two years, to work out and adopt a detailed plan of action for the progressive implementation, within a reasonable number of years, to be fixed in the plan, of the principle of compulsory education free of charge for all.

Article 15

1. The States Parties to the present Covenant recognize the right of everyone:

(a) To take part in cultural life;

(b) To enjoy the benefits of scientific progress and its applications;

(c) To benefit from the protection of the moral and material interests resulting from any scientific, literary or artistic production of which he is the author.

2. The steps to be taken by the States Parties to the present Covenant to achieve the full realization of this right shall include those necessary for the conservation, the development and the diffusion of science and culture.

3. The States Parties to the present Covenant undertake to respect the freedom indispensable for scientific research and creative activity.

4. The States Parties to the present Covenant recognize the benefits to be derived from the encouragement and development of international contacts and co-operation in the scientific and cultural fields.

PART IV

Article 16

1. The States Parties to the present Covenant undertake to submit in conformity with this part of the Covenant reports on the measures which they have adopted and the progress made in achieving the observance of the rights recognized herein.

2.

(a) All reports shall be submitted to the Secretary-General of the United Nations, who shall transmit copies to the Economic and Social Council for consideration in accordance with the provisions of the present Covenant;

(b) The Secretary-General of the United Nations shall also transmit to the specialized agencies copies of the reports, or any relevant parts therefrom, from States Parties to the present Covenant which are also members of these specialized agencies in so far as these reports, or parts therefrom, relate to any matters which fall within the responsibilities of the said agencies in accordance with their constitutional instruments.

Article 17

1. The States Parties to the present Covenant shall furnish their reports in stages, in accordance with a programme to be established by the Economic and Social Council within one year of the entry into force of the present Covenant after consultation with the States Parties and the specialized agencies concerned.

2. Reports may indicate factors and difficulties affecting the degree of fulfilment of obligations under the present Covenant.

3. Where relevant information has previously been furnished to the United Nations or to any specialized agency by any State Party to the present Covenant, it will not be necessary to reproduce that information, but a precise reference to the information so furnished will suffice.

Article 18

Pursuant to its responsibilities under the Charter of the United Nations in the field of human rights and fundamental freedoms, the Economic and Social Council may make arrangements with the specialized agencies in respect of their reporting to it on the progress made in achieving the observance of the provisions of the present Covenant falling within the scope of their activities. These reports may include particulars of decisions and recommendations on such implementation adopted by their competent organs.

Article 19

The Economic and Social Council may transmit to the Commission on Human Rights for study and general recommendation or, as appropriate, for information the reports concerning human rights submitted by States in accordance with articles 16 and 17, and those concerning human rights submitted by the specialized agencies in accordance with article 18.

Article 20

The States Parties to the present Covenant and the specialized agencies concerned may submit comments to the Economic and Social Council on any general recommendation under article 19 or reference to such general recommendation in any report of the Commission on Human Rights or any documentation referred to therein.

Article 21

The Economic and Social Council may submit from time to time to the General Assembly reports with recommendations of a general nature and a summary of the information received from the States Parties to the present Covenant and the specialized agencies on the measures taken and the progress made in achieving general observance of the rights recognized in the present Covenant.

Article 22

The Economic and Social Council may bring to the attention of other organs of the United Nations, their subsidiary organs and specialized agencies concerned with furnishing technical assistance any matters arising out of the reports referred to in this part of the present Covenant which may assist such bodies in deciding, each within its field of competence, on the advisability of international measures likely to contribute to the effective progressive implementation of the present Covenant.

Article 23

The States Parties to the present Covenant agree that international action for the achievement of the rights recognized in the present Covenant includes such methods as the conclusion of conventions, the adoption of recommendations, the furnishing of technical assistance and the holding of regional meetings and technical meetings for the purpose of consultation and study organized in conjunction with the Governments concerned.

Article 24

Nothing in the present Covenant shall be interpreted as impairing the provisions of the Charter of the United Nations and of the constitutions of the specialized agencies which define the respective responsibilities of the various organs of the United Nations and of the specialized agencies in regard to the matters dealt with in the present Covenant.

Article 25

Nothing in the present Covenant shall be interpreted as impairing the inherent right of all peoples to enjoy and utilize fully and freely their natural wealth and resources.

PART V

Article 26

1. The present Covenant is open for signature by any State Member of the United Nations or member of any of its specialized agencies, by any State Party to the Statute of the International Court of Justice, and by any other State which has been invited by the General Assembly of the United Nations to become a party to the present Covenant.

2. The present Covenant is subject to ratification. Instruments of ratification shall be deposited with the Secretary-General of the United Nations.

3. The present Covenant shall be open to accession by any State referred to in paragraph 1 of this article.

4. Accession shall be effected by the deposit of an instrument of accession with the Secretary-General of the United Nations.

5. The Secretary-General of the United Nations shall inform all States which have signed the present Covenant or acceded to it of the deposit of each instrument of ratification or accession.

Article 27

1. The present Covenant shall enter into force three months after the date of the deposit with the Secretary-General of the United Nations of the thirty-fifth instrument of ratification or instrument of accession.

2. For each State ratifying the present Covenant or acceding to it after the deposit of the thirty-fifth instrument of ratification or instrument of accession,

the present Covenant shall enter into force three months after the date of the deposit of its own instrument of ratification or instrument of accession.

Article 28

The provisions of the present Covenant shall extend to all parts of federal States without any limitations or exceptions.

Article 29

1. Any State Party to the present Covenant may propose an amendment and file it with the Secretary-General of the United Nations. The Secretary-General shall thereupon communicate any proposed amendments to the States Parties to the present Covenant with a request that they notify him whether they favour a conference of States Parties for the purpose of considering and voting upon the proposals. In the event that at least one third of the States Parties favours such a conference, the Secretary-General shall convene the conference under the auspices of the United Nations. Any amendment adopted by a majority of the States Parties present and voting at the conference shall be submitted to the General Assembly of the United Nations for approval.

2. Amendments shall come into force when they have been approved by the General Assembly of the United Nations and accepted by a two-thirds majority of the States Parties to the present Covenant in accordance with their respective constitutional processes.

3. When amendments come into force they shall be binding on those States Parties which have accepted them, other States Parties still being bound by the provisions of the present Covenant and any earlier amendment which they have accepted.

Article 30

Irrespective of the notifications made under article 26, paragraph 5, the Secretary-General of the United Nations shall inform all States referred to in paragraph I of the same article of the following particulars:

(a) Signatures, ratifications and accessions under article 26;

(b) The date of the entry into force of the present Covenant under article 27 and the date of the entry into force of any amendments under article 29.

Article 31

1. The present Covenant, of which the Chinese, English, French, Russian and Spanish texts are equally authentic, shall be deposited in the archives of the United Nations.

2. The Secretary-General of the United Nations shall transmit certified copies of the present Covenant to all States referred to in article 26.

Appendix IV

Draft Optional Protocol to the International Covenant on Economic, Social and Cultural Rights

The States Parties to the present Protocol,

Noting that the Charter of the United Nations reaffirms faith in fundamental human rights and in the dignity and worth of the human person,

Also noting that the Universal Declaration of Human Rights proclaims that all human beings are born free and equal in dignity and rights and that everyone is entitled to all the rights and freedoms set forth therein, without distinction of any kind,

Recalling that the International Covenant on Economic, Social and Cultural Rights and the International Covenant on Civil and Political Rights recognize that the ideal of free human beings enjoying freedom from fear and want can only be achieved if conditions are created whereby everyone may enjoy civil, cultural, economic, political and social rights,

Also recalling that the World Conference on Human Rights, in the Vienna Declaration and Programme of Action adopted in 1993, reaffirmed that all human rights are universal, indivisible and interdependent and interrelated,

Considering that in order further to achieve the purposes of the International Covenant on Economic, Social and Cultural Rights (hereinafter referred to as the Covenant) and the implementation of its provisions it would be appropriate to enable the Committee on Economic, Social and Cultural Rights (hereinafter referred to as the Committee) to receive and consider, as provided in the present Protocol, communications concerning violations of any of the rights set forth in the Covenant.

Have agreed as follows:

Article 1
The competence of the Committee

1. A State Party to the Covenant that becomes a Party to the present Protocol recognizes the competence of the Committee to receive and consider communications and to conduct inquiries as provided for by the provisions of the present Protocol.

Article 2
Individual communications

1. Communications may be submitted by or on behalf of individuals or groups of individuals, subject to the jurisdiction of a State Party, claiming to be victims of a violation of any of the rights set forth in [Parts II and III of] the Covenant by that State Party. Where a communication is submitted on behalf of individuals or groups of individuals, this shall be with their consent.
2. Each State Party may, at the time of signature or ratification of the present Protocol or accession thereto, declare that it does not recognize the competence of the Committee to consider individual communications under certain provisions of articles 2 (1) and 6 to 15 of the Covenant.

Article 3
Collective communications

1. The States Parties to the present Protocol recognize the right of international nongovernmental organizations with consultative status before the United Nations Economic and Social Council to submit communications alleging unsatisfactory application of any of the rights set forth in the Covenant by a State Party.
2. Any State Party may also, at the time of ratification or accession to the present Protocol, or at any moment thereafter, declare that it recognizes the right of any representative national nongovernmental organization within its jurisdiction, which has particular competence in the matters covered by the Covenant, to submit collective communications against it.

Article 4
Admissibility

1. The Committee shall not consider a communication unless it has ascertained that all available domestic remedies have been exhausted. This shall not be the rule where the application of such remedies is unreasonably prolonged or unlikely to bring effective relief.

2. The Committee shall declare a communication inadmissible where:

(a) It is not submitted within six months after the exhaustion of domestic remedies, except in cases where the author can demonstrate that it had not been possible to submit the communication within that time limit;

(b) The facts that are the subject of the communication occurred prior to the entry into force of the present Protocol for the State party concerned unless the facts can be shown to amount to a violation of the Covenant after that date;

(c) The same matter has already been examined by the Committee or has been or is being examined under another procedure of international investigation or settlement;

(d) It is incompatible with the provisions of the Covenant;

(e) It is manifestly ill founded or not sufficiently substantiated;

(f) It is an abuse of the right to submit a communication;

(g) It is anonymous or not in writing.

Article 5
Interim measures

At any time after the receipt of a communication, the Committee may request the State party concerned to take such measures of interim protection as may be necessary to avoid possible irreparable damage to the victim of the alleged violation, when the risk of such damage is sufficiently substantiated.

Article 6
Transmission of the communication

1. Unless the Committee considers a communication inadmissible without reference to the State Party concerned, the Committee shall bring any communication submitted to it under the present Protocol confidentially to the attention of the State Party concerned.

2. Within six months, the receiving State Party shall submit to the Committee written explanations or statements clarifying the matter and the remedy, if any, that may have been provided by that State Party.

Article 7
Friendly settlement

1. The Committee shall make available its good offices to the parties concerned with a view to reaching a friendly settlement of the matter on the basis of the respect for the obligations set forth in the Covenant.

2. Any agreement on a friendly settlement shall be deemed to close consideration of the communication under the present Protocol.

Article 8
Consideration of the merits

1. The Committee shall consider communications received under articles 2 and 3 of the present Protocol in the light of all information made available to it by the parties concerned.
2. The Committee shall hold closed meetings when examining communications under the present Protocol.
3. When examining communications under the present Protocol, the Committee shall give due consideration to relevant decisions and recommendations of other United Nations mechanisms as well as of bodies belonging to regional human rights systems.
4. When examining communications under the present Protocol concerning article 2, paragraph 1 of the Covenant, the Committee will assess the reasonableness of the steps taken by the State Party, to the maximum of its available resources, with a view to achieving progressively the full realization of the rights recognized in the present Covenant by all appropriate means.
5. After examining a communication, the Committee shall transmit its views on the merits together with its recommendations on the remedies, if any, to the parties concerned.
6. The State Party shall give due consideration to the Views of the Committee, together with its recommendations on the remedies, if any, and shall submit to the Committee, within six months, a written response, including information on any action taken in the light of the Views and recommendations of the Committee.
7. The Committee may invite the State Party to submit further information about any measures the State Party has taken in response to its Views or recommendations, if any, including as deemed appropriate by the Committee, in the State Party's subsequent reports under articles 16 and 17 of the Covenant.

Article 9
Inter-State communications

1. A State Party to the present Protocol may at any time declare under this article that it recognizes the competence of the Committee to receive and consider communications to the effect that a State Party claims that another State Party is not fulfilling its obligations under the Covenant. Communications under this article may be received and considered only if submitted by a State Party that has made a declaration recognizing in regard to itself the competence of the Com-

mittee. No communication shall be received by the Committee if it concerns a State Party which has not made such a declaration. Communications received under this article shall be dealt with in accordance with the following procedure:

(a) If a State Party to the present Protocol considers that another State Party is not fulfilling its obligations under the Covenant, it may, by written communication, bring the matter to the attention of that State Party. The State Party may also inform the Committee of the matter. Within three months after the receipt of the communication the receiving State shall afford the State that sent the communication an explanation, or any other statement in writing clarifying the matter which should include, to the extent possible and pertinent, reference to domestic procedures and remedies taken, pending or available in the matter;

(b) If the matter is not settled to the satisfaction of both States Parties concerned within six months after the receipt by the receiving State of the initial communication, either State shall have the right to refer the matter to the Committee, by notice given to the Committee and to the other State;

(c) The Committee shall deal with a matter referred to it only after it has ascertained that all available domestic remedies have been invoked and exhausted in the matter, in conformity with the generally recognized principles of international law. This shall not be the rule where the application of the remedies is unreasonably prolonged or unlikely to bring effective relief;

(d) Subject to the provisions of subparagraph (c) of the present paragraph, the Committee shall make available its good offices to the States Parties concerned with a view to a friendly solution of the matter on the basis of the respect for the obligations set forth in the Covenant;

(e) The Committee shall hold closed meetings when examining communications under the present article;

(f) In any matter referred to it in accordance with subparagraph (b) of the present paragraph, the Committee may call upon the States Parties concerned, referred to in subparagraph (b), to supply any relevant information;

(g) The States Parties concerned, referred to in subparagraph (b) of the present paragraph, shall have the right to be represented when the matter is being considered by the Committee and to make submissions orally and/or in writing;

(h) The Committee shall, with all due expediency after the date of receipt of notice under subparagraph (b) of the present paragraph, submit a report, as follows:

(i) If a solution within the terms of subparagraph (d) of the present paragraph is reached, the Committee shall confine its report to a brief statement of the facts and of the solution reached;

(ii) If a solution within the terms of subparagraph (d) is not reached, the Committee shall, in its report, set forth the relevant facts concerning the issue between the States Parties concerned. The written submissions and record of the oral submissions made by the States Parties concerned shall be attached to the report. The Committee may also communicate only to the States Parties concerned any views that it may consider relevant to the issue between them.

In every matter, the report shall be communicated to the States Parties concerned.

2. A declaration under paragraph 1 of the present article shall be deposited by the States Parties with the Secretary-General of the United Nations, who shall transmit copies thereof to the other States Parties. A declaration may be withdrawn at any time by notification to the Secretary-General. Such a withdrawal shall not prejudice the consideration of any matter that is the subject of a communication already transmitted under the present article; no further communication by any State Party shall be received under the present article after the notification of withdrawal of the declaration has been received by the Secretary-General, unless the State Party concerned has made a new declaration.

Article 10
Inquiry procedure

1. If the Committee receives reliable information indicating grave or systematic violations by a State Party of the rights set forth in the Covenant, the Committee shall invite that State Party to cooperate in the examination of the information and to this end to submit observations with regard to the information concerned.
2. Taking into account any observations that may have been submitted by the State Party concerned as well as any other reliable information available to it, the Committee may designate one or more of its members to conduct an inquiry and to report urgently to the Committee. Where warranted and with the consent of the State Party, the inquiry may include a visit to its territory.
3. Such an inquiry shall be conducted confidentially and the cooperation of the State Party shall be sought at all stages of the proceedings.
4. After examining the findings of such an inquiry, the Committee shall transmit these findings to the State Party concerned together with any comments and recommendations.
5. The State Party concerned shall, within six months of receiving the findings, comments and recommendations transmitted by the Committee, submit its observations to the Committee.

6. After such proceedings have been completed with regard to an inquiry made in accordance with paragraph 2, the Committee may, after consultations with the State Party concerned, decide to include a summary account of the results of the proceedings in its annual report.

Article 11
Follow-up to the inquiry procedure

1. The Committee may invite the State Party concerned to include in its report under articles 16 and 17 of the Covenant details of any measures taken in response to an inquiry conducted under article 10 of the present Protocol.
2. The Committee may, if necessary, after the end of the period of six months referred to in article 10, paragraph 5, invite the State Party concerned to inform it of the measures taken in response to such an inquiry.

Article 12
Protection measures

A State Party shall take all appropriate steps to ensure that individuals subject to its jurisdiction are not subjected to ill-treatment or intimidation as a consequence of communicating with the Committee pursuant to the present Protocol.

Article 13
International assistance and cooperation

The Committee shall transmit, as it may consider appropriate, to United Nations specialized agencies, funds and programmes and other competent bodies, its views or recommendations concerning communications and inquiries that indicate a need for technical advice or assistance, along with the State party's observations and suggestions, if any, on these views or recommendations. The Committee may also bring to the attention of such bodies any matter arising out of communications considered under the present Protocol which may assist them in deciding, each within its field of competence, on the advisability of international measures likely to contribute to assisting States Parties in achieving progress in implementation of the rights recognized in the Covenant.

Article 14
Special fund

1. To support the implementation of recommendations on remedies of the Committee under any of the procedures set forth in the present Protocol, and

for the benefit of victims of violations of the Covenant, a special fund shall be set up by decision of the General Assembly, to be administered in accordance with the financial regulations and rules of the United Nations, to provide economic assistance, when requested, to States parties that lack the financial means to implement effective remedies.

2. The Special Fund may be financed through voluntary contributions made by Governments, intergovernmental and non-governmental organizations and other private or public entities.

Article 15
Annual report

The Committee shall include in its annual report a summary of its activities under the present Protocol.

Article 16
Dissemination and information

Each State Party undertakes to make widely known and to disseminate the Covenant and the present Protocol and to facilitate access to information about the Views and recommendations of the Committee, in particular, on matters involving that State Party, and to do so in accessible formats.

Article 17
Rules of procedure

The Committee shall develop its own rules of procedure to be followed when exercising the functions conferred on it by the present Protocol.

Article 18
Signature, ratification and accession

1. The present Protocol shall be open for signature by any State that has signed, ratified or acceded to the Covenant.

2. The present Protocol shall be subject to ratification by any State that has ratified or acceded to the Covenant. Instruments of ratification shall be deposited with the SecretaryGeneral of the United Nations.

3. The present Protocol shall be open to accession by any State that has ratified or acceded to the Covenant.

4. Accession shall be effected by the deposit of an instrument of accession with the SecretaryGeneral of the United Nations.

Article 19
Entry into force

1. The present Protocol shall enter into force three months after the date of the deposit with the Secretary-General of the United Nations of the tenth instrument of ratification or accession.
2. For each State ratifying the present Protocol or acceding to it after its entry into force, the present Protocol shall enter into force three months after the date of the deposit of its own instrument of ratification or accession.

Article 20
The Committee's competence regarding the inquiry procedure

1. Each State Party may, at the time of signature or ratification of the present Protocol or accession thereto, declare that it does not recognize the competence of the Committee provided for in articles 10 and 11.
2. Any State Party having made a declaration in accordance with paragraph 1 of the present article may, at any time, withdraw this declaration by notification to the Secretary-General.

Article 21
Reservations

[No reservations to the present Protocol shall be permitted.]

Article 22
Amendments

1. Any State Party may propose an amendment to the present Protocol and file it with the Secretary-General of the United Nations. The Secretary-General shall thereupon communicate any proposed amendments to the States Parties with a request that they notify her or him whether they favour a conference of States Parties for the purpose of considering and voting on the proposal. In the event that at least one third of the States Parties favour such a conference, the Secretary-General shall convene the conference under the auspices of the United Nations. Any amendment adopted by a majority of the States Parties present and voting at the conference shall be submitted to the General Assembly of the United Nations for approval.
2. Amendments shall come into force when they have been approved by the General Assembly of the United Nations and accepted by a two-thirds majority of the States Parties to the present Protocol in accordance with their respective constitutional processes.

3. When amendments enter into force, they shall be binding on those States Parties that have accepted them, other States Parties still being bound by the provisions of the present Protocol and any earlier amendments that they have accepted.

Article 23
Transfer of competences

A Conference of States Parties to the present Protocol may decide, by two-thirds majority, whether it is appropriate to transfer to another body, without excluding any possibility, the competences attributed to the Committee by the present Protocol.

Article 24
Denunciation

1. Any State Party may denounce the present Protocol at any time by written notification addressed to the Secretary-General of the United Nations. Denunciation shall take effect one year after the date of receipt of the notification by the Secretary-General.
2. Denunciation shall be without prejudice to the continued application of the provisions of the present Protocol to any communication submitted under articles 2, 3 and 9 before the effective date of denunciation.

Article 25
Notification by the Secretary-General

The Secretary-General of the United Nations shall notify all States referred to in article 26, paragraph 1, of the Covenant of the following particulars:
    (a) Signatures, ratifications and accessions under the present Protocol;
    (b) The date of entry into force of the present Protocol and of any amendment under article 22;
    (c) Any denunciation under article 24.

Article 26
Official languages

1. The present Protocol, of which the Arabic, Chinese, English, French, Russian and Spanish texts are equally authentic, shall be deposited in the archives of the United Nations.

2. The Secretary-General of the United Nations shall transmit certified copies of the present Protocol to all States referred to in article 26 of the Covenant.

Appendix V

The Declaration on the Right to Development

Adopted by General Assembly resolution 41/128 of 4 December 1986

The General Assembly,

Bearing in mind the purposes and principles of the Charter of the United Nations relating to the achievement of international co-operation in solving international problems of an economic, social, cultural or humanitarian nature, and in promoting and encouraging respect for human rights and fundamental freedoms for all without distinction as to race, sex, language or religion,

Recognizing that development is a comprehensive economic, social, cultural and political process, which aims at the constant improvement of the well-being of the entire population and of all individuals on the basis of their active, free and meaningful participation in development and in the fair distribution of benefits resulting therefrom,

Considering that under the provisions of the Universal Declaration of Human Rights everyone is entitled to a social and international order in which the rights and freedoms set forth in that Declaration can be fully realized,

Recalling the provisions of the International Covenant on Economic, Social and Cultural Rights and of the International Covenant on Civil and Political Rights,

Recalling further the relevant agreements, conventions, resolutions, recommendations and other instruments of the United Nations and its specialized agencies concerning the integral development of the human being, economic and social progress and development of all peoples, including those instruments concerning decolonization, the prevention of discrimination, respect for and observance of, human rights and fundamental freedoms, the maintenance of international peace and security and the further promotion of friendly relations and co-operation among States in accordance with the Charter,

Recalling the right of peoples to self-determination, by virtue of which they have the right freely to determine their political status and to pursue their economic, social and cultural development,

Recalling also the right of peoples to exercise, subject to the relevant provisions of both International Covenants on Human Rights, full and complete sovereignty over all their natural wealth and resources,

Mindful of the obligation of States under the Charter to promote universal respect for and observance of human rights and fundamental freedoms for all without distinction of any kind such as race, colour, sex, language, religion, political or other opinion, national or social origin, property, birth or other status,

Considering that the elimination of the massive and flagrant violations of the human rights of the peoples and individuals affected by situations such as those resulting from colonialism, neo-colonialism, apartheid, all forms of racism and racial discrimination, foreign domination and occupation, aggression and threats against national sovereignty, national unity and territorial integrity and threats of war would contribute to the establishment of circumstances propitious to the development of a great part of mankind,

Concerned at the existence of serious obstacles to development, as well as to the complete fulfilment of human beings and of peoples, constituted, inter alia, by the denial of civil, political, economic, social and cultural rights, and considering that all human rights and fundamental freedoms are indivisible and interdependent and that, in order to promote development, equal attention and urgent consideration should be given to the implementation, promotion and protection of civil, political, economic, social and cultural rights and that, accordingly, the promotion of, respect for and enjoyment of certain human rights and fundamental freedoms cannot justify the denial of other human rights and fundamental freedoms,

Considering that international peace and security are essential elements for the realization of the right to development,

Reaffirming that there is a close relationship between disarmament and development and that progress in the field of disarmament would considerably promote progress in the field of development and that resources released through disarmament measures should be devoted to the economic and social development and well-being of all peoples and, in particular, those of the developing countries,

Recognizing that the human person is the central subject of the development process and that development policy should therefore make the human being the main participant and beneficiary of development,

Recognizing that the creation of conditions favourable to the development of peoples and individuals is the primary responsibility of their States,

Aware that efforts at the international level to promote and protect human rights should be accompanied by efforts to establish a new international economic order,

Confirming that the right to development is an inalienable human right and that equality of opportunity for development is a prerogative both of nations and of individuals who make up nations,

Proclaims the following Declaration on the Right to Development:

Article 1

1. The right to development is an inalienable human right by virtue of which every human person and all peoples are entitled to participate in, contribute to, and enjoy economic, social, cultural and political development, in which all human rights and fundamental freedoms can be fully realized.

2. The human right to development also implies the full realization of the right of peoples to self-determination, which includes, subject to the relevant provisions of both International Covenants on Human Rights, the exercise of their inalienable right to full sovereignty over all their natural wealth and resources.

Article 2

1. The human person is the central subject of development and should be the active participant and beneficiary of the right to development.

2. All human beings have a responsibility for development, individually and collectively, taking into account the need for full respect for their human rights and fundamental freedoms as well as their duties to the community, which alone can ensure the free and complete fulfilment of the human being, and they should therefore promote and protect an appropriate political, social and economic order for development.

3. States have the right and the duty to formulate appropriate national development policies that aim at the constant improvement of the well-being of the entire population and of all individuals, on the basis of their active, free and meaningful participation in development and in the fair distribution of the benefits resulting therefrom.

Article 3

1. States have the primary responsibility for the creation of national and international conditions favourable to the realization of the right to development.

2. The realization of the right to development requires full respect for the principles of international law concerning friendly relations and co-operation among States in accordance with the Charter of the United Nations.

3. States have the duty to co-operate with each other in ensuring development and eliminating obstacles to development. States should realize their rights and fulfil their duties in such a manner as to promote a new international economic order based on sovereign equality, interdependence, mutual interest and co-operation among all States, as well as to encourage the observance and realization of human rights.

Article 4

1. States have the duty to take steps, individually and collectively, to formulate international development policies with a view to facilitating the full realization of the right to development.

2. Sustained action is required to promote more rapid development of developing countries. As a complement to the efforts of developing countries, effective international co-operation is essential in providing these countries with appropriate means and facilities to foster their comprehensive development.

Article 5

States shall take resolute steps to eliminate the massive and flagrant violations of the human rights of peoples and human beings affected by situations such as those resulting from apartheid, all forms of racism and racial discrimination, colonialism, foreign domination and occupation, aggression, foreign interference and threats against national sovereignty, national unity and territorial integrity, threats of war and refusal to recognize the fundamental right of peoples to self-determination.

Article 6

1. All States should co-operate with a view to promoting, encouraging and strengthening universal respect for and observance of all human rights and fundamental freedoms for all without any distinction as to race, sex, language or religion.

2. All human rights and fundamental freedoms are indivisible and interdependent; equal attention and urgent consideration should be given to the implementation, promotion and protection of civil, political, economic, social and cultural rights.

3. States should take steps to eliminate obstacles to development resulting from failure to observe civil and political rights, as well as economic social and cultural rights.

Article 7

All States should promote the establishment, maintenance and strengthening of international peace and security and, to that end, should do their utmost to achieve general and complete disarmament under effective international control, as well as to ensure that the resources released by effective disarmament measures are used for comprehensive development, in particular that of the developing countries.

Article 8

1. States should undertake, at the national level, all necessary measures for the realization of the right to development and shall ensure, inter alia, equality of opportunity for all in their access to basic resources, education, health services, food, housing, employment and the fair distribution of income. Effective measures should be undertaken to ensure that women have an active role in the development process. Appropriate economic and social reforms should be carried out with a view to eradicating all social injustices.

2. States should encourage popular participation in all spheres as an important factor in development and in the full realization of all human rights.

Article 9

1. All the aspects of the right to development set forth in the present Declaration are indivisible and interdependent and each of them should be considered in the context of the whole.

2. Nothing in the present Declaration shall be construed as being contrary to the purposes and principles of the United Nations, or as implying that any State, group or person has a right to engage in any activity or to perform any act aimed at the violation of the rights set forth in the Universal Declaration of Human Rights and in the International Covenants on Human Rights.

Article 10

Steps should be taken to ensure the full exercise and progressive enhancement of the right to development, including the formulation, adoption and implementation of policy, legislative and other measures at the national and international levels.

Bibliography

CHAPTER 1

Kitty Arambulo. *Strengthening the Supervision of the International Covenant on Economic, Social, and Cultural Rights—Theoretical and Procedural Aspects.* Antwerpen/Groningen/Oxford: Intersentia-Hart, 1999.

Noam Chomsky. "The United States and the Challenge of Relativity," Pp. 32–39 in *Human Rights Fifty Years On: A Reappraisal*, edited by Tony Evans. Manchester University Press, 1998.

S.T. Coleridge. *Religious Musings.* 1796.

Matthew Craven. *The International Covenant on Economic, Social, and Cultural Rights.* Oxford, UK: Clarendon Press, 1995.

Discussion Paper, "Re-Evaluation of the Human Rights Protections in New Zealand," October, 2000, 21–22.

Asbjorne Eide. *Economic and Social Rights in Human Rights: Concepts and Standards*, edited by Janusz Symonides. UNESCO, 2000.

Tony Evans. *Trading Human Rights in Global Trade and Global Social Issues.* Routledge, 1999.

David Forsythe. *Human Rights and Development.* St. Martin's Press, 1989.

Francis Fukuyama. *The End of History and the Last Man.* Avon Books Inc., 1992.

Yash Ghai. "Rights, Social Justice, and Globalization in East Asia" in the *East Asian Challenge for Human Rights*, edited by Joanne R. Bauer and Daniel A. Bell. Press Syndicate of the University of Cambridge, 1999.

Mario Gomez. "Social Economic Rights and Human Rights Commissions." *Human Rights Quarterly* 17, 1995.

Robin Gwynn. *The Denial of Democracy.* Cosmos Publishing, 1998.

Te Rau Hinengaro. The New Zealand Mental Health Survey, edited by Mark Brown et al, Ministry of Health, Wellington, September 19, 2006. http:// www.moh.govt.nz/ moh.nsf/pagesmh/5223 (accessed April 15, 2008).

"Human Rights in New Zealand Today," New Zealand Human Rights Commission, 2004.

Paul Hunt. "Human Rights—How Are They Best Protected?" New Zealand Human Rights Commission, December, 1998.

Felix Kirchmeier. "The Right to Development—Where Do We Stand?" *Dialogue on Globalization* 23 (July 2006). (http://library.fes.de/pdf-files/icz/global/50288.pdf (accessed March 2, 2008)).

Paul Lauren, "Men of vision with right on their side," *New Zealand Herald*, December 10, 1998, A15.

John Stuart Mill. *On Liberty*. Harvard Classics, Vol. 25, 1909. Released in the Public Domain 1993, Chapter 2(11). http://www.csulb.edu/~jvancamp/free/excerpts.htm (accessed April 15, 2008).

Reins Mullerson. "Perspectives on Human Rights and Democracy in the Former Soviet Republics," in *Human Rights in Eastern Europe*, edited by Istvan Pogamy. Edward Elgar Publishing, 1995.

"New Zealand Values Survey 1998," Human Rights in New Zealand Today, New Zealand Human Rights Commission, 2004, 101.

Richard Nordahl. "A Marxian Approach to Human Rights," in *Human Rights in Cross-Cultural Perspectives—A Quest for Consensus*, edited by Abdullahi Ahmed An Na'im. University of Pennsylvania, 1992.

Sir Geoffrey Palmer. "Human Rights and New Zealand Government's Treaty Obligations," Address to the International Law Association on 30 April 1998.

Power to the People: The Report of Power, an independent inquiry into Britain's democracy, The Power Inquiry, United Kingdom, 2006, 9–10 *htt;://www.parliament.uk/commons/lib/research/notes/snpc-03948.pd*f (accessed April 15, 2008)

Report of the High Commissioner for Human Rights to the fifty-fifth session of the UN General Assembly, 'a mid-term global evaluation' of the UN Decade for Human Rights Education (1995–2004) (A/55/360), 20, 129(a), September 7, 2000. http://www.ohchr.org/Documents/AboutUs/annualreport2004.pdf (accessed April 15, 2008).

E. Rose et al., New Zealand Values Survey, Centre for Social and Health Outcomes, Massey University, Auckland, New Zealand, December 2005, 32. *http://www.shore.ac.nz/projects/Public_Life_Values.pdf* (accessed April 15, 2008).

Nils Rosemann. "Human Rights Education—Towards the End of the UN Decade." Mennesker & Rettigheter, *Nordic Journal of Human Rights*, no. 4 (Autumn 2003) (http://www.hrea.org/erc/Library/rosemann03.pdf (accessed March 3, 2008)).

Margot Salomon. "The Significance of the UN Task Force on the Right to Development," WorldBank Development Outreach, 2006.

Henry Shue. *Basic Rights*. Princeton University Press, 1980.

Keith Sinclair. *A History of New Zealand*. Pelican Books, 1991.

Voices of the Poor, World Bank Series, 2000 (http://www.worldbank.org/poverty/voices/reports.htm #crying (accessed March 2, 2008)).

CHAPTER 2

David Beetham. "What Future for Economic and Social Rights." (Political Studies series Vol. 43, Issue s1), 1995, 41–60.

Audrey Chapman and Sage Russell. *Core Obligations: Building a Framework for Economic, Social, and Cultural Rights.* Intersentia, 2002.

H. Charlesworth. Writing in Rights, (UNSW Press, 2002), 68–69.

Noam Chomsky. "The United States and the Challenge of Relativity," in *Human Rights Fifty Years On: A Reappraisal*, edited by Tony Evans. Manchester University Press, 1998.

Maurice Cranston. *What are Human Rights?* The Bodley Head Ltd., 1973.

Tony Evans. "Trading Human Rights," in *Global Trade and Global Social Issues*, edited by Annie Taylor and Caroline Thomas. Routledge, 1999.

William Felice. *Taking Suffering Seriously.* State University of New York, 1996.

David Forsythe. *Human Rights and Comparative Foreign Policy*, edited by David Forsythe. United Nations University, 2000.

Francis Fukuyama. *The End of History and the Last Man.* Avon Books Inc., 1992.

General Comment No. 3 (8), The nature of State parties obligations, UN Document E./C. 12/1990/8, UN Office of the High Commissioner for Human Rights, 14th December, 1990.

Human Development Report 2005, International cooperation at a crossroads, published for the United Nations Development Program, 21.

"Human Rights and Poverty Reduction—A Conceptual Framework," Office of the United Nations High Commissioner on Human Rights, 2004 (http://www.ohchr.org/Documents/Publications/Poverty_Reductionen.pdf (accessed December 5, 1994)).

Paul Hunt. *Reclaiming Social Rights.* Dartmouth Publishing, 1996.

Stephen Lendman. Global Research, "Predatory Capitalism, Corruption and Militarism: What Lies Ahead in the Age of Neocon Rule?" Global Research.ca, Center for Research on Globalization, January 1, 2007. (http://www.globalresearch.ca/index.php?context=viewArticle&code=LEN20070102&articleId=4293 (accessed March 2, 2008)).

Nelson Mandela. 'While poverty persists, there is no freedom' *The Guardian,* November 4, 2006 (http://www.guardian.co.uk/commentisfree/2006/nov/04/developmen tinternationalaidanddevelopment (accessed April 15, 2008).

T.H. Marshall. *Citizenship and Social Class.* Cambridge University Press, 1950.

Dexter Perkins. *The New Age of Franklin Roosevelt, 1932–45.* University of Chicago Press, 1965.

Paul Rishworth. 'A core to freedom of expression,' (forthcoming) cited in the Status Report, New Zealand Plan of Action for Human Rights, New Zealand Human Rights Commission, 2004, 4.

Bernard Robertson. Economic, Social, and Cultural Rights, Time for Reappraisal, A Study for the New Zealand Business Round Table, 1997.

R.J. Rummel, *Democratic Peace*, World Freedom, February 26, 2008. http://free-domspeace.blogspot.com (accessed April 15, 2008).

Henry Shue. *Basic Rights*. Princeton University Press, 1980.

The Social Report 2006, Income Inequality, New Zealand Ministry of Social Development, 60–61.

Status report, NZ Plan of Action for Human Rights, New Zealand Human Rights Commission, 2004, 4.

H.J. Steiner and P. Alston. "International Human Rights" in *Context: Law, Politics, Morals.* Oxford: Clarendon Press, 1996.

Brady Tyson and Abdul Azizi Said. "Human Rights: A Forgotten Victim of the Cold War." *Human Rights Quarterly* 15, (1993).

CHAPTER 3

Margaret Bedggood. "Constitutional Rights and Responsibilities in Aotearoa/New Zealand." *Otago Law Review* (1998).

David Beetham. "Democracy and Human Rights: Civil, Political, Economic, Social and Cultural." *Polity* (1999).

Toby Boraman. "Struggles Against Neo liberalism in Aotearoa/New Zealand in the 1990s," January 26, 2006. (http://www.anarkismo.net/newswire.php?story.id=2277 (accessed March 3, 2008)).

Pierre Bourdieu. *Act of Resistance.* New York Press, 1998.

"Child Abuse Figures Unacceptably High in New Zealand," Press release, Save the children New Zealand. September 19, 2003. http://www.savethechildren.org.nz/new_zealand/newsroom/child_abuse_deaths.html (accessed April 15, 2008)

Noam Chomsky. September 11 Znet Composite Interview 2, September 21, 2001.

Helen Clark. New Zealand Prime Minister, Interview. The Electoral Finance Bill, Interview on Newstalk ZB with Mike Hosking, November 19, 2007.

Simon Collins. 'Terror law 'faulty', admits Clark,' *New Zealand Herald*, November 9, 2007. http://www.nzherald.co.nz/section/1/story.cfm?c_id=1&objectid=10475054 (accessed April 15, 2008).

Jack Donnelly. Universal Human Rights in Theory and Practice. Ithaca: Cornell University Press, 1989, 180.

Roger Douglas. *There's Got to Be a Better Way.* Fourth Estate Books Ltd., 1980.

William F. Felice. *Taking Suffering Seriously.* Albany: State University of New York Press, 1996, 65.

Yash Ghai. "Rights, Social Justice, and Globalization," in *East Asia in the East Asian Challenge for Human Rights*, edited by Joanne R. Bauer and Daniel A. Bell. Press Syndicate of the University of Cambridge, 1999.

"Human rights agency's outcry gains it new respect on the Rights," *New Zealand Herald*, November 13, 2007, A4.

Michael Ignatieff. *Human Rights Politics and Ideology*, edited by Amy Gutmann. Princeton University Press, 2001.

Colin James. "The Political History and Framework since 1980," in *Building the Constitution*, edited by Colin James. Brebner Print, 2000.

——. "Introduction," in *Building the Constitution*, edited by Colin James. Brebner Print, 2000.

Jane Kelsey. "The Closure of Critique: Embedding the New Regime," 1996 University of Auckland Winter Lecture Series, August 13, 1996 (http://www.uow.edu.au/arts/sts/bmartin/dissent/documents/kelsey.html (accessed March 1, 2008)).

——. "Hatched, Thatched, and Dispatched," *The Guardian Weekly*, October 27, 1996. (http://www.jobsletter.org.nz/jb104919.htm (accessed April 15, 2008)).

Norman Lewis. "Human Rights, Law and Democracy in an Unfree World," in *Human Rights Fifty Years On—A Reappraisal*, edited by Tony Evans. Manchester University Press, 1998.

Karl Marx and Friedrich Engels. "Manifesto of the Communist Party," P. 49 in *Marx and Engels*, edited by Lewis S. Feuer. Anchor Books, 1959.

David McLoughlin. "Broken Welfare?" *North and South Magazine* (May 2000): 34–43.

National Business Review. Crony Watch Special, the Sims, November 17, 2007. http://www.nbr.co.nz/home/column_article.asp?id=19184&cid=15&cname=Politics (accessed April 15, 2008).

Richard Nordahl. "A Marxian Approach to Human Rights," in *Human Rights in Cross-Cultural Perspectives—A Quest for Consensus*, edited by Abdullahi Ahmed An-Na'im. University of Pennsylvania, 1992.

Thomas Paine. *The Human Rights Reader*, edited by Micheline R. Ishay. Routledge, 1997.

Louis-Edmond Pettiti and Patrice Meyer-Bisch. "Human Rights and Extreme Poverty," in *Human Rights: New Dimensions and Challenges*, edited by Janusz Symonides. Dartmouth Publishing Company Ltd., 1998.

Thomas Pogge. "World Poverty and Human Rights, Symposium." *Ethics & International Affairs* 19, no. 1 (2005).

Sir Ivor Richardson. "Rights Jurisprudence—Justice For All?," in *Essays on the Constitution*, edited by Philip A. Joseph. Brooker's, 1995.

Paul Rishworth. *Rights and Freedoms*, edited by Grant Huscroft and Paul Rishworth. Brooker's Ltd., 1995.

Carne Ross. First Secretary at the UK Permanent Mission to the UN from 1999 to 2003, Select Committee on Economic Affairs, Comprehensive UN sanctions–Iraq 1990–2003, the United Kingdom Parliament, Chapter 3 (34). http://www.publications.uk/pa/idselect/ldeconaf.96/96i.pdf (accessed April 15, 2008).

Keith Sinclair. *A History of New Zealand.* Pelican Books, 1991.

'2000 march against Electoral Bill,' *New Zealand Herald*, November 17, 2007. http://www.nzherald.co.nz/section/1/story.cfm?c_id=1&objectid=10476662 (accessed April 15, 2008).

CHAPTER 4

Colin Aikman. "New Zealand and the origins of the Universal Declaration," *Victoria University of Wellington Law Review* 29 (1999).

Kitty Arambulo. *Strengthening the Supervision of the International Covenant on Economic, Social, and Cultural Rights.* Intersentia, 1999.

G. E. Aylmer. *A Short History of the 17th Century England 1603–1689.* Blandford Press Ltd., 1963.

David Beetham. "What Future for Economic and Social Rights?," *Political Studies* (1995). George Boyer. Cornell University, English Poor Laws, EH Net. Encyclopedia, 2002 (http://eh.net/encyclopedia/article/boyer.poor.laws.england (accessed March 1, 2008)).

Miriam Bell. New Zealand's Contribution to the Early Post-War Development of International Human Rights, Human Rights Commission, December 1998. http://www.hrc.co.nz/index.php?p=452 (accessed April 15, 2008).

Paul Brian. Introduction to 19th-Century Socialism, Washington State University, http://wsu.edu/~brians/hum_303/socialism.html.

Bill Browning. "Human Rights in Russia: Discourse of Emancipation or only a Mirage?," *Human Rights in Eastern Europe*, edited by Istvan Pogany. Elgar Publishing Ltd., 1995.

Noam Chomsky. "The United States and the Challenge of Relativity," *Human Rights Fifty Years On: A Reappraisal*, edited by Tony Evans. Manchester University Press, 1998.

Cicero. "The Laws Book I," *Human Rights Reader*, ed. Micheline R. Ishay (Routledge, 1997).

Maurice Cranston. *What Are Human Rights?* (The Bodley Head Ltd., 1973).

Matthew Craven. *The International Covenant on Economic, Social, and Cultural Rights* Oxford: Clarendon Press, 1995.

Scott Davidson. *Human Rights.* Open University Press, 1993.

Ivo Duchacek. *Rights and Liberties in the World Today: Constitutional Promise and Reality.* Clio Press, 1973

Richard M. Ebeling. "A Liberal World Order," *Essay in Freedom Daily*, 1991. http://www.fff.org/fredom/0991b.asp (accessed April 15, 2008).

Asbjorne Eide. "Economic and Social Rights," in *Human Rights: Concepts and Standards*, edited by Janusz Symonds. UNESCO, 2000.

Tony Evans. "Trading Human Rights," in *Global Trade and Global Social Issues*, edited by Annie Taylor and Caroline Thomas. Routledge, 1999.

——. *Human Rights Fifty Years On: A Reappraisal*, ed. Tony Evans (Manchester University Press, 1998).

——. *The Politics of Human Rights.* Pluto Press, 2001.

William F. Felice. *The Global New Deal: Economic and Social Human Rights.* Rowman and Littlefield, Inc., 2003.

——. *Taking Suffering Seriously.* State University of New York, 1996.

Robert C. Frederiksen. Florida State University, Tallahassee, FL 32308, Alexis de Tocqueville (http://www.crimiology.fsu.edu/crimtheory/tocqueville.htm (accessed January, 2007)).

Michael Freeman. "The Philosophical Foundations of Human Rights," *Human Rights Quarterly* 16 (1994): 491.

Harris Friedburg. Masterless Men, 2002. (http://hfriedberg.web.wesleyan.edu/engl205/wshakespeare/riotandliberties.htm (accessed March 1, 2008)).

Erich Fromm. *The Fear of Freedom.* ARK Paperbacks, 1984.

Francis Fukuyama. *The End of History and the Last Man.* Avon Books, Inc., 1992.

Johan Galtung. "The Third World and Human Rights in the Post-1989 World Order," in *Human Rights Fifty Years On: A Reappraisal*, edited by Tony Evans. Manchester University Press, 1998.

Mahatma Gandhi. *Human Rights: A Symposium Prepared by UNESCO.* Allan Wingate Publishers, 1949.

Louis Henkin. "Human Rights: Ideology and Aspiration, Reality and Prospect," in *Realising Human Rights*, edited by Samantha Power, Graham Allison. St. Martin's Press, 2000.

"High Commissioner backs work on Mechanism to consider complaints of breaches of economic, social and cultural rights," Speeches and Statements by the High Commissioner, Office of the United Nations High Commissioner for Human Rights. UN Press Release, Geneva, July 16, 2007 (http://www.2.ohchr.org/english/issues/escr/escr-general-info.htm (accessed April 15, 2008)).

Human Rights Commission. Celebrating the 50th Anniversary of the UDHR, History of the UDHR, 1998. http//www.hrc.co.nz/index.php?p=451&format=text (accessed April 15, 2008).

Paul Hunt. *Reclaiming Social Rights.* Dartmouth Publishing, 1996.

Micheline R. Ishay. *The History of Human Rights: From Ancient Times to the Globalisation Era.* University of California Press, 2004.

Philip Joseph. "The Legal History and Framework of the Constitution," in *Building the Constitution*, edited by Colin James. Brebner Print, 2000.

Paul Lauren. *The Evolution of International Human Rights: Visions Seen.* University of Pennsylvania Press, 2003.

Andrew Little. New Zealand and the Soviet Union Kotare: New Zealand Notes and Queries, 6, ed. Patricia McLean. Review. 2006. (http://www.nzetc
.org/tm/scholarly/tei-whi06Kota-t/-gl-t7.html (accessed April 15, 2008)).

John Locke. *An Essay Concerning Human Understanding* [1690], 3, vi, 12.

Arthur Lovejoy. *The Great Chain of Being: A Study of the History of an Idea.* Harvard University Press, 2006, 20.

Karl Marx. "On the Jewish Question," in *The Human Rights Reader*, edited by Micheline R. Ishay. Routledge, 1997.

Susan Mendes. "Human Rights in Political Theory," *Political Studies*, XLIII (1995).

Rein Mullerson. *Human Rights Diplomacy.* Routledge, 1997.

Kenneth Pennington. The History of Natural Law, The Catholic University of America, Washington, D.C. (http://faculty.cua.edu/Pennington/Canon%20Law/Natural Law.htm (accessed March 1, 2008)).

Thomas Pogge. "World Poverty and Human Rights: Symposium," *Ethics and International Affairs* 19, no. 1 (2005):1–2. (http://www.cceia.org/resources/journal/19_1/ sympos ium/5109.html (accessed April 15, 2008)).

Samantha Power and Graham Allison. *Realising Human Rights* (New York: St. Martin's Press, 2000), xiiv.

"Revolutions in Europe 1848–1852" (5), *The Encyclopedia of World History, Sixth Edition*, Peter N. Stearns, General Editor, 2001 (http://www.bartleby.com/67/ 1081.html (accessed March 1, 2008)).

Jerome Shestack. "The Philosophic Foundations of Human Rights," *Human Rights Quarterly* 20 (1998).

Henry Shue. *Basic Rights: Substance Affluence, and U.S. Foreign Policy* (Princeton University Press, 1980).

Lejo Sibbel. ILO Conventions and the Covenant on Economic, Social and Cultural Rights: One Goal, Two Systems, 2001 (http://library.fes.de/pdf-files/iez/global /02078.pdf (accessed March 1, 2008)).

H. J. Steiner & P. Alston. "International Human Rights," in *Context: Law, Politics, Morals.* Oxford: Clarendon Press, 1996.

Paul Wade. Enclosure, History 1450–1789, *Encyclopedia of the Early Modern World*, The Gale Group, Answers.com, 2004. http://www.answers.com/topic/enclosure-4 (accessed April 15, 2008).

Jeremy Waldron. "Foreign Law and the Modern Ius Gentium," *Harvard Law Review* Vol. 119, 129–134, http://www.harvardlawreview.org/issues/119/Nov05/Waldron 05.shtml (accessed March 1, 2008).

Robert H. Walker. "Equality and Human Rights," http://www.cosmos-club.org/web/ journals/2001/Walker.html (accessed March 1, 2008).

H. G. Wells. "The Common Man's Life Under the Early Roman Empire," in *An Illustrated Short Story of the World.* Web and Bower Publishers Ltd., 1987.

CHAPTER 5

Amanda Abrams. Freedom in the World 2007: Year Marked by Global "Freedom Stagnation," Setbacks for Democracy in Asia, Washington, D.C., January 17, 2007 (http://www.freedomhouse.org/template.cfm?page=70+release=457 (accessed March 1, 2008)).

Catarina Albuquera. Chairperson of the OEWG for the OP for ICESCR, Responses to the nine questions posed by the chairperson, question 6, Choike.org., a portal on Southern civil societies, 2004.http://www.choike.org/Nuevo_eng/mformes/ 1728.html. (accessed April 15, 2008)

"Al Qaeda Terrorist Attacks," Information Please, 2007. (http://www.infoplease.com/ ipa/ A0884893.html (accessed March 1, 2008)).

Zebra Arat. *Democracy and Human Rights in Developing Countries.* London: Lagneia Publishers, 1991.

Louise Arbour. United Nations High Commissioner for Human Rights, Economist.com, The inbox, April 4, 2008. http://www.economist.com/blogs/theinbox/ 2007/04/01-week/ (accessed April 15, 2008).

Audrey R. Chapman. "A 'Violations Approach' for Monitoring the International Covenant on Economic, Social, and Cultural Rights," *Human Rights Quarterly* 18 (1996).

Christine Chinkin. "International Law and Human Rights," in *Human Rights Fifty Years On: A Reappraisal*, edited by Tony Evans. Manchester University Press, 1998.

Noam Chomsky. "The United States and the Challenge of Relativity," in *Human Rights Fifty Years On: A Reappraisal*, edited by Tony Evans. Manchester University Press, 1998.

Fons Coomans. "The Role of the UN Committee on Economic, Social, and Cultural Rights in Strengthening Implementation and Supervision of the International Covenant on Economic, Social, and Cultural Rights," Centre for Human Rights, Maastricht University, the Netherlands (http://www.uu.nl/uupublish/homerechts geleer/onderzockcholen/rechtenvandemens/english/publications/publication/srese/uu/303.85main.pdf (accessed March 1, 2008)).

Ruth Cunniff. "Democrats Split over Sanctions-Sanctions against Iraq," *The Progressive*, June, 2000 (http://www.commondreams.org.views/053000-103.htm (accessed March 1, 2008)).

Scott Davidson. *Human Rights.* Open University Press, 1993.

Jack Donnelly. "Universal Human Rights," in *Theory and Practice.* Cornell University Press, 1989.

Cecile Fabre. *Social Rights Under the Constitution.* Oxford University Press, 2000.

William F. Felice. *The Global New Deal.* Rowman and Littlefield Publishers, Inc., 2003.

Michael Freeman. *Key Concepts Human Rights.* Blackwell Publishers Ltd., 2002.

Francois Gianviti. General Counsel, International Monetary Fund, Economic, Social and Cultural Rights and the IMF, 2002. (http://www.imf.org/external/np/leg/sem/2002/cdmfl/eng/gianv3.pdf (accessed April 15, 2008)).

Ruth Gledhill, religion correspondent. "Anti-American Feelings Soar among Muslims, Study Finds," *The Times*, February 21, 2007 (http://www.timesonline.co.uk/tol/news/ world/US_and_americas/article1415550 (accessed March 1, 2008)).

'High Commissioner backs work on mechanism to consider complaints of breaches of economic, social and cultural rights,' Speeches and Statements by the High Commissioner, Office of the United Nations High Commissioner for Human Rights, July 16, 2007. http://www2.ohchr.org/english/issues/escr/escr-general-info .htm (accessed April 15, 2008).

Ted Honderich. *After the Terror.* Edinburgh University Press Ltd., 2002.

Lyndon Hood and Selwyn Manning. "PM, Foreign Minister Announce Fiji Sanctions," *Scoop*, December 6, 2006 (http://www.scoop.co.nz/stories/1th0612/500116.htm (accessed March 1, 2008)).

Paul Hunt. Statement of Fifth Annual Meeting of the Asia Pacific Forum of the National Human Rights Institutions, August, 2000 (http://www.asiapacificforum.net/about/annual-meetings/5th-new-Zealand-2000/downloads/keynote-speeches/hunt.pdf).

Caroline Lambert. International Council of Human Rights Policy and International Commission of Jurists Workshop, 2005 (http://www.ichrp.org/paperfiles/12ow01.doc (accessed March 1, 2008)).

Stephen Marks. "The Human Right to Development: Between Rhetoric and Reality," *Harvard Human Rights Journal*, 17 (http://www.law.harvard.edu/students/orgs/hrj/iss/7/marks.pdf).

Michael McLure. Working Paper Series, Dualistic Distinctions, and the Development of Pareto's General Theories of Economic and Social Equilibrium, 2003 (http://www.ces mep.unito.if/WP/2003/2_WP_cesmep.pdf (accessed March 1, 2008)).

Open-ended Working Group for the Optional Protocol to the International Covenant on Economic, Social and Cultural Rights, 23 Feb to 5 March, 10/03/2004, fidh networking human rights defenders.

Heidi Ost. Fourth Session of OEWG, March 16–27, 2007. Aland Islands Peace Institute and the Institute for Human Rights at Abo Akademi University (http://www.Peace. aland.fi/HeidiOst%20Report%20170907.pdf (accessed March 1, 2008)).

Vilfredo Pareto. *The Rise and Fall of Elites*. Transaction Publishers, 1991.

John Pilger. *The New Rulers of the World*. Verso, 2002.

———. 2005 (http://dissidentvoice.org/June05/Pilger0623.htm (accessed March 1, 2008)).

"PM, Foreign Minister Announce Fiji Sanctions," Lyndon Hood and Selwyn Manning, *Scoop*, December 6, 2006 (http://www.scoop.co.nz/stories/lth0612/500116.htm (accessed March 1, 2008)).

Arch Puddington. "The Pushback Against Democracy," *Journal of Democracy*, 18, no. 2 (April 2007) (http://muse.jhu.edu/login?uri=/journals/journal_of_democracy/V018/18.2puddington.html (accessed March 1, 2008)).

Eibe Riedel. The Draft Optional Protocol to the International Covenant on Economic, Social, and Cultural Rights, "The Right to Development and Economic, Social, and Cultural Rights," Universität Mannheim Winter Semester, 1998/1999 (http://www.dey erler.de/seiten/semdata/sem00005.htm (accessed March 2, 2008)).

Bernard Robertson. *Economic, Social, and Cultural Rights: A Reappraisal* (New Zealand Business Round Table Publishers, 1997 (http://www.nzbr.org.nz/documents/publica tions-1997/nzbr-rights.doc.htm (accessed March 1, 2008)).

Geoffrey Robertson. *Crimes Against Humanity*. Allan Lane, Penguin Press, 1999.

Carne Ross. Select Committee on Economic Affairs Second Report, Chapter 3: Comprehensive UN Sanctions—Iraq 1990–2003, The United Kingdom Parliament, 128.

Peter Schwarb and Adamantia Pollis. *Globalization's Impact on Human Rights: Human Rights New Perspectives, New Realities*, edited by Adamantia Pollis and Peter Schwarb. Lynne Rienner Publishers, 2000.

Sigrun Skogley. *The Human Rights Obligations of the World Bank and the International Monetary Fund*. Cavendish Publishers Ltd., 2001.

H. J. Steiner & P. Alston. "International Human Rights," in *Context: Law, Politics, Morals*. Oxford: Clarendon Press, 1996.

R. Stevens, P. Frater, and C. Waldegrave. *Below the Line: An Analysis of Income Poverty in New Zealand* (1984–1998).

Straight UN Facts, 2006 (http://www.eyeontheun.org/facts.asp?1=l+p=54 (accessed March 1, 2008)).

Gary Teeple. *The Riddle of Human Rights*. Garamond Press Ltd., 2004.

Wouter Vandenhole. Working Paper: An Optional Protocol to the International Convenant on Economic, Social, and Cultural Rights, Institute for Human Rights, Catholic University of Leuven, Belgium, 36 (http://www.escr net.org/resources_more _show.htm?doc-id.431276 (accessed March 3, 2008)).

Onuma Yasuaki. "Towards an Intercivilisation Approach to Human Rights," in *The East Asian Challenge for Human Rights*, edited by Joanne R. Bauer and Daniel A. Bell. Press Syndicate of the University of Cambridge, 1999.

Hans L. Zetterberg. "Introduction," *Vilfredo Pareto: The Rise and Fall of Elite*. Transaction Publishers, 1991.

CONCLUSION

Helen Clark. "Clark to meet East Asia's leaders ahead of Summit," cited in 'New Zealand could lead in Human Rights in the proposed East Asia Regional Bloc,' by Anthony Ravlich, December 12, 2005. http://www.hrc2001.org.nz (accessed April 15, 2008).

Harris Friedberg. Masterless Men, "Riot and Liberties" Section, Wesleyan College, 2002. http://hfriedberg.web.wesleyan.edu/eng1205/wshakespeare/riotand liberties.htm. (accessed April 15, 2008).

Erich Fromm. *The Fear of Freedom.* ARK Paperback, 1984.

Ted Honderich. *After the Terror.* Edinburgh University Press Ltd., 2002.

Edward Kannyo. *Uganda International Handbook of Human Rights*, edited by Jack Donnelly and Rhoda E. Howard. Greenwood Press, 1987.

Tony Karon. "How Hunger Could Topple Regimes," *Time* in partnership with CNN, April 11, 2008.http://www.time.com/time/world/article/0,8599, 1730107,00.html? xid=feed-yahoo-full-world (accessed April 15, 2008).

Errol Kiong and Jerrod Booker. 'Wealth gap leaves our youngest at most risk,' *New Zealand Herald*, November 27, 2007, A3.

Bert Massey. Chairperson of the Disability Rights Commission, 'Britons don't know their human rights,' Evening news, *The Edinburgh Paper*, July 7, 2006. http://news .scotsman.com/latestnews/Britons-dont-know-their-human.2790451.jp (accessed April 15, 2008).

C. W. Mills. *White Collar* (New York: Pioneer, 1951), cited in *Economic, Social, and Cultural Rights: A Reappraisal*, edited by Bernard Robertson. New Zealand Business Round Table, 1997, footnote 21.

Rose Nakayi. 'Government has duty to feed its starving children,' *The New Vision*, January 17, 2007 (http://allafrica.com/stories/200701180066.html (accessed March 3, 2008)).

Winston Peters. Minister of Foreign Affairs, "Peters Speech: Human Rights Priorities," *Scoop*, October 19, 2007 (http://www.scoop.co.nz/stories/P190710/ 500375.htm (accessed March 3, 2008)).

Anthony Ravlich. "The Need for Shelter-A 'Core' Human Rights Obligation," Indymedia, March 31, 2004 (http://indymedia.org.nz/newswire/display/16829/index.php (accessed April 15, 2008)).

———. New Zealand Could Lead in Human Rights in the Proposed East Asia Regional Bloc (http://www.hrc2001.org.nz).

Select Committee on Economic Affairs, Second Report, Chapter 3: Comprehensive UN Sanctions-Iraq 1990–2003, The United Kingdom Parliament (http://www.publi cations.parliament.uk/pa/ld200607/ldeconaf/96/9606.htm (accessed March 1, 2008)).

Henry Shue. *Basic Rights.* Princeton University Press, 1980.

Susan St. John. Families Get Boost—Child Poverty Set to Deepen, Monday, April 3, 2006, Press Release: Child Poverty Action Group (http://jobsletter.org.nz/jbl24900. htm (accessed March 1, 2008)).

H. J. Steiner & P. Alston. "International Human Rights," in *Context: Law, Politics, Morals.* Oxford: Clarendon Press, 1996.

Wayne Thompson. "McDonald's workers win 'supersize' deal," *New Zealand Herald*, December 5, 2006.

Victory in Homeless Rights Case, ACLU, April 14, 2006 (http://www.aclu-sc.org/News/Releases/2006/101775 (accessed March 1, 2008)).

Index

About the Author

Anthony Ravlich was born in Auckland, New Zealand in 1949. Ravlich attended St Peter's College in Epsom, Auckland, and later obtained degrees in politics (MA), statistics (BSc) and criminology (Dip Crim (Hons)) at Auckland University. He became fully involved in human rights in 1991 and pioneered the promotion of economic, social, and cultural rights in New Zealand writing articles, giving talks in the community, and hosting a human rights show on Planet Radio for eighteen months. Part-time work such as dishwashing and tutoring English helped finance my activities. Ravlich formed a close relationship with Psychiatric Survivors Inc. in 1992 and in 2001 formed the Human Rights Council Inc. (New Zealand) of which he is Chairperson.